Creative Music
Composition

Creative Music Composition

The Young Composer's Voice

Margaret Lucy Wilkins

Routledge
Taylor & Francis Group
New York   London

Routledge is an imprint of the
Taylor & Francis Group, an informa business

Published in 2006 by
Routledge
Taylor & Francis Group
270 Madison Avenue
New York, NY 10016

Published in Great Britain by
Routledge
Taylor & Francis Group
2 Park Square
Milton Park, Abingdon
Oxon OX14 4RN

Printed in the United States of America on acid-free paper
10 9 8 7 6 5 4 3 2 1

International Standard Book Number-10: 0-415-97467-4 (Softcover)
International Standard Book Number-13: 978-0-415-97467-7 (Softcover)
Library of Congress Card Number 2005030527

Library of Congress Cataloging-in-Publication Data

Wilkins, Margaret Lucy.
    Creative music composition : the young composer's voice / Margaret Lucy Wilkins.
        p. cm.
    Includes bibliographical references (p.) and index.
    ISBN 0-415-97466-6 (hb) -- ISBN 0-415-97467-4 (pb) 1. Composition (Music) I. Title.

MT40.W56 2006
781.3--dc22   2005030527

Taylor & Francis Group
is the Academic Division of Informa plc.

Visit the Taylor & Francis Web site at
http://www.taylorandfrancis.com

and the Routledge Web site at
http://www.routledge-ny.com

Contents

ACKNOWLEDGMENTS   VII

KEY TO TERMINOLOGY   IX

INTRODUCTION   I

CHAPTER 1   YOUNG COMPOSERS AND A CREATIVE
ENVIRONMENT   7

CHAPTER 2   CONCEPTS OF THE IMAGINATION: GETTING
STARTED   15

CHAPTER 3   STRUCTURES: TRADITIONAL/INVENTED   23

CHAPTER 4   MUSICAL LANGUAGES: MULTIPLICITY OF
STYLES   43

CHAPTER 5   TECHNICAL EXERCISES   103

CHAPTER 6   EXPLORING INSTRUMENTS   117

CHAPTER 7   COMPOSING FOR TRADITIONAL ENSEMBLES   151

CHAPTER 8   COMPOSING FOR VOICES   199

CHAPTER 9   COMPOSING FOR A MONODIC INSTRUMENT   235

CHAPTER 10 MOVING AHEAD   255

NOTES   265

BIBLIOGRAPHY   267

INDEX   275

ACKNOWLEDGMENTS

The writing of this book was made possible by a Learning Teaching Support Network "Palatine Award," 2002–2003, funded by the British Government. This award was further supported by a grant from the University of Huddersfield, UK.

Permissions to use the musical extracts were granted by the following music publishers: Associated Music Publishers, Boosey & Hawkes, Chesters, Durand, Faber, Lengnick, Novello, Oxford University, Press Peters, PWM (Poland), Schott, Sikorski, Stockhausen-Verlag, Wilhelm Hansen, and Universal Edition. In addition, my thanks go to the family of Ruth Crawford Seeger.

I am indebted to Professor Clyde Binfield, Emeritus Professor of History, University of Sheffield, UK, for kindly providing the photograph of Gaudí's *Sagrada Familia*.

Also, my grateful thanks for reading drafts and for helpful advice go to Andrew Lucas, Clarence Schofield, and Dr. Duncan Druce. In addition, I would like to thank Routledge Executive Editor Richard Carlin for his assistance and support.

KEY TO TERMINOLOGY

Note Values

American Usage	British Usage
Whole note	Semibreve
Half note	Minim
Quarter note	Crotchet
Eighth note	Quaver
Sixteenth note	Semiquaver
Thirty-second note	Demisemiquaver
Sixty-fourth note	Hemidemisemiquaver

Intervals

M = Major
m = minor
P = perfect
A = augmented
D = diminished

Thus:

P1 = unison
m2 = minor second
M2 = major second
m3 = minor third
M3 = major third
P4 = perfect fourth
A4 = augmented fourth
D5 = diminished fifth
P5 = perfect fifth
A5 = augmented fifth
D6 = diminished sixth
m6 = minor sixth
M6 = major sixth
D7 = diminished seventh
m7 = minor seventh
M7 = major seventh
P8 = perfect octave

INTRODUCTION

It has often been claimed that composition cannot be taught. While it is true that no teacher can endow the student with musical talent and imagination, good teachers can provide a stimulating environment in which creativity can flourish. This is best done within an institution that has the resources to provide opportunities for listening to and studying new music, as well as by providing performers (both professionals and students) who are willing and able to rehearse emerging composers' works.

This book is the outcome of more than a quarter of a century of experience in teaching young composers at the University of Huddersfield, United Kingdom. A composer myself, I taught free composition between 1976 and 2003 at the University of Huddersfield, and was Composition Leader for fourteen years.

As the largest university department of music in the United Kingdom, with up to 400 undergraduate and postgraduate music students, the University of Huddersfield has provided important opportunities for the development of young composers. Most of the undergraduate students have taken free composition as part of their honors degree program. Some students enter the music program as specialist young composers, while others discover their talent for composing *en route*, and choose to specialize in composition for their final year. Approximately a third of undergraduates select free composition as part of their final year of study.

Unusually, composition is a core activity for at least the first year of the undergraduate music program at the University of Huddersfield. In many music institutions, students are not encouraged to freely compose until later in their courses, and a year or two of valuable guided creativity is lost. The object at Huddersfield is not necessarily to produce *bona fide* composers (although this does happen), but to produce educated musicians. Experience in composing informs all the other musical activities: performance, musicology, and electroacoustic music studies.

The term "free composition" implies creative work that is not stylistically based within historical eras. In practice, it has come to mean composing within a twentieth- and twenty-first century Western European style, open to individual interpretation.

Throughout the course at the University of Huddersfield, students of composition have the experience of actually composing, and of hearing their works performed by professional and student performance groups. Not only is this activity an essential aspect of the learning process for composers, but it also informs performers of the excitement of bringing to life music that has never been heard before. This part of the education process is immediately audible. Less obvious are three ingredients that are vital to the development of composers:

- Stimulus to the imagination
- Technical skill
- Knowledge of the musical context in which they wish to work

These form the basis of the teaching of free composition and of the materials in this book.

The teaching of free composition can best take place in a variety of formats, ranging from small class groups to individual tutorials. Specialist composers enjoy one-on-one tutorials with a mature composer, as well as regular studies in composition classes. These latter classes can be taught to a group of composers as a forum for the analysis of particular works of interest and for debates on æsthetic issues.

Workshops, in which students hear their compositions rehearsed by professional performers, may be arranged for each year of the course. In this way, student composers learn by the experience of coming into contact with the "real thing." There is no substitute for the excitement (and anxiety) of baring your musical soul before your peers! In addition, there are opportunities for enthusiastic student composers to organize their own performance groups, working with their talented contemporaries.

Notable successes among composers who have studied music at the University of Huddersfield include prizewinners in national and international composition competitions as well as numerous performances via the Society for the Promotion of New Music (SPNM). A team of a dozen established composers, all of whom have international reputations, undertakes the teaching of this mass of creativity, either as full-time or part-time members of the staff. Although potentially this is a recipe for disagreements, given the individual nature of each composer's outlook, in fact members of the team work harmoniously together. The educational vision, ethos, and tradition of the music department inspire all who teach there.

This pioneering vision for the development of young composers grew from the mostly inadequate musical education that many British composers received at universities during the middle of the twentieth century. In the second and third decades of the twentieth century, inspirational composers taught at various conservatories of music. Nadia Boulanger taught at the Paris Conservatoire and attracted an entire generation of young composers from Europe and America to her classes. In Britain, Ralph Vaughan Williams taught for 20 years at the Royal College of Music, London. However, in the decade immediately following World War II, there were few professional composers teaching in British universities. Young composers were advised to seek instruction from European and American masters, including Babbit in the United States, Donatoni in Italy, Messiaen in France, Stockhausen in Germany, and, towards the end of the century, Andriessen in the Netherlands. Although individuals can provide a mentoring role for younger composers, particularly at the postgraduate stage, there are essential opportunities that can best be accessed via an institution. These include a good library of contemporary musical scores, recordings, and critical books, as well as resources for workshops. These requirements were in part met by the postwar rise of summer schools of music, notably Darmstadt in Germany, Tanglewood in the U.S., and Dartington in England. In addition, organizations such as the Society for the Promotion of New Music (SPNM) emerged in England in 1943, and the International Society of Contemporary Music (ISCM) has become established as both a national and international platform for new music. In North America, organizations such as the Society of Composers, Inc. (SCI), the Society for Electro-Acoustic Music (SEA-MUS), the Electronic Music Foundation (EMF), Broadcast Music, Inc. (BMI), and The American Society of Composers, Authors, and Publishers (ASCAP) all offer opportunities to emerging composers.

During the twentieth century, undergraduate music degrees seemed to be founded on a nineteenth century model: stylistic composition was the order of the day. Young composers were expected to thrive on a diet of weekly exercises in which the styles of the classical composers of the past (Palestrina, Bach, Mozart, Schubert) were imitated. When these old techniques were mastered, young composers were "allowed" to compose freely, though by then they were nearing the end of their higher education. The vast leap from tonal musical thinking to the exciting new modernism was left to the floundering student to make, unaided. Frustration and disappointment were the only outcomes of this musical education system, especially for those who aspired to be composers. There were few opportunities for young composers to actually hear their own compositions, unless they organized their own performances to be given by cooperative fellow students. Although this was a lesson in creating one's own chances, it left students woefully ignorant of the real standards of professional performance, as well as of the business of being a composer. The result was that, instead of being stimulated, creative imaginations were stifled.

Other subjects in the arts have adopted different educational models. An aspiring writer is not expected to undergo the rigors of learning to write in the style of past authors and poets. How many successful present-day writers were required to master the language of Chaucer, Shakespeare, Milton, or Dickens before being "allowed" to write in the language of their own time? On the other hand, young painters can be seen in art galleries painstakingly copying the work of Michelangelo, Rubens, Turner, or Renoir.

During the latter quarter of the twentieth century, access to higher education expanded throughout Europe and America. Conservatories and universities appointed professional composers as lecturers in such numbers that almost every music department in higher education now has at least one composer as a member of the teaching staff. Indeed, universities have become the new patrons of the arts, replacing the former historical patronage of the church and the aristocracy.

Interest in the study and practice of composition has been encouraged so that it is no longer the prerogative of the gifted few. Access to the experience of composing has been widened to include pupils at primary and secondary levels. In this, it reflects the practice of painting and creative writing that have always existed in the school curriculum. So, at the tertiary level, composition tutors are teaching students who come to the university with some composing experience on which to build.

Determined not to pass on their own debilitating experiences to the next generation, present composition instructors in universities and conservatories have devised a musical education that is more suited to the needs of developing young composers. Of course, there is some point in studying your chosen art as practiced by successful exponents of the past. Classical composers have set the standards for artistic integrity and technical command. Both of these should remain as desirable goals, and be applicable to any current musical language. However, the in-depth study of musical tonality has now become the realm of musicology, as well as being essential for the performer of music from the past; it is no longer a prerequisite for a composer. Indeed, mastering all aspects of tonality is such a lengthy process that, with the passage of the centuries and the ever-increasing wealth of knowledge, students are in danger of never arriving at the music of their own time. So, to concentrate on the study of contemporary music, with occasional glances back to some interesting ideas from the past, seems a good way for young composers to develop their own techniques and knowledge of the context in which they will operate.

The musical examples discussed in this book are among those that have inspired the current generation of young composers. They have been selected to illustrate particular techniques and musical ideas. They are not intended to be imitated, but rather to demonstrate a standard of musical thinking and expertise. They are by no means exclusive. There are many more contemporary musical masterpieces to discover.

The book has been written with developing composers in mind: composers who have some experience of composing and who want to make further progress. Typically, they might be undergraduates, high school students, or adults who have discovered composing later in life.

1

YOUNG COMPOSERS AND A
CREATIVE ENVIRONMENT

Discovering that you can compose music is very exciting and can lead to a lifetime of creative fulfillment. You will embark on a journey of exploration to find your own composing voice, and, on the way, you will encounter stimulating ideas and techniques that have fascinated other composers. Helping you to develop as a composer is the object of this book. A postgraduate has likened the process of discovering your own voice to that of sculpting: the voice is hidden inside the block of marble, and the task is to chip away until the sculpture, or the voice, is revealed. The Italian sculptor, Antonio Canova (1757–1822), famous for his beautiful *The Three Graces* (marble, 1814–1817), offered the following advice to his students: "Study Nature, consult the works of the great masters of Antiquity, and, after careful comparisons, arrive at your own original style."[1]

It's common nowadays for young musicians to have some experience of composing during their school education. In England, the music education system provides for creative experience in both primary and secondary schools. Thus, in the United Kingdom, students who choose to study music in further or higher education (college, conservatory, or university) will have already started on the road of discovery. The ability to have musical ideas and to imagine sounds, and the desire to create new music, have been awakened. For some, this becomes a life-long passion; for others, the spirit of inquiry, musical exploration, and discovery is a life-enhancing experience. Free composition can be studied as a specialty subject, or may be taken as a component of a music degree, together with performance, musicology, electroacoustic music, and music theory.

The experience of composing can provide insights into the other fields of musical activity. Performers who have composed can better understand, for example, the limits of musical notation. Their own performance can benefit by assimilating the often improvisatory nature of a work, which otherwise appears to be a fixed entity on a printed page. The ability to make an imaginative leap into the mind of other composers (because of the experience of having composed) can produce a stunning performance. All the same, the idea of undertaking free composition (that is, composing in your own style, rather than in the style of a composer of the past) can be daunting. Rest assured that almost every musician is capable of composing, to a greater or lesser extent, given the opportunity of doing so.

The object of including free composition in a music course on equal terms with the other areas of musical study is not necessarily to produce *bona fide* composers (although this has happened many times), but to produce educated musicians. Through composition, you are able to give expression to your own ideas, and to learn about the musical issues of the twentieth and twenty-first centuries. This in turn enhances your understanding of all music and produces more thoughtful performances and historical insights. Examples of musicians who are, or were, both composers and performers are overwhelmingly numerous: Claudio Monteverdi, Bar-

bara Strozzi, Johann Sebastian Bach, Wolfgang Amadeus Mozart, Ludwig van Beethoven, Clara Schumann, Amy Beach, Cécile Chaminade, Claude Debussy, Gustav Mahler, Rebecca Clarke, Serge Rachmaninov, Paul Hindemith, Otto Klemperer, Pablo Casals, Pierre Boulez, André Previn, and Leonard Bernstein, to mention just a few.

Pianist Murray Perahia expressed that he felt that composition is the center of musical activity, and that performing needs a basis in composition. Music teachers need composing experience in order to be able to lead their pupils, at both primary and secondary school levels. The tasks of the aspiring composer are actually to compose, to undertake the "search," to be true to one's own integrity, and to learn about the work of other composers. Composing should not be a navel-gazing activity (that is, concentrating exclusively on your own work), but should embrace knowledge and appreciation of other composers' ideas. The latter can often spark creative ideas that can be modified and utilized in your own work.

Professional Opportunities

In modern society, all composers are freelance: there are no salaried positions for composers, unlike during the Classical era when male musicians were hired as *Kappelmeisters* by the Christian Church, or as court composers by the aristocracy; this was how J. S. Bach, Mozart, and Haydn, for example, were employed. In the twenty-first century, composers can earn an income by writing for film, television, and other media, or by writing to commission for the concert hall (or other performance venues), or by publishing recordings of their music, or by publishing music for educational use, for example. Apart from working in the pop industry, it is rare for composers to be able to earn their entire incomes from composing activities alone, and many choose to have a multiplicity of income-generating employment.

Finding the Right Teaching/Learning Environment

It is important to find the right teaching/learning environment that will encourage and support composing activity. Try to find a course that includes as many of these ingredients as possible:

- Experienced composition instructors (preferably a choice)
- Opportunities to hear your compositions (in organized workshops, for example)
- A fellowship of composers (including undergraduate, postgraduate, and mature staff composers)
- Access to scores and recordings of new music, as well as to opportunities to attend live concerts and musical events

It is an advantage to be surrounded by contemporaries at different stages of creative development. Belonging to a group of understanding and supportive colleagues, who can offer advice and encouragement, is much better than trying to develop in isolation.

Workshops

The importance of learning through doing, and through hearing the results of your efforts, cannot be overstressed. Workshops, in which your pieces can be tried out, are fundamental to the learning experience of composers. They are the crucible in which composers learn if their ideas can prove to be practical. Perhaps the most difficult aspect of composing is to judge the effectiveness of the structure and whether it appears to be convincing. Although some computing music software programs allow the composer to hear a work-in-progress, the artificial sounds are not the same as those obtained from real acoustic instruments. The advantage of a good computer music program is that you can test the rhythmic flow and structural effectiveness of your work in real time, ahead of a rehearsal or performance situation. The disadvantage is that the electronic sounds are artificial because, unlike acoustic instruments, they are lacking in harmonic resonance and timbral beauty. As there is no human element involved in the performance of electronically produced sounds, composers can acquire a false impression of what is really possible when human musicians perform the music. In addition, composers need to build their "inner ear" from the real sounds of the instruments rather than artificial ones.

A variety of performance situations can be arranged, ranging from workshops provided by students through to professional performers who are hired especially for composers' workshops. Student groups can involve small ensembles, graded through to the college orchestra, brass band, and symphonic wind orchestra. For composers developing outside formal education, there are other opportunities for accessing resources and workshops. National music centers exist in many countries. For example, the British Music Information Centre in London and the Scottish Music Centre in Glasgow house scores and recordings of most national composers. Opportunities for composers' workshops are offered each season by the Society for the Promotion of New Music (SPNM) in England, or the national branches of the International Society for Contemporary Music (ISCM) in many other countries.

The use of a choir in workshop situations has proved more problematic than the use of instrumental ensembles. This is because student and amateur singers need much more time to learn new works than competent instrumentalists, who are capable of sight-reading music very quickly. Unfortunately, this can lead to a situation in which young composers tend not to have the same learning experience in writing for voices as they have in writing for instruments. Composing for voices needs special care, because the singers have to pitch their notes, not only horizontally (melodically), but vertically (harmonically) in relation to the other singers. Of course the need to pre-hear the notes is not exclusive to singers, because instrumentalists also need this ability. A solution to this practical problem might be to write a work for a local choir or church choir.

Composers who are learning need performers who are sympathetic and able to offer constructive criticism. Feedback from performing musicians can also indicate what is rewarding to play. Composers are understandably nervous about the first hearing of a new work, especially if the piece contains an element of experimentation. In fact, composers may use the workshop to try out experimental ideas, so that encouraging and helpful comments will assist the young composer's development.

Stylistic versus Free Composition

In some institutions, there is a debate surrounding the issue of the teaching/learning of stylistic or free composition. This stems from a widespread twentieth-century practice of teaching the tonal musical language via the completion of exercises that imitate the styles of various "old masters." This educational model was appropriate at the time — that is, before non-tonal musical styles had been developed. Now, the teaching/learning of stylistic composition could be regarded as a branch of musicology, useful for learning the mechanisms of the tonal musical language. It should not be regarded as a substitute for, or an alternative to, guided experience of free composition, particularly for those intending to be specialist composers. Having said this, competence in composing stylistic music could be a useful accomplishment for composers intending to write incidental music for period plays or films.

The term "free composition" implies creative work that is not stylistically based within historical eras. In practice, it has come to mean composing within a twentieth- and twenty-first century Western European style, open to individual interpretation.

The Teaching Offered

Ideally, a program of teaching/learning that offers a combination of composers' classes, workshops, and individual tuition is the most desirable. "Studies in Composition" classes can impart much stimulating information, provide opportunities for analysis, and provoke æsthetic discussion among the group as a whole. They enable composers (who tend to work otherwise as solitary figures) to meet as a group for the exchange of ideas, under the direction of a mature composition tutor.

Regular individual instruction should be given by experienced composers in order to discuss the work-in-progress of each student. Matters of viable musical ideas, how to develop them, and the practicalities of notating them can be guided on an individual basis.

Listening to New Music

The best way of learning about new music — the sound of it, the ideas, the philosophies— is to take every opportunity to listen to it. By attending concerts and by visiting festivals of contemporary music, you experience the excitement that goes with hearing new music. Radio programs, occasional television programs, and recordings can all be experienced without leaving home. Specialist sites on the Internet are another means by which new music recordings may be purchased.

Artists have always developed by learning from their predecessors. The ideas of the previous generations might be used directly, or developed in a new way, or rejected, but ignorance of them is not to be commended.

2

CONCEPTS OF THE IMAGINATION

Getting Started

When you first started to compose, you probably had little idea of what you were trying to create. It was sufficient just to find some sounds. Then came the task of how to notate them. As you develop, you may become aware that you want to have more control over what you are creating.

In the past, classical structures dictated the form and character of the work. Nowadays, it is more usual for composers to determine a concept, or basic idea, around which to build their work. From a strong concept will flow much information about the essential parameters of musical composition. The concept might determine the overall structure, for example, or the tempo, or the mood and character of the musical ideas.

It is likely that the concept will fall into one of two categories: programmatic or abstract. Programmatic music takes its inspiration from an extra-musical idea. A popular source of inspiration might be found in a phenomenon of nature, for example. Vivaldi's violin concerto *The Four Seasons* (c.1730), Beethoven's Symphony No. 6, *Pastoral* (1808), and Debussy's *Voiles*, *Des Pas sur la Neige*, *La Cathédrale Engloutie* and *La Fille aux Cheveux de Lin* (from *Douze Préludes* Book 1 for solo piano, 1910) are all examples of programmatic ideas represented in musical terms. Abstract concepts concern purely technical musical ideas. They might embrace, for example, the idea of a piece that gradually increases in speed throughout, or a movement that slowly progresses from the lowest pitches to the highest. Such a work would require mastery of technique and imaginative use of the musical forces involved. Górecki's Symphony No. 3, *Symphony of Sorrowful Songs* (1976), uses a folk-like melody in canon throughout Movement I, which winds its way from low double basses to high strings and back again. Igor Stravinsky, in his *Symphony of Psalms* (1930), wrote chorale-like parts for the chorus and included a fugal Movement II, in a tribute to Bach. Similarly, Béla Bartók composed a fugue for Movement I of his *Music for Strings, Percussion and Celesta* (1936).

Stimuli to the Imagination

Ideas that spark the imagination can be found in a variety of contexts, including pictorial, scientific, literary, mathematical, architectural, spiritual, historical, and so on. Here are some texts that might fire your imagination. They are taken from descriptions of particular works by the composers themselves, or from reviewers' comments.

> … there is the extraordinary haunting and intoxicating magic of its sound. There is often startling imagery, with its undercurrents of association, and frequent allusion to things animate and inanimate, or to other music.[1]

> Rhythm is organised linearly and is easy to hear: things get steadily faster or slower, durations steadily expand and contract, and the number of durations increases or decreases around 12. In section X the tempos (written out against the conductor's constant beat) move

from slow to fast. In Y they start at a median and get alternately slower and faster. In Z they do the same but the two tempos are played simultaneously.[2]

… it can be considered on the same level as the stars, the numbers, and the riches of the human brain, as it was in the great periods of the ancient civilizations.[3]

In the 'Cantar del alma' the number seven (last words) first comes to prominence with seven trumpet calls from the gallery; beginning with one trumpet sounding for one bar, the series adds a trumpet and a bar to each call. 'El descenso' then alternates seven blocks of seven-part counterpoint with seven blocks, increasingly loud and fast, of echoing and re-echoing wind chords, most of them triadic.[4]

… I wanted the players at times to be independent of the bar-line and also, at times, independent of the conductor. I wanted to be able to give them the freedom that a virtuoso cadenza or lyrical rubato can have without the texture as a whole lapsing into anarchy. It was a considerable notational headache working out how to synchronize events simply and practically, leaving the players free to concentrate on presenting their lines in an uninhibited way.[5]

Just as this music tests the virtuosity of the soloist to the limit, so does it dare the audience to hang on tight as it takes them on the high-energy roller-coaster ride of their lives. […] His music speaks of 'now,' in bold, exuberant, manic, at times raucous terms that reflect the world in which we live. We shouldn't be surprised by the pile-driving dynamics and rhythms of rock that leap from his scores. Nor should we be surprised that his musical language seems ever in a state of flux. […] Rouse will lull the listener with a wash of quasi-tonal harmony before shattering the mood with a clamorous burst of ratchet and Chinese opera gongs. It's not music for the faint of heart, or ear.[6]

[In Cantigas] he unleashes a riotous, Dionysiac processional of erup-tive brass and pulverising percussive throbs. There are hints of church chorales in the string lines that soar intermittently above the melée.[7]

[…] – massive slow-moving blocks of sound, which sometimes coalesce into a single melodic line, and anarchic rapid figurations.

The two alternate and are never reconciled, but the effect is luminous and compelling.[8]

Listening for what is not yet sounded, like a fisherman waiting for a nibble or a bite. Pull the sound out of the air like a fisherman catching a fish, sensing its size and energy — when you hear. When you hear the sound, play it. Move to another location if there are no nibbles or bites. There are sounds in the air like sounds in the water. When the water is clear, you might hear the sounds.[9]

EWA7 was inspired by machine and factory sounds: the scrapes, squeaks and bangs of metal, the ambient buzzes and whines of electric devices, and the imperfect rhythmic repeats of heavy machinery.... I was particularly fascinated by the ever-changing sonic landscapes that occur in each factory as sounds shift, overlap and echo in the distance.... Machine rhythms went in and out of phase, dynamics varied wildly, and in an environment of constantly shifting activity and noise, the frequency spectrum fluctuated from sub-audio rumbles to barely audible high-pitched whines....[10]

Improvisation

Programmatic ideas are often easier for composers to handle in the early stages of their development. Abstract ideas tend to need knowledge of particular forms and disciplined technique.

Having decided on the concept for the piece, improvisation can be the starting point for the musical materials. Try improvising your way through the whole piece as you envisage it, without attempting to write anything down. As an illustration, you might improvise your way through the poem "Jabberwocky," from Lewis Carroll's *Through the Looking Glass and What Alice Found There* (1871). Select an instrument on which to experiment.

The language, though apparently in English, uses many nonsense words. The first verse, for example, successfully conjures a magical scene, populated by strange creatures, while using mostly invented words. What, for example, are "slithy toves," and how do they "gyre and gimble in the wabe"? What does the "jubjub" bird sound like and what is a "vorpal" sword? Nevertheless, despite the invented language we detect a story similar to that of

"St. George and the Dragon." Apart from the ancillary creatures, there are three main characters: the Old Man, the Young Man (St. George), and the Jabberwocky (Dragon). Each of these needs a musical motto. There are a number of scenes: the wood (?), the conversations, the hunt, the fight, the galumphing (triumphant) march. These are couched in a clever palindromic structure of seven verses: verses 1 and 7 set the scene and are identical; in verses 2 and 6 the Old Man speaks to the Young Man; verses 3 and 5 represent the hunt and the fight; and in the central fourth verse the Jabberwocky makes its first appearance, "whiffling through the tulgey wood, And burbled as it came!"

v.1   'Twas brillig, and the slithy toves

              Did gyre and gimble in the wabe;

              All mimsy were the borogroves,

              And the mome raths outgrabe.

v.2   "Beware the Jabberwock, my son!

              The jaws that bite, the claws that catch!

              Beware the jubjub bird and shun

              The frumious Bandersnatch!"

v.3   He took his vorpal sword in hand:

              Long time the manxome foe he sought —

              So rested he by the Tumtum tree,

              And stood awhile in thought.

v.4   And as in uffish thought he stood,

              The Jabberwock, with eyes of flame,

              Came whiffling through the tulgey wood,

              And burbled as it came!

v.5   One two! One, two! And through and through

              The vorpal blade went snicker-snack!

              He left it dead, and with its head

              He went galumphing back.

v.6   "And hast thou slain the Jabberwock?

Come to my arms, my beamish boy!

O frabjous day! Callooh! Callay!"

He chortled in his joy.

v.7   'Twas brillig, and the slithy toves

Did gyre and gimble in the wabe;

All mimsy were the borogroves,

And the mome raths outgrabe.

Lewis Carroll,
Through the Looking Glass and What Alice Found There (1871), p. 22

In your improvisation, try to match the nonsense English with an invented musical language of your own, which nevertheless manages to convey the mythical scenario. You will have a very good memory indeed if you can make the last verse sound exactly the same as the first verse, as the structure of the poem suggests. It is often the case that the fingers alight upon some impressive ideas, but that it is difficult to recapture them. The best ideas seem to escape through the window! If this proves to be a problem, try recording your improvisation sessions so that you can later recall your best ideas.

The task here is not to set the text as a song, but to use it as the springboard for a programmatic exploration of sounds and musical ideas of your own invention. Having worked on an improvisation, you might like to note down a few of the ideas, as an *aide memoire*, before presenting your improvisation to the class.

Titles

Choosing a suitable title for your work is often problematic. Sometimes, the abstract nature of the concept does not itself suggest an attractive title. Prior to the twentieth century, composers were often content to use the name of the form as the title of their works—for example, sonata, suite, symphony, and so forth—using numbers and keys to differentiate them. Occasionally, particular works acquired a nickname to distinguish them from the thousands of other sonatas and symphonies. Haydn's Symphony No. 45 in F#, "Farewell" (1772), and Beethoven's Sonata in C#, op. 27, no. 2, "Moonlight" (1801) are two well-known examples of nicknames that were added post-composition.

However, it is possible to begin with a title, which in turn has implications for the content of the piece. Here are some suggestions for titles that might be used as starting points:

Wind, Rain, Steam
Time Zone
Time Is, Time Was, Times Past
Speed, Flight
Blow, Trumpet, Blow
Celestial Harmonies
Musical Games for Two

3

STRUCTURES

Traditional/Invented

During the eras of the Baroque, Classical, and, to some extent, Romantic epochs, Western composers used various traditional forms for the structure of their works. In a sense, their task was made easier than in modern times by the availability of classical forms. Each dance that made up a suite (*allemande, courante, bourrée, sarabande, gavotte, minuet,* and *gigue*) had its own rhythmic character and tempo, and all were in binary form. Other forms—including fugue, *chaconne, passacaglia*, sonata, minuet and trio, rondo, and aria—had their particular prototypes that composers adapted or developed, thus stamping their individuality upon the particular structures. All of these forms utilized the key system of tonality—with its hierarchy of tonic, dominant, and their subsidiaries—and acted as "moulds" into which composers "poured" their music.

Though the advent of the twentieth century heralded a new open-
ness to alternatives to the prior all-pervasive tonal system, it is possible to adapt the traditional forms to new musical languages. Michael
Tippett and Elliott Carter are just two twentieth century composers
who have written sonatas for the piano. Paul Hindemith tasked himself with writing a sonata for every orchestral instrument, as a duo with
piano. The sonata form can easily be adapted to a non-tonal system.
The exposition of the first subject will always be based on a "tonic,"
or "pitch center," however this might be deduced. The second subject
can be placed anywhere other than the initial pitch center. The two
ideas may then be developed, ideally avoiding the original pitch center.
At the conclusion, the first and second subjects are recapitulated, both
sounding at the original pitch center. The form of this work is the classic sonata form: exposition, development, and recapitulation. This is a
model that any developing composer might like to emulate.

Nowadays, however, apart from the adaptation of old forms, modern
composers are faced with inventing a new structure for every work that
they write. The structure for a composition is akin to an architect's plan
for a building. There are basic models, such as a square divided into
four unequal spaces that are to be used as rooms. The number of levels/
floors is adaptable, according to the proposed function of the building.

Then there are architectural designs for special buildings. A Christian cathedral is modeled on the shape of the cross placed on the
ground. Added to the basic plan are designs for the upper structures,
with degrees of elaboration and decoration that reflect the spiritual
aspirations/wealth of the commissioners.

Without the architect's drawings and instructions, the builders could
not begin their work. Piling one stone on top of another and waiting
to see how the building would turn out is not an option when dealing
with bricks, mortar, steel, and concrete!

The work of the famous Spanish architect Antoní Gaudí (1852–
1926) can be seen in Barcelona, where he mainly worked. The cathedral, *Sagrada Familia*, which occupied him for most of his working life,
is built upon the fundamental model of a cross, familiar since the first
century A.D. Yet the superstructure speaks of the contemporary gothic
and *art nouveau* styles in which he participated. The slender pinnacles,

Gaudí, *Sagrada Familia* (c. 1883–c. 1926). Photo: Clive Binfield.

encrusted with stunning and elaborate decoration, are a match for any Norman cathedral. Typically, Gaudí worked by supplying the basic architectural plans, and then almost intuitively deciding on the particular decorations as the building progressed.

Intellectual Control versus Free Flow

Gaudí's approach to planning could be a model for a composer. While some might advocate working in an entirely intuitive fashion, others might prefer to plan, in advance, at least the main pillars of the work. The intuitive approach will inevitably result in some kind of structure. It is impossible to place sonic events in time without a structure emerging. However, the structure in this circumstance is governed by chance and has not been under the control of the composer. (If this were bricks and mortar, it might collapse!) This is the debate about the degree of intellectual control versus the free flow of ideas that is needed to create a successful musical composition. Perhaps the Gaudí model provides a good balance between complete control over every facet of the construction and the opportunity to allow creative inspiration to adorn the basic structure.

Because classical composers were entirely familiar with the forms of their day, they carried the prototypes around in their heads and did not need to write down their structural planning in advance of composing. Thus there are no extant structural sketches. Past composers' sketchbooks contained ideas for themes and motives with projected developments rather than formal sketches. Contemporary composers, however, often need to undertake structural planning as part of the compositional process.

Structure Determined by Concept

Sometimes, the concept determines the structure of the work. Karlheinz Stockhausen's *MANTRA* (1970) is for

- Two pianists, each with 12 antique cymbals
- Piano 1 with a shortwave radio receiver
- Special modulator to regulate 3 microphone amplifiers, a compressor, filters, a sine-wave generator, and a particularly refined ring modulator

As its title implies, the work is based upon a mantra, or ever-repeating formula — in this case, a musical motto (see Example 3.1a).

In Jonathan Cott's *Stockhausen: Conversations with the Composer* (1974), Stockhausen explains the meaning of his initial musical mantra, and how it is used throughout the 70-minute work. The mantra consists of four phrases, separated by rests that are proportionally linked: 3: 2: 1: 4. Similarly, the number of beats in each phrase is expressed proportionally: 10: 6: 15: 12. There are 13 pitches (12 different pitches with the first repeated at the end) that are exposed at the beginning by the right hand of Piano 1:

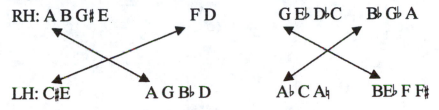

Stockhausen, *MANTRA* (1970): Pioano 1 opening statement.

Simultaneously, the left hand of Piano 1 plays the inversion of phrase 2 under phrase 1, the inversion of phrase 1 under phrase 2, the inversion of phrase 4 under phrase 3, and the inversion of phrase 3 under phrase 4.

Each note is allotted a specific character:

Note 1: regular repetition
Note 2: accent at the end
Note 3: normal
Note 4: *appoggiatura*
Note 5 + 6: *tremolo*
Note 7: accent at the beginning
Note 8: chromatic (embryonic *glissando*)
Note 9: *staccato*
Note 10: irregular repetition (embryonic morse code)
Note 11: embryonic trill
Note 12: *sfz* (embryonic echo)
Note 13: *arpeggio*

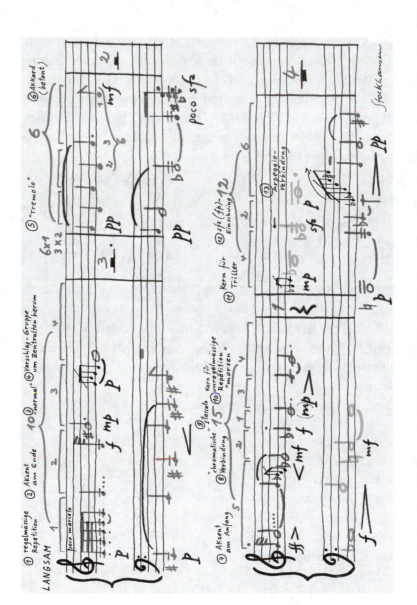

Example 3.1a The mantra for Stockhausen's *MANTRA* (1970). All Stockhausen CDs, scores, books, and videos may be ordered directly from the Stockhausen-Verlag, 51515 Kürten, Germany (www.stockhausen.org).

The 13 pitches, together with their characteristic articulations, form the bases of the 13 large sections that make up the piece. For each of these 13 sections, the mantra itself evolves via a scheme of "expanded scales," which allows for the metamorphosis of the initial mantric pitches. The mantra is read off each new scale in turn, thus transforming itself into a new set of pitches per section. Following the final section is a coda in which all the notes of the previous sections are played, as fast as possible, in a flurry of virtuosity. In Jonathan Cott's book, Stockhausen describes, in great detail, the complex calculations that he employed in the generation of the materials and structure of *MANTRA*. The result is a masterpiece of perpetual transformation, not least in the use of the live electronics that produce scintillating *glissandi* that, of course, are not possible to perform on acoustic pianos. Stockhausen insists that the work is not a set of variations. Rather, that the mantra is altered by size, in the way that Alice in Wonderland grew larger or smaller by drinking a potion.

This type of detailed forethought needs careful planning. Stockhausen created a "Form Scheme" for *MANTRA* (see Example 3.1b).

The concept for Thea Musgrave's Horn Concerto (1970–1971) involves the solo horn interacting with the four orchestral horns. These are placed around the auditorium, so that the audience experiences the answering horns in an unusual spatial arrangement, akin to that heard in the diffusion of electroacoustic music. In fact, the orchestral horns move their positions during the course of the work. Horn 1 begins offstage, behind the platform, and then moves to the back of the hall. Horns 2 and 3 start in their usual positions in the body of the orchestra, and then move to the front of the hall, on the right and left sides respectively. Horn 4 remains centrally positioned in the body of the orchestra. Similarly, the two trumpets begin at the back of the orchestra and later move to the front.

Because the spatial aspect is so fundamental to this particular concerto, the seating plan of the orchestra, soloist, four orchestral horns, and two trumpets had to be determined in advance of composing the work (see Example 3.2).

The structure for Harrison Birtwistle's opera *The Mask of Orpheus* (1973–1983) is both complex and fascinating. Fundamentally, the opera

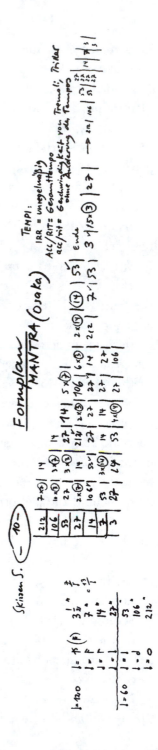

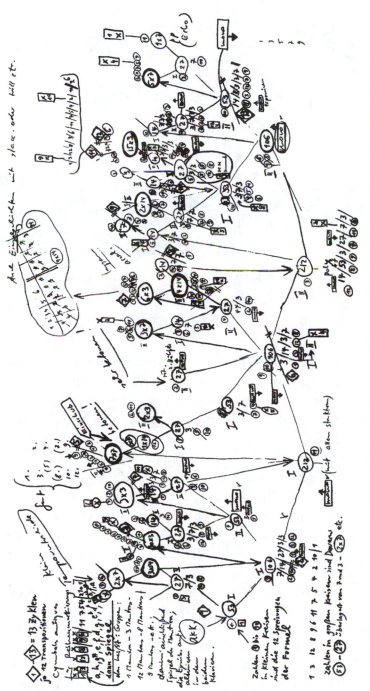

Example 3.1b Stockhausen's form scheme for *MANTRA* (1970). All Stockhausen CDs, scores, books, and videos may be ordered directly from the Stockhausen-Verlag, 51515 Kürten, Germany (www.stockhausen.org).

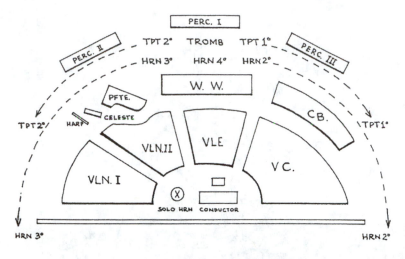

Seating Plan for Thea Musgrave's Horn Concerto

Example 3.2 Seating plan for Thea Musgrave's Horn Concerto (1974). Copyright © 1974 Chester Music Ltd.

is concerned with the psychological states of fulfillment/loss, grief, and acceptance/renewal. These are portrayed in the ancient Greek legend about Orpheus and Euridice, part of the cultural heritage of the West, a "given" object that is well known. The libretto and dramatic narrative, by Peter Zinovieff, provides the type of many-layered scenario that captured Birtwistle's imagination. The signification is worked on a myriad of levels that are juxtaposed, cut into, and reassembled. A third, and major, collaborator in the Orpheus project was Barry Anderson, who created the electronic music at IRCAM, Paris.

There is much "triplicity" conveyed in many guises throughout this work. Each of the three main characters, Orpheus, Euridice, and Aristaeus, is represented in three manifestations: singer, mime, and puppet. The opera retells the ancient story from different angles. There are three plots afoot:

1. The classical story: Orpheus' love for Euridice; his vain attempts to bring her back to life following her early death; his renown as a teacher and rival, as a musician, to Dionysus; and his appalling death at the hands of the Maenads in Northern Greece.
2. Apollo gave Orpheus the gift of music, but finally removed this power after Orpheus's skull became a famous oracle on Lesbos.

3. Aristaeus's seduction of Euridice, resulting in the loss of his power to cultivate bees and vines (honey and wine), which, however, he manages to regain after appeasing the gods.

Aspects of these three plots are woven throughout the structure (see Example 3.3a).

The diagram of the dramatic structures reveals three acts, each subdivided into three scenes of unequal duration, preceded by a *Parados* and succeeded by an *Exodos*. Each act represents a season: summer (representing fulfillment/loss), winter (representing grief), and spring (representing acceptance/renewal). Scattered amongst these parts are five dramatic threads: the Metamorphoses, the Journeys, the Ceremonies, Arches & Tides, and Passing Clouds & Allegorical Flowers. All of these, except for Arches & Tides, make three appearances. The three Metamorphoses (Man, Hero, Myth) occur in Act I, Scene 3; Act II, Scene 1; and Act III, Scene 3. The Arches take up the entirety of Act II, and the Tides occupy the whole of Act III. The first Journey (Love) takes place in Act I, Scene 1; and the second and third Journeys (Underworld, Death) both take place in Act II.

Of the three Ceremonies, the Wedding and the Funeral occur in Act I, with the Sacrifice occurring in Act III. Likewise, there are three sets of Passing Clouds & Allegorical Flowers; PC1, PC2, and AF1 float through Act I; AF2 appears at the end of the Arches in Act II; and PC3 and AF3 float through Act III. The duration of each of these six appearances is approximately 3 minutes. In all, there are 126 (3 × 42) discrete events. The effect is not unlike that of a film scenario that contains a number of disconnected narratives, which are intercut with flashbacks.

A clear and fascinating example of the detail of the structuring is to be found in Act II, the Arches (see Example 3.3b). It consists of seventeen mini-scenes, with durations of between 2 and 2.5 minutes each. Broken down like this, the composing task is much more approachable than creating a block of music lasting for 42 minutes.

The drawing of the Arches (akin to an aqueduct) and the stage diagram indicate the nature and "meaning" of each of the arches. As the central section of the opera, Act II represents the darkest journey, the doomed attempt by the grief-stricken Orpheus to enter the Underworld

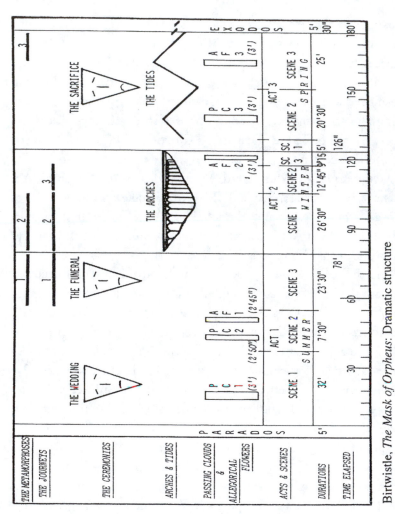

Birtwistle, *The Mask of Orpheus*: Dramatic structure

Example 3.3a Birtwistle and Zinovieff: dramatic structure for *The Mask of Orpheus* (1973–1983). Copyright Universal Edition (London). Reproduced by permission. All rights reserved.

in a hopeless effort to bring his love, Euridice, back to life. In dreams and nightmares, he descends into the lowest depths of despair. It is a metaphor for the grieving process: despair, loss, anger, anguish, denial, fantasy in the attempt to recover the loved one, and the final acceptance of the loss.

Birtwistle matches the layered dramatic scenario with layering techniques in the music. Once again, there are three musical strands, which are interwoven and clearly audible in Act II:

1. Vocal lines:
   Orpheus has both a comprehensible text and an invented language.
   Euridice sings lyrical lines.
   Charon, who rows the boat across the River Styx, has interjections.
   In addition, there is the trio of the Three Furies.
2. The orchestra:
   Woodwind flourishes, chordal melodic lines, *glissandi.*
   Horn bursts.
   Vibraphone and xylophone *roulades.*
   Harp and strings matched in *pizzicato.*
   Low brass and double bass whoops and stabs.
3. The electronic music (which marks the end of each Arch) is created from three types of sound:
   Harp, recorded playing two chords, one high note and one low note, which were analyzed, resynthesized, and transformed.
   "Electronic aura" evoking the rustle of natural sounds, bees, etc., created by hundreds of oscillators.
   Invented language derived from the phonemes in the names "Orpheus" and "Euridice," made using the CHANT program at IRCAM, Paris.

This collaborative effort has created a highly sophisticated, elaborate, and moving masterpiece. Clearly, the larger the scale of the enterprise and forces involved, the greater is the need for detailed planning.

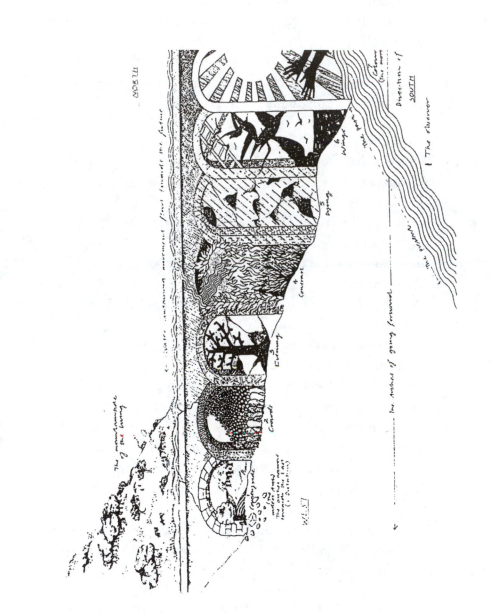

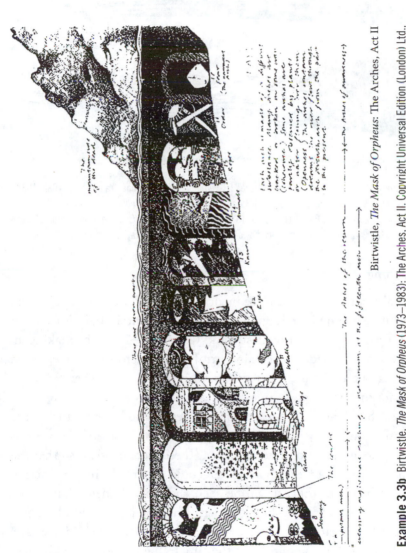

Birtwistle, *The Mask of Orpheus*: The Arches, Act II

Example 3.3b Birtwistle, *The Mask of Orpheus* (1973–1983): The Arches, Act II. Copyright Universal Edition (London) Ltd., London. Reproduced by permission. All rights reserved.

Kaija Saariaho

First sketches of the global form of *Verblendungen* for orchestra and tape.

Example 3.4a Kaija Saariaho: first sketches for *Verblendungen* for orchestra and tape (1982–1984). © 1987 from Kaija Saariaho, "Timbre and Harmony: Interpolations of Timbral Structures," *Contemporary Music Review*, Vol. 2, Part 1 (1987) 93–133, Editor-in-Chief, Nigel Osborne, issue editor, Stephen McAdams (www.tandf.co.uk). Reproduced by permission of Routledge/Taylor & Francis Books, Inc.

Graphing

Several composers start a piece by drawing the concept for their work. The Finnish composer Kaija Saariaho created the initial idea for her work *Verblendungen*, for orchestra and tape (1982–1984), by making an image: a brush, loaded with paint, firmly drawn across the canvas, then petering out as the paint is used up. This provided the overall framework for the piece (see Example 3.4a).

Kaija Saariaho (1987) has described her method of structuring the several parameters utilized in her piece. The shapes of the various layers were graphed on tracing paper. These were overlaid so that the proposed curves of each parameter could be "read" in conjunction with each other. Thus, it can be seen that the Orchestra and Tape parts begin simultaneously (along with the Dynamics and Homophony curves), creating the impression of the loaded brush image. The Tape part dips in the middle of the timeframe to reveal the Orchestra, then reemerges and is all-pervasive at the end, submerging the Orchestra. The pitch curve begins in the low register and ends in the high, being realized at this point by the Tape part. At the end, the

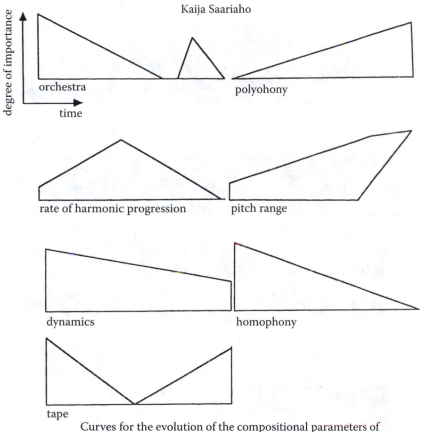

Curves for the evolution of the compositional parameters of *Verblendungen*. For each curve, time is represented on the vertical axis.

Example 3.4b Kaija Saariaho: first sketches for *Verblendungen* for orchestra and tape (1982–1984). © 1987 from Kaija Saariaho, "Timbre and Harmony: Interpolations of Timbral Structures," *Contemporary Music Review*, Vol. 2, Part 1 (1987) 93–133, Editor-in-Chief, Nigel Osborne, issue editor, Stephen McAdams (www.tandf.co.uk). Reproduced by permission of Routledge/Taylor & Francis Books, Inc.

aural result is a magical ascent of the strings that seamlessly melt into the Tape solo (see Example 3.4b).

When I came to compose my symphony in 1989, I eschewed the classical symphonic forms and created my own integrated structures. The starting point for the structure of the sound world for this symphony was very visual. Drawings were made of the pitch terrain and relative durations of the basic musical ideas. The work was fashioned into three continuous movements, the first and third being the positive and negative of each other. The titles of the movements describe their functions.

Margaret Lucy Wilkins: SYMPHONY

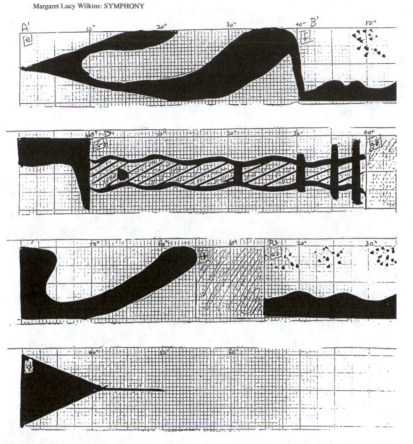

Example 3.5 Graph of Movement I, *Exposition*, of Margaret Lucy Wilkins' Symphony (1989). Reproduced by permission of the composer.   (continued)

I   *Exposition* (a setting forth of ideas)

II   *Juxtaposition* (a placing side by side)

III   *Opposition* ("contrast, antithesis, a relationship between two propositions with the same subject and predicate, but differing in quality" [*Oxford English Dictionary*])

Movement I, *Exposition*, is dramatic with its orchestral *glissandi* and sculptured textures. There are four sculptural types of musical material: A, B, C, and D. At the first exposition, each type has a duration of 40". Subsequently, the repetitions of the materials are shorter by approximately 50 percent; that is, the same amount of music is packed into a

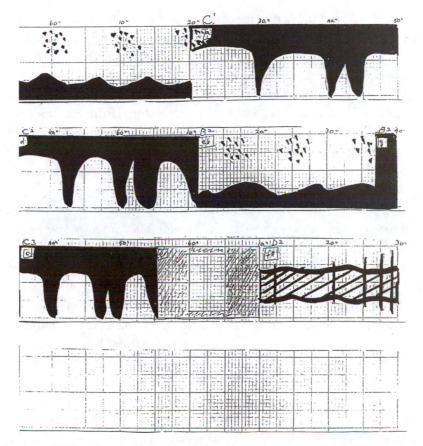

Example 3.5 (continued) Graph of Movement I, *Exposition*, of Margaret Lucy Wilkins' Symphony (1989). Reproduced by permission of the composer.

reduced space of time: 40" × 4 = 160"; 27" × 3 = 81"; 20" × 2 = 40"; 20" × 1 = 20". The repetitions of the materials are interrupted four times by unrelated music, the interruptions becoming additively longer: 5", 10", 15", 20", thus ending with the same duration as the final versions of the B, C, and D types of sculptured texture. In addition, each section is transposed, following an intervallic scheme: E + F, A+B flat, D+E flat, G+A flat, C+F sharp (G+A). The fundamental pitch is E (see Example 3.5).

This idea of creating a special structure is part of the composition process. It provides the scaffolding that supports the composition. It is a good idea to plot the pitch centers on the graph. This will ensure that the composition moves away from its starting point (the equivalent of modulation). To use another metaphor, plotting a composition is rather like planning a journey. The more ambitious the expedition, the greater is the need for preparation. If you are going exploring (to the Antarctic, or the Amazon, for example) you will not be able to keep returning home for vital equipment that you have forgotten. Forethought and imagination are vital to a successful undertaking. If the essentials for survival have been planned for, then enjoyment of the discoveries will be greater. Even a holiday to another country has to be planned and booked; however, a simple walk around the park can be pleasurably undertaken without much effort.

It is worth considering where you want to end the work, that is, whether you decide to return to the same pitch center as you began (the tonic), or whether you are actually moving the house! In general, it is best not to keep returning "home" once you've started your journey. In other words, once the piece is under way, avoid your initial pitch center, by modulating or transposing your musical materials.

Judging the success of your structural planning is often the most difficult aspect of composing. Ultimately, the real test is heard in a live performance of your work. Now, it is possible to "hear" your work on a computer in advance of experiencing a live performance. Most often, the inexperienced composer will tend to pack too much musical information into too short a space of time. This results from the fact that the task of writing down the music, by whatever method, is slow, so that the composer loses the feeling of just how long (or short) the music appears to last, in terms of experienced time, as opposed to the actual duration in seconds. Young composers can underestimate just how much music the listener can enjoy without becoming "bored." In fact, moving too quickly to yet another new idea can result in "overload." Arriving at an appropriate balance between too much and too little musical information is often a matter of experience and fine, instinctive judgment.

4

MUSICAL LANGUAGES

Multiplicity of Styles

The musical language that best expresses your musical persona is often intertwined with the concept and structure of a particular composition. No longer is there a *lingua franca* such as existed in the era of Western tonality. There appears to be a bewildering multiplicity of choices of musical language, ranging from the conservative to the exploratory. Nevertheless, viewed from the perspective of the twenty-first century, the styles that occupied composers in the twentieth century might fall into two broad camps: either tonal or non-tonal.

The essence of world music, folk music, and popular music is an emphasis on rhythm. The supremacy of melody is also a characteristic of all these styles. The unique contribution of Western Europe to the development of classical music has been that of harmony, which resulted from the contrapuntal combination of melodic lines. To this, recent Western composers have added the exploration of *timbre*, texture, and spectral music (which involves the use of microtones).

The various schools of thought that emerged and developed during the twentieth century may be broadly summarized as follows:

- Twelve-tone (Arnold Schoenberg, Anton Webern)
- *Avant garde* (Pierre Boulez, Karlheinz Stockhausen)
- Post-serial techniques (Harrison Birtwistle)
- Post-modernism (Henryk Górecki, Galina Ulstvol'skaya)
- Experimental (John Cage, Pauline Oliveros)
- Minimalism (Steve Reich, John Adams, Louis Andriessen)
- The new tonality (Judith Weir)
- Polystylicity (Alfred Schnittke)
- Spectralism (Tristan Murail, Livia Teodorescu)
- Gesture (Sofia Gubaidulina)
- Spatialization (Thea Musgrave)
- Microtonality (Iannis Xenakis, Giacinto Scelsi)
- The new complexity (Brian Ferneyhough)
- Sonic composition (Rebecca Saunders)

Just one or two composers have been suggested to represent each aesthetic school, although, in each category, there are many others. Some of these composers worked in more than one area. Xenakis's music, for example, embraces gesture and sonic composition as well as microtonality; and Gubaidulina's broad approach uses "the new tonality" and polystylicity in addition to gesture. As well as the composers mentioned, there are hundreds of other composers who work within a more conservative tradition, based on tonality or modality. Stravinsky, Prokofiev, Shostakovitch, and Messiaen are just four composers whose music has mass appeal, possibly because of their more traditional musical aesthetic.

Developing composers might choose to experiment with various styles before finding their true voice. Natural inclination will lead you to the musical style that eventually marks your identity. Indeed, some composers have developed more than one style. Igor Stravinsky's musical *oeuvre* can be divided into three distinct phases: Russian; neo-classic; and serial works. Arvo Pärt and Górecki are two composers whose early music was serial and *avant garde*, but whose later music adopted simpler styles based on Orthodox Christian music and East European folk music, respectively.

Apart from aesthetic considerations, composers need to take account of the particular performers of their work. Normally, amateur and young musicians will not be able to perform the technically demanding music of the *avant garde*, which is composed with specialist virtuoso performers in mind. Thus, it is prudent for composers to build styles that are appropriate to the capacities of the intended performers.

Parameters

The components, or parameters, of a musical style comprise the following elements:

- Rhythm (pulse)
- Pitch (line, melody; horizontal)
- Counterpoint (addition of horizontal lines, creating verticals)
- Harmony (conglomerate of vertical pitches)
- *Timbre* (individual sounds)
- Texture (counterpoint, combination of *timbres*)

At the same time that one is considering each parameter independently, it has to be borne in mind that each note, or group of notes, contains combinations of several components. Pitch, for example, cannot exist without rhythm and *timbre*. Counterpoint will involve rhythm, pitch, harmony, texture, and *timbre*.

Rhythm

Rhythm *is* music. It is the most fundamental element, yet it is often the least controlled parameter in the composing of music. Rhythm can fall into one of three categories: intuitive, functional, or constructed.

Intuitive Rhythm. A rhythm may be arrived at intuitively, that is, by accepting whatever floats into the mind at the moment of composing. In this instance, it will probably be the case that the rhythm itself is a reflection of one that is stored in the memory from hearing other pieces of music. In other words, it is not likely to be "original," but rather a (possibly distorted) memory of something previously heard.

Functional Rhythm. Functional rhythm is one that is dictated by the demands of the particular piece of music. A march, for instance, has to have four audible pulses to a bar and move at a human walking speed (left, right, left, right), precisely because the function of this particular piece of music is to move a group of people from one place to another in an orderly fashion. Marching in rhythmic unison is an effective way of doing this, with a drum providing the basic beat and speed. Similarly, folk dances have characteristic rhythms. The waltz, samba, and tango each have their own particular rhythms and *tempi* that are essential to their identities.

Constructed Rhythm. Constructed rhythm, as its name implies, is built by the composer. A particular number series, such as the *Fibonacci* (a twelfth century mathematician), might be utilized. A *Fibonacci* series progresses by adding two numbers together. Taking the last two numbers in the series and adding those together creates the next number:

$$0 + 1 = 1 \qquad 1 + 1 = 2 \qquad 1 + 2 = 3$$
$$2 + 3 = 5 \qquad 3 + 5 = 8 \qquad 5 + 8 = 13, \text{etc.}$$

Another *Fibonacci* series:

$$0 + 2 = 2 \qquad 2 + 2 = 4 \qquad 2 + 4 = 6$$
$$4 + 6 = 10 \qquad 6 + 10 = 16 \qquad 10 + 16 = 26, \text{etc.}$$

The numbers might be used to build the rhythmic units themselves. The lower numbers in the series lend themselves to this, whereas the higher numbers could be used to determine the overall number of pulses in a section, or as durations measured in seconds. Sofia Gubaidulina uses the *Fibonacci* numbers 3, 5, 8, and 13 in the opening section of her *Seven Words* (1982) for bayan, cello, and strings. Here, they indicate the durations (in seconds) of the phrases and the pauses between the *pathétique* utterances of the bayan and cello (see Example 4.1).

Alternatively, you might invent your own method of rhythmic construction.

Sieben Worte
für Violoncello, Bajan und Streicher

I. Vater, vergib ihnen, denn sie wissen nicht, was sie tun.

Sofia Gubaidulina

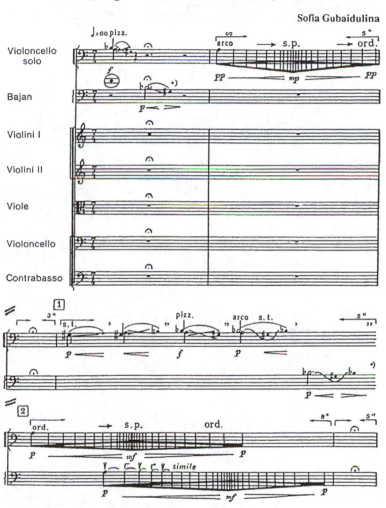

*)Nicht temperiertes Glissando. dabei Blasebalg ziehen und Taste loslassen.
Portamento: pull the bellows and release key.

Example 4.1 Sofia Gubaidulina, *Seven Words* (1982). © Copyright Musikverlag Hans Sikorski, Hamburg. Sole publishers for the United Kingdom, British Commonwealth (ex Canada), Eire and South Africa: Boosey & Hawkes Music Publishers Ltd. Reproduced by permission of Boosey & Hawkes Music Publishers Ltd.

(continued)

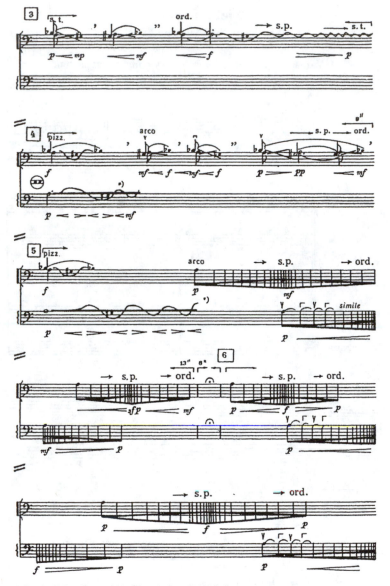

*)Der eine Unisoso-Ton macht ein Glissando, der andere bleibt liegen.
  One unison note glissando, the other held.

Example 4.1 (continued)   Sofia Gubaidulina, *Seven Words* (1982). © Copyright Musikverlag Hans Sikorski, Hamburg. Sole publishers for the United Kingdom, British Commonwealth (ex Canada), Eire and South Africa: Boosey & Hawkes Music Publishers Ltd. Reproduced by permission of Boosey & Hawkes Music Publishers Ltd.

(continued)

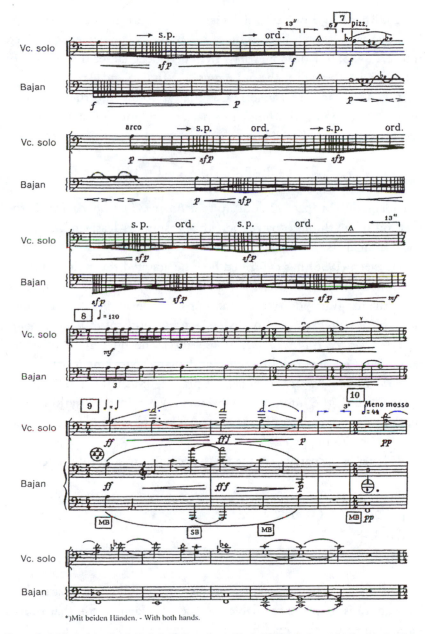

*)Mit beiden Händen. - With both hands.

Example 4.1 (continued) Sofia Gubaidulina, *Seven Words* (1982). © Copyright Musikverlag Hans Sikorski, Hamburg. Sole publishers for the United Kingdom, British Commonwealth (ex Canada), Eire and South Africa: Boosey & Hawkes Music Publishers Ltd. Reproduced by permission of Boosey & Hawkes Music Publishers Ltd.

Additive Rhythm and Subdivisions. Western music is character-ized by the rhythmic subdivision of the beat. The beat may be divided into 2, 3, 4, 5, 6, 7 or more parts. In general, the larger the number of subdivisions, the slower the pulse must be. Indian and African musics, on the other hand, use rapid pulses that are built into rhythmic pat-terns. Try clapping the following pattern, taking a fast tempo and accenting the first of each group:

$$2 + 3 + 2 + 5 + 3 + 2 + 1 + 3$$

(Incidentally, this pattern adds up to a *Fibonacci* number!) This is the method of rhythmic construction that inspired Messiaen as well as the Minimalists.

Messiaen (1956) has described how he adapted the style of Hindu rhythms for his own use. Principally, his rhythms are constructed from the irregular addition of small units, for example, the sixteenth note. Here is an example from Messiaen's *Quatuor pour la fin du temps* (*Quartet for the End of Time*; 1940–1941), the quartet in this case comprising clarinet, violin, cello, and piano. Movement VI, *Danse de la fureur, pour les sept trompettes*, is played, unusually, in unison and octaves. Thus, the interest in Movement VI is in the rhythmic and melodic development, rather than in Messiaen's unique, radiant har-monies (see Example 4.2).

At letter F, the patterns of the rhythmic units (in sixteenth notes) are:

Bar 1:   3, 5, 8, 5, 3 (a *Fibonacci* series)
Bar 2:   4, 3, 7, 3, 4
Bar 3, 4:   7, 5, 7
Bar 5, 6, 7: 5, 3, 5

This rhythmic pattern is then repeated in the following 7 bars. Each bar pattern is "non-retrogradable," to use Messiaen's term, that is, it is palindromic: whether read from left to right or from right to left, the rhythm remains the same. In addition, the pitches of this passage make a 16-note row. This row is repeated several times, being superimposed upon the rhythm. Because the number of notes in the rhythm pattern is not the same as the number of notes in the pitch row, they do not coincide. Thus, what has been created are two rows of unequal length (one of rhythm and the other of pitch) that encircle each other. Mathematically, they would eventually meet after a number of repetitions: you could multiply the number of notes in each row to find out how many times that would be.

Minimalism. A different interpretation of the influence of African and Indian music, and the use of the rapid pulse, results in minimalist music. The term "minimal" was first used in connection with a movement in the visual arts during the latter part of the twentieth century. It implies the least of every parameter, the reduction to the barest of materials. In music, the movement became identified with the pulsing pieces of American composers Steve Reich, Philip Glass, and John Adams, and in Europe with the music of Louis Andriessen. The constant repetition and pulsing have a hypnotic effect on the listener, especially because many of the works in this style have durations of approximately an hour. Steve Reich's *Drumming* (1970–1971), for example, lasts for 65 minutes.

Though the repeated patterns appear to be static for considerable time spans, they often comprise subtly altered "phasing." This is a technique whereby two or more "series" are set in motion simultaneously, then one strand becomes slightly quicker than the other, moving ahead by one pulse, or so. It is a technique that was experienced in the analog electronic music studio. Two identical tapes were played on two reel-to-reel tape recorders, starting off exactly together. Before long, one of the tape recorders, being mechanical, would play back a little ahead of the other, creating phasing. Steve Reich had the idea of transposing this technique to human performers, a challenging proposition that can be heard in his *Piano Phase* (1967) for two pianos (or two marimbas).

Piano 1 begins with a repeated figure containing 12 notes (6 + 6), which are divided between the two interlocking hands:

RH plays 2 notes × 3; LH plays 3 notes × 2.

Piano 2 joins in, playing exactly the same notes as piano 1. Then, after a few repetitions, piano 2 effects a slight *accelerando* (indicated in the score by the dotted bars) until note 2 of piano 2 coincides with note 1 of piano 1. Herein lies the difficulty in performance! This process is

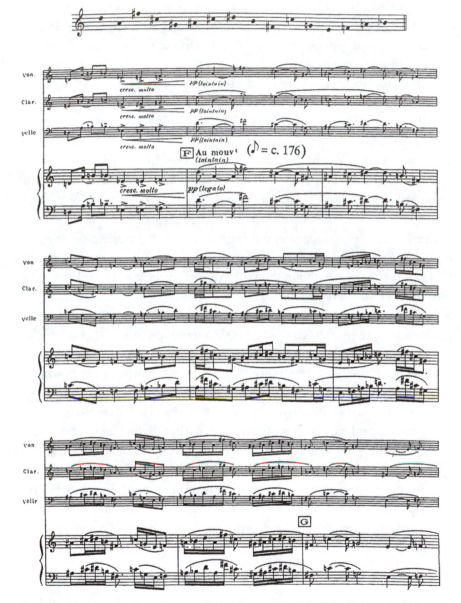

Example 4.2 Oliver Messiaen, *Quatuor pour la fin du temps* (1940–1941): VI *Danse de la fureur, pour les sept trompettes.* (continued)

Messiaen, *Quatuor pour la fin du temps*

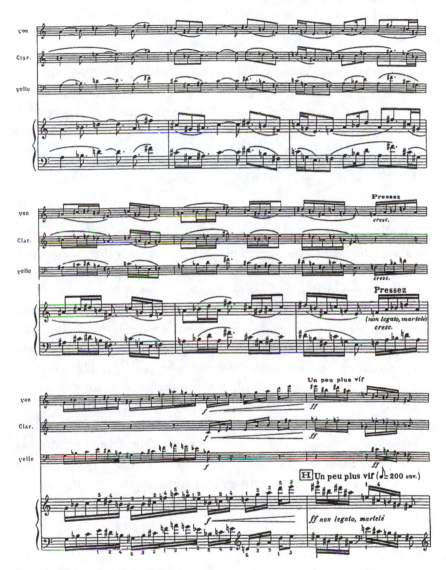

Example 4.2 (continued) Oliver Messiaen, *Quatuor pour la fin du temps* (1940–1941): VI *Danse de la fureur, pour les sept trompettes.*

repeated 12 times until note 1 coincides again in both pianos. At this point (bar 16), the 12-note figure is reduced to 8 interlocking notes: piano 1 RH plays 2 + 2; LH plays 4 × 1. At bar 17, piano 2 rejoins piano 1, but with a different set of 8 interlocking notes, creating the first harmonic change. The phasing process is repeated 8 times, until note 1 coincides in both pianos. Here (bar 27), the 8-note figure is reduced to 4 interlocking notes: piano 2 RH plays 2 × 1; LH plays 2 × 1. These 4 notes are the remnant of the second chord. At bar 28, piano 1 rejoins piano 2 with the same pitches, and the phasing process is repeated 4 times, until, once again, note 1 coincides in both pianos.

This process creates an interesting proportional structure:

12 notes	8 notes	4 notes
3:	2:	1

Thus, each of the three sections reduces by a third. However, the mathematical neatness is blurred by the fact that each "bar" is repeated a number of times, within a suggested range (for example, × 16–24), which is determined in advance by the performers.

Piano Phase demonstrates the essence of minimalism: two instruments, but one *timbre*; the pitch range remains entirely within the span of one octave, in the middle register; only five pitch classes are used; only two harmonies; one tempo; and one pulse (see Example 4.3).

Louis Andriessen has established a minimalist presence in Europe. Working with the Dutch ensembles *De Ijsbreker* and *De Volharding*, he has developed a rhythmic pulsing technique. His early work, *Hoketus* (1975–1977), for two groups of six instruments, demonstrates his approach. Referencing the medieval technique of the hoquet, the two groups alternate note by note, in rapid succession. The opening section sets up a simple rhythmic pattern:

Notes:	2]	3]	3]	4]	4]	5]	5]	6]	6]	7]	7
Silences:	8]	7]	7]	6]	6]	4]	4]	3]	3]	2]	1
Addition:	10					9					

As the number of sounding notes increases, the number of silent pulses decreases, until eventually there are continuous sounding notes. The players select their pitches from the given chord according to the

Steve Reich, *piano phase*

Example 4.3 Steve Reich, *Piano Phase* (1967).

range of their instruments, which include two each of panpipes, pianos, electric pianos, bass guitars, alto saxophones, and sets of bongos. The total effect is antiphonal, the two groups being spatially separated, but, because of the similarity of instrumentation, their identities gradually become blurred (see Example 4.4).

The setting up of processes can be enticing. However, judging when and how to break the pattern, so as to avoid mathematical predictability, is an acquired skill.

Metric Modulation. At the opposite end of the rhythmic spectrum, another American composer, Elliott Carter, works with metric modulation. This is a temporal technique that causes the underlying pulse to change speed.

Hoketus

Louis Andriessen

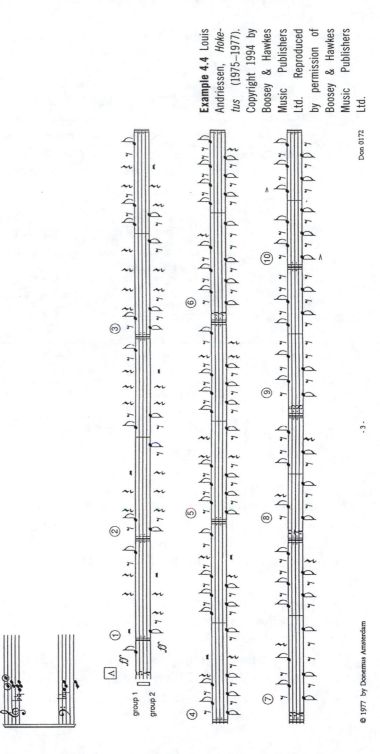

Example 4.4 Louis Andriessen, *Hoketus* (1975–1977). Copyright 1994 by Boosey & Hawkes Music Publishers Ltd. Reproduced by permission of Boosey & Hawkes Music Publishers Ltd.

Don 0172

- 3 -

Movement I of Carter's String Quartet No. 2 (1959; see Example 4.5a) makes great play of metric modulation. At bar 57, the pulse is a moderate tempo of quarter note = 112 mm., with a time signature of 3/4. The quarter note beat is subdivided into quintuplet sixteenth notes for violin I, violin II, and cello, for two bars. At bar 59, violin I continues with the quintuplet pattern, which is here notated as 2 groups of 5 sixteenth notes in a 10/16 time signature. The next bar, bar 60, sees another time signature change to 15/16, with the indication that a sixteenth note = sixteenth note. In fact, the sixteenth notes sound at the same speed between bars 58 and 60, even though the pulse has moved from simple time (quarter note beat) to compound time (dotted eighth note beat). At bar 60, there are five dotted eighth notes in the bar. At bar 61, the time signature changes yet again to 12/16 (four dotted eighth notes per bar), where it settles until bar 73.

The effect is that the pulse becomes quicker. The pulse in bar 57 is quarter note = 112 mm., with 3 quarter notes per bar. At bar 60, the pulse has become 186.7 mm. (to be precise!) with 5 dotted eighth notes per bar. The new pulse is equal to the first 3 notes of the sixteenth note quintuplet. Though the tempo changes during the course of this transition, the speed of the sixteenth note remains the same. Despite the fact that the notation (and this verbal explanation) appears to be complicated, the actual performance of this, and similar metrical modulations found in this String Quartet, is not so difficult. This is because the small subdivision of the pulse remains constant, so that the performers do not have to worry about accurately reaching mm. = 186.7 because this will occur automatically. This method is an excellent way of composing and notating accurate tempo changes, without resorting to the use of imprecise verbal instructions, such as *meno mosso, più allegro*, and so on.

Movement II of the same string quartet (see Example 4.5b) demonstrates the technique of sounding two different time signatures simultaneously. The *Presto scherzando* begins with the violin II part sounding four quarter notes per bar, while the other three parts have five quarter notes per bar. Mathematically, multiplying 4 × 5 will provide the common number, 20 (sixteenth notes), which can be divided into 4 groups of 5, or 5 groups of 4. So, the 4/4 time signature in a 5/4 bar can be

Elliott Carter, String Quartet No. 2 (1959), Movement I, Bars 54-64

Example 4.5a Elliott Carter, String Quartet No. 2 (1959): Movement I. Copyright 1961 (Renewed) by Associated Music Publishers, Inc. (BMI) International Copyright Secured. All Rights Reserved. Reprinted by permission.

Elliott Carter, String Quartet No. 2

* Alternate rhythmic notation for Violin II indicating how its part should sound, within itself. This alternate notation also indicates the correct length of resonance of each note, regardless of the note-values which appear in the actual part.

* Die zusätzliche Notenlinie gibt das eigentliche Metrum der 2. Violine an. Für die genaue Länge der einzelnen Noten sind ebenfalls die Notenwerte dieser zusätzlichen Linie und nicht die der regulären Stimme maßgebend.

AMP-9609 62

Example 4.5b Elliott Carter, String Quartet No. 2 (1959): Movement II. Copyright 1961 (Renewed) by Associated Music Publishers, Inc. (BMI) International Copyright Secured. All Rights Reserved. Reprinted by permission.

sounded by placing an accent on every fifth sixteenth note. Carter notates the violin II part like this, but also adds the 4/4 version underneath so that his original intention becomes clear to the performer.

Pitch/Line

Next to be considered is the pitch parameter. A *scale* or *mode* traditionally governs the choice of pitch material. Other systems developed during the twentieth century have included the creation of *rows* (12-notes, or other sizes), and arising from this, *note cells* and the application of *serial variants*. These represent the raw materials from which the building is constructed.

Scales and Modes. Common to all musical systems, the scale is a series of notes that usually progresses by small pitch intervals, for

Example 4.6 Scales and modes.

example, a minor 2nd or a Major 2nd (m2, M2) in Western tuning. Example 4.6 shows the scales that define the Western tonal system, familiar to all who have been brought up with this large corpus of music. Prior to the development of this system, composers employed by the mediaeval Christian Church used modes, which themselves evolved from the early pre-Christian Greek modes. Secular music, in the form of folk songs from many European countries, also uses these modes. Non-Western countries have developed yet other modes that are tuned according to their own systems, which do not necessarily correspond to the equal temperament tuning of Western music. All are available for use by any composer.

The pattern of m2 and M2 determines the medieval mode. The Phrygian mode is characterized by the m2 between notes 1/2 and 5/6, the remainder being M2. The Lydian mode has a m2 between notes 4/5 and 7/8, the remainder being M2. The Ionian mode became the major scale of the tonal system. The Aeolian mode became the descending form of the melodic minor scale. This appears to be the only Western scale that is different in the ascending and descending forms. The chromatic scale consists entirely of m2, while the Whole Tone scale comprises six intervals of a M2, as its name suggests. There are five forms of the Pentatonic (5-note) scale, much used in music of the Far East. These depend on the starting note. A Pentatonic scale is made up of three intervals of a M2 and 2 intervals of a m3.

Some Scottish folk songs also use the Pentatonic scale. *Auld Lang Sine* can be played on the black notes of a keyboard (which represent one form of the Pentatonic scale), beginning C#, F#. All of the scales and modes may be transposed to any starting note.

Ave Generosa, Hymn to Saint Mary (twelfth century), by Hildegard von Bingen, is a typical example of her free-flowing melodic lines. Written to be sung by the nuns in the Convent at Rupertsberg where she was Abbess, it uses the mediaeval modal system of the time. Verse 1 is clearly in the Aeolian mode, A–A. However, verses 2–7, with the B flats, are in the Phrygian mode on A, the "tonic." Characteristic of Hildegard's melodic lines are the leaps of P5 and P4, unusual for the time, which outline the tonic and dominant of the mode.

Hindustani scale types

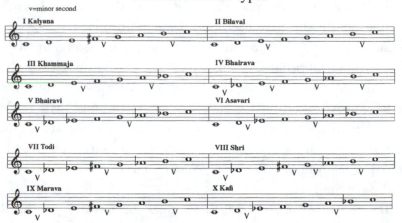

Example 4.7 Ten scale types found in Hindustani music theory.

Non-Western Scales and Modes. Scales and modes from non-Western music are also stimulating. Example 4.7 shows ten scale types found in Hindustani music theory. As can be observed, several are the same as Western modes:

I   Kalyána is the same as the Lydian mode
II   Bilával is the same as the Ionian mode (which became the Major scale)
III   Khammája is the same as the Mixolydian mode
V   Bhairaví is the same as the Phrygian mode
VI   Ásávarí is the same as the Aeolian mode
X   Káfí is the same as the Dorian mode

However, numbers IV, VII, VIII, and IX are quite distinct from the pattern of the Western modes. Four intervals of a M2 within a scale create a distinctive character, as in the Bhairava and Shri modes.

These modes play a unique role in Indian music. They can also be used by composers from other cultures in their own explorations of alternative tonalities.

Twentieth Century Use of Scales and Modes. Leaping to the twentieth century, Claude Debussy's famous *Syrinx* (1913) for solo flute is an expressive single line that takes into account the particular *timbral* qualities of the instrument. The husky lower register, utilizing bottom E flat, D, D flat, and C of the flute, occupies the middle of the piece as pitch centers. Debussy makes use of a combination of scales within the line: Pentatonic between bars 10 and 12; Chromatic between bars 13 and 16; Whole Tone in the last 2 bars. The opening motif, which appears several times, B flat–A flat–G flat, suggests the key of G flat major, but is decorated with B–A–G, suggesting G major and producing bitonality: G + G flat majors. Here, a limpid, liquid line for one instrument alone is created from the most basic of musical pitch materials, yet it is haunting in its beauty (see Example 4.8).

Quarter Tone Scales. Per Nørgård's *The Secret Melody* (Movement I from *Libro per Nobuko*, 1993; see Example 4.9) for violin solo is entirely made from arcs that outline chromatic scales. Also incorporated are quarter tones, which divide the smallest interval of Western music (a semitone) into two. Of particular interest are Nørgård's inventive rhythms, which include metric modulation.

Invented Scales. In addition to these traditional scale forms, it is possible to invent your own. Because the conventional scales are built from small intervals, you might try creating your own pattern of tones and semitones (see Messiaen 1956, Chapter 16). Messiaen has created his own "Seven Modes of Limited Transposition." As their name suggests, these are modes that, because of their construction, can be transposed only a few times. They are created logically from note cells consisting of only a few intervals.

Mode 1 is, in fact, the Whole Tone scale, built from one interval: M2.
Mode 2 is built from a 3-note cell containing m2, M2.
Mode 3 is built from a 4-note cell: M2, m2, m2.
Mode 4 is built from a 5-note cell: m2, m2, m3, m2.
Mode 5 is built from a 4-note cell: m2, M3, m2.
Mode 6 is built from a 5-note cell: M2, M2, m2, m2.
Mode 7 is built from a 6-note cell: m2, m2, m2, M2, m2.

The intervallic pattern is repeated from the last note of each cell, until the octave is reached. Thus, there are different numbers of notes per octave: 6 in Modes 1 and 5; 8 notes (known as the octatonic scale)

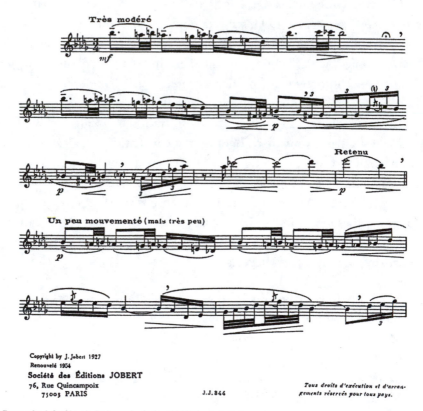

Example 4.8   Claude Debussy's *Syrinx* (1913) for solo flute.

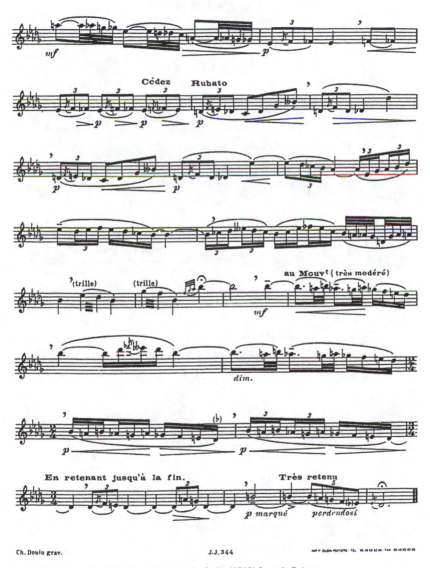

Example 4.8 (continued) Claude Debussy's *Syrinx* (1913) for solo flute.

LIBRO PER NOBUKO

for violin solo

SONATA
THE SECRET MELODY

I
PROLOGUE

*) According to the mood of the soloist, the prologue may or may not be repeated.
By repetition stop playing at a freely chosen moment before reaching the last bar.

WH 30388   Copyright © 1997 by Edition Wilhelm Hansen, Copenhagen   ISBN 87 598 0909 4

Example 4.9 Per Nørgård, *The Secret Melody* (1997), Movement I from *Libro per Nobuko*. Copyright 1993 Edition Wilhelm Hansen AS, Copenhagen.

in Modes 2, 4, and 6; 9 notes in Mode 3; and 10 notes in Mode 7 (see Example 4.10a).

Returning to Messiaen's *Quatuor pour la fin du temps*, we can observe his "Modes of Limited Transposition" in context (see Example 4.10b). Movement VII, *Fouillis d'arcs-en-ciel, pour l'Ange qui annonce la fin du temps* (*Gatherings of Rainbows, for the Angel Who Announces the End of Time*) begins with a melody played high on the "passionate" A-string of the cello. Accompanying the cello is the piano, which plays chords that appear to be tonal. In fact, both the cello melody and the harmonies are derived from Messiaen's Mode 2 in its first transposition (see Example 4.10a).

Divisions of the Octave. The traditional scales and modes occupy the space within one octave. The most common division of the octave is into 7 different pitch classes. The exceptions are :

- Pentatonic scale, dividing the octave into 5 pitch classes
- Whole tone scale, dividing the octave into 6 pitch classes
- Chromatic scale, dividing the octave into 12 pitch classes

Messiaen's Modes of Limited Transposition

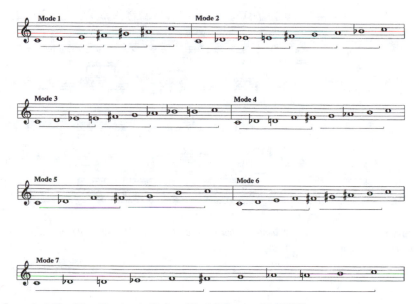

Example 4.10a Oliver Messiaen's *Modes of Limited Transposition* (1956).

Messiaen, *Quatuor pour la fin du temps*

VII. Fouillis d'arcs-en-ciel, pour l'Ange qui annonce la fin du Temps

Example 4.10b Oliver Messiaen *Quattuor pour la fin du temps* (1945): VII *Fouillis d'arcs-en-ciel, pour l'Ange qui annonce la fin du Temps.*

Invented Scales

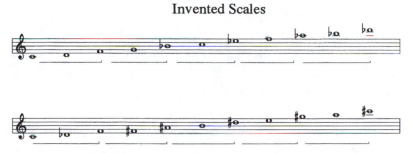

Example 4.11 Invented scales.

Added to the above are Messiaen's modes that divide the octave into 6, 8, 9, and 10 pitch classes. However, scales need not be limited to encompass one octave. Using intervals larger than the M2, it is possible to construct scales that exceed the octave range. Scale 1 (see Example 4.11) is built from a cell of M2, m3; scale 2 below is built from a cell of m2, M3.

Twelve-Tone Method. An alternative method of organizing pitch material, apart from using scales and modes (traditional or invented), was developed by Arnold Schoenberg at the start of the twentieth century. It arose from the extreme chromaticism of the music of the late nineteenth century (for example, Wagner, Liszt, César Franck) that stretched the tonal system to its limits. In adopting the chromatic scale, Schoenberg's new system equalized the notes, abandoning the hierarchic structure of tonic, dominant, and so on. Indeed, the equality of the twelve-tone system could be interpreted as reflecting the new trend towards social democracy that was sweeping Europe at the turn of the twentieth century.

In the strictest manifestation of the twelve-tone method, all twelve chromatic notes are arranged to form a *row*, which is used in place of the scale or mode. Each chromatic note is used only once within the row. The entire composition is built from the invented row and its variants. Schoenberg's Wind Quintet (1924) was an early large-scale work in which he used his new method. Example 4.12a shows the row that Schoenberg developed for this work.

It is interesting to observe how Schoenberg used his twelve-tone row in the opening bars of his Wind Quintet (see Example 4.12b). First, we need to establish that the score is notated at sounding pitch; that is, the

Schoenberg, Wind Quintet: Row

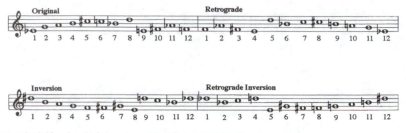

Example 4.12a Arnold Schoenberg, Wind Quintet (1924): The Row.

clarinet and horn parts are not transposed. Next, we need to determine what is the original row (review Example 4.12a). Then, we should work out the variants of the row:

- The *retrograde* is the original row written backwards.
- The *inversion* is obtained by going in the opposite direction to the original, by the same interval. For example, the first interval is a M3 ascending (E flat–G), so the inversion is a M3 descending (E flat–C flat, or D sharp–B enharmonically changed). This is the variant that needs the most care in working out.
- The *retrograde inversion* is the inversion written backwards.
- All four variants can be transposed 12 times, making 48 available in total.

The full original row is played linearly by the flute (bars 1–6). This is accompanied in such a way that tones 1–6 (played by the flute) are played against tones 7–12 scattered amongst the other four instruments and sustained to form chords (bars 1–3). Starting in bar 3, the oboe, clarinet, horn, and bassoon sound tones 1–6 against tones 7–12 played by the flute (bars 3–6). In bar 6, the entire original row is heard as a chord progression:

The clarinet plays tones 1, 2, 3
The oboe plays tones 4, 5, 6
The horn plays tones 7, 8, 9
The flute plays tones 10, 11, 12

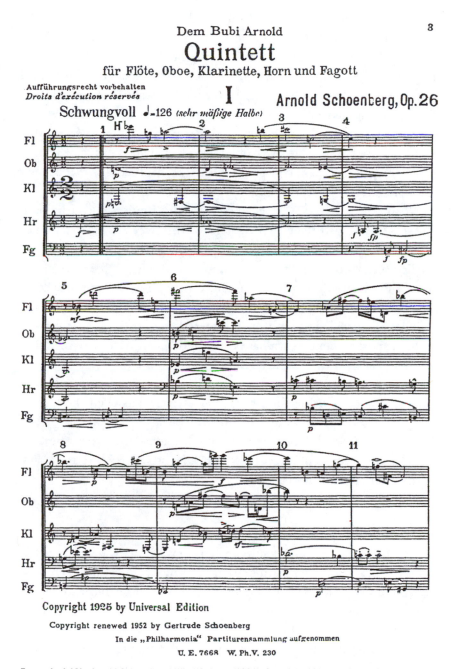

Example 4.12b Arnold Schoenberg, Wind Quintet (1924). Copyright 1925, renewed 1952 by Universal Edition A. G. Vienna. Reproduced by permission. All rights reserved.

The last tone of the original row (F) becomes the first tone of the retrograde, which is played in its entirety by the flute in bars 7–9. This is accompanied contrapuntally by the retrograde tones 7–12 heard in the horn (bars 7–8); original tones 7, 8, 9, then retrograde tones 7–12 heard in the bassoon (bars 7–8); retrograde tones 1–9 heard in the clarinet (bars 8-9) and completed with tones 10–12 played above by the flute (bar 9); and retrograde tones 1–6 heard in the oboe (bar 9). Thus, it can be seen that the row is used to generate a web of interconnected note cells that are used contrapuntally or as harmonic progressions. (See Brindle [1977] and Rufer [1954] for more complete information about the twelve-tone method.)

Notable composers, for example, Pierre Boulez and Elisabeth Lutyens, developed their own versions of the twelve-tone system, not using it as strictly as Schoenberg initially indicated. Several others applied serial techniques to every parameter. After much experience of using this system during the twentieth century, many composers came to the conclusion that the use of all twelve tones was not essential, and individually decided to limit pitch materials to more manageable note cells. Almost a circular path has been trodden, curiously arriving, via a different route, at the invented scales made out of repeated note cells.

Perhaps the most enduring compositional legacy to emerge from the experience of using the twelve-tone system has been the importance of the interval as a fundamental building block. Instead of using scales or modes, or even rows, pitch materials can be generated by selecting a series of intervals which may be inverted, retrograded, permutated, or transposed.

Pitch/Harmony

Piling up notes vertically results in harmony. Perhaps more than any other musical parameter, harmony suggests mood and atmosphere. The collection of vertical intervals determines the consonant or dissonant effect of any particular chord.

Tonal Chords. The tonal system was based on the *overtone series*; that is, the harmonics obtained from any fundamental tone. However, equal temperament produces pitches that only approximately match the "natural" harmonics. Apart from the interval of the P8 (the octave), the other intervals that make up an overtone series (that is, the fifth, third, seventh, second, fourth, and sixth, followed by microtonal intervals above the fundamental tone) are close to, but not the same as, the normal notational spellings. The chords of the tonal system principally use triads comprising intervals of the P8/P1, P5/P4, M3/m6, and m3/M6.

Added Note Chords. Taking the tonal triad as the starting point, other notes may be added, such as the 7th and 9th. Added to a dominant triad, these become the dominant 7th and dominant 9th chords. However, the 7th and 9th can be added to *any* tonal triad, not only to the dominant chord. In addition, why stop at the 9th? Try adding the 11th, 13th, and 15th. For example, the 15th is the same pitch class as the root of the chord, but two octaves higher (see Example 4.13). Carrying this process of piling up the interval of a third (M or m) to its conclusion, it becomes possible to build a chord of all twelve pitch classes.

Almost any vertical collection of pitches can be classified in terms of the tonal system. It is possible to create a harmony from any number of degrees of the chord. Harmonies comprising 3 + 9 + 13, or 5 + 11 + m15 + m19 above a root, will result in interesting chords. In addition, each pitch may be transposed into a different octave (this is called *octave displacement*). Because it became increasingly difficult and contorted to analyze these chords in terms of the tonal system, it was generally thought unnecessary to attempt do so.

Non-Tonal Harmony: Intuitive or Constructed. If we decide not to use the tonal system, what governs our choice of intervals with which to build chords? We can arrive at some interesting chords quite intuitively, simply by placing our hands on a keyboard and "finding" some harmonies. By using our ears, we can decide whether or not the particular conglomeration of notes is satisfactory for our purpose. The effect of the harmony can be changed by altering one or more notes of the chord. This method can produce some interesting results that otherwise might not have been discovered.

Alternatively, chords can be constructed in a more intellectual way, by inventing a logical method. The starting point could be the tonal system. A tonal triad consists of M3 + m3, producing a major triad, or reversed, m3 + M3, producing a minor triad. Logically following from this, it is possible to construct chords that use intervals other than the third (see Example 4.14a, Example 4.14b, and Example 4.14c).

Added Note Chords

Example 4.13 Added note harmony.

Chords

Built from one interval

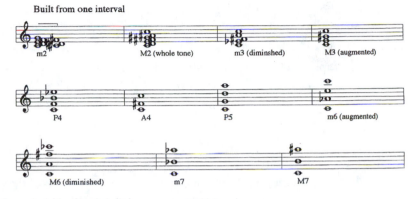

Example 4.14a Chords built from one repeated interval.

Built from 2 intervals

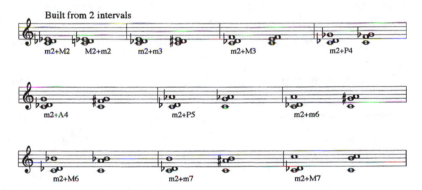

Example 4.14b Chords built from two intervals.

Combined intervals

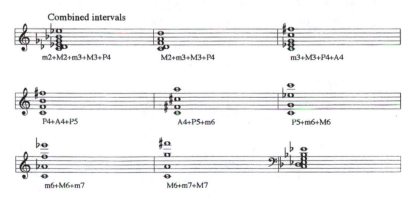

Example 4.14c Chords built from a combination of interval

Inversions. The first inversion of a major chord consists of m3 + P4, and for the minor chord, M3 + P4. The second inversion consists of P4 + M3, or P4 + m3, for major and minor triads, respectively. Following from this, the next logical step would be to construct chords from two intervals; Example 4.14b uses a m2 plus one other interval. Next, you could work out a series of chords based on M2 plus one other interval, and so on, until you have a list of all possible chords using this logical system.

As with the tonal system, each of the chords can be placed in inversion, that is, the bottom note is put on top. See Example 4.15 for the first chord of the Combined Intervals in inversion. There will be as many inversions as there are notes in the chord.

The aural effect of the chord appears to alter according to its register and position, even though the same pitch classes are involved. In addition to the inversions, each of these chords can be transposed twelve times. (See Hindemith [1945] for a very full account of the construction of chords.)

Harmonic Progressions. A *harmonic progression*, or succession of chords, can be created by following any of the methods that we've discussed. If stylistic consistency is a consideration, then chords using the same intervallic construction will produce the required result. If a consonant mood is aimed for, select "consonant" intervals. Generally, these will include: M2, M3, m6, m3, M6, P4, P5, P8, and P1. "Dissonant" intervals will create a harsher effect, useful for suggesting moods of anger, conflict, fear, or mystery. These include m2, A4/D5, m7, and M7. Always, the ear should be the final judge of the result.

An interesting use of an unusual progression of tonal chords can be heard in Ralph Vaughan Williams's *Sinfonia Antarctica* (1949). Other-

Chords in Inversion

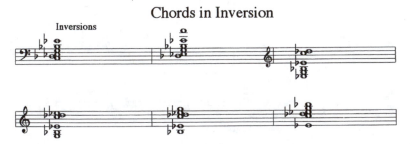

Example 4.15 Chords in inversion.

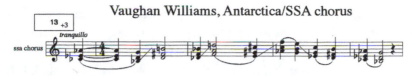

Example 4.16a Ralph Vaughan Williams, *Sinfonia Antarctica* (1949): SSA chorus.

Vaughan Williams, Antarctica

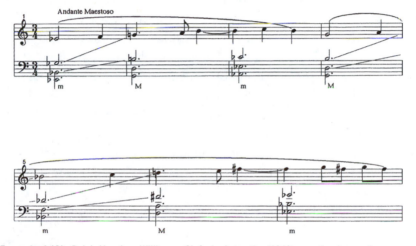

Example 4.16b Ralph Vaughan Williams, *Sinfonia Antarctica* (1949): opening harmonic progression. Copyright Oxford University Press 1953. Extracts reproduced by permission.

wise known as Symphony No. 7, it was developed from Vaughan Williams's score for the film *Scott of the Antarctic* (1947). The icy wastes of the Antarctic are suggested by the use of a wind machine as part of the orchestral palette, and the loneliness is conjured with the sound of the disembodied female choir floating over the desolate soundscape (see Example 4.16a).

The haunting effect is created by the parallel first inversion triads, as well as the false relations between the alto part and the soprano 1 part. In bar 2, the alto B flat is contradicted in the next beat by the B natural of soprano 1. This pattern is repeated in bar 3 (alto D flat to soprano 1 D natural) and bars 3–4 (alto E to soprano 1 F/E sharp). A descending form is heard in bar 4 (soprano 1 E to alto E flat).

The opening melody (see Example 4.16b) outlines a whole tone scale in the first phrase, followed by an ascending melodic minor scale in the second phrase. This is accompanied by parallel tonal triads that alternate between minor and major. Once again, a series of false relations is heard. The progression of the tonal chords is characterized by rises of the interval of a third: bars 1–2, E flat m – GM = M3; bars 4–5, GM – B flat m = m3; bars 5–6, B flat m – DM = M3.

Benjamin Britten's atmospheric *Sea Interludes*, from his opera *Peter Grimes* (1945), also use tonal chords to create the effect of spaciousness. However, Britten superimposes tonal triads in different keys upon each other, a technique known as *bitonality*. Bitonality indicates that two keys are sounded together, whereas *polytonality* indicates many keys sounding together.

Sea Interlude No. 1, Dawn, makes use of widely separated tonal chords, the bass line suggesting the key of D, while the horn and trombone harmonies of AM and BM could belong to the key of EM (see Example 4.17).

This movement comprises just three musical ideas: the opening melody played high by the flute and violins in unison and decorated with grace notes; an *arpeggio* sixteenth-note figure played by clarinets, harp, and violas in unison; and the brass chords. The sixteenth note *arpeggio* figure is built from the interval of a third.

Harmonic Fields. Scottish composer James MacMillan demonstrates the expressivity of the technique of *harmonic fields* in his orchestral work *The Confession of Isobel Gowdie* (1990). The opening 64 bars, with a duration of over five minutes, gradually build a chord of the Lydian mode on C. Starting with C + D sounding together in clarinets, bassoons, and horns, the third note to be added is G, in bar 7. The most characteristic note of the Lydian mode, the raised fourth-degree F sharp, follows in bar 9. The lower five notes of the mode are completed with the addition of the E in bar 11 (C, D, G, F sharp, E). The remaining two notes of the mode, the B followed by the A,

Example 4.17 Benjamin Britten, *Sea Interlude* (1945): No. 1, *Dawn*, bars 10–13. Copyright 1945 by Boosey & Hawkes Music Publishers Ltd. Reproduced by permission of Boosey & Hawkes Music Publishers Ltd.

are added in the two *divisi* cello parts, bars 16 and 17, sounding below the middle range modal cluster. With the notes of the mode complete at this point, MacMillan works with only this material until bar 64. The choice of the Lydian mode symbolizes traditional seventeenth century Scottish folk music, pertinent to the extra musical program of the work.

Searing *glissandi* played by the strings, and a particularly prominent scurrying figure for the violas, create the dour and tragic atmosphere suggested by the subject matter. From the opening, centered in the middle of the pitch territory, the texture fans outwards, eventually to encompass a range of over six octaves at the intense climax, bars 54–56 (see Example 4.18).

Counterpoint

The simultaneous sounding of two or more independent musical lines results in *counterpoint*. MacMillan's *The Confession of Isobel Gowdie* (see Example 4.18) has ten parts, all *divisi* strings, each independent of the others. While the lines work horizontally, they will automatically create vertical harmonies. It is important to take account of the vertical results of the horizontal combinations. In the case of the MacMillan example, the vertical combinations all fit the overall harmonic field, outlined by the Lydian mode that has operated since the start of the work, plus a few passing chromatic notes.

Attributes of counterpoint include the following:

- Combination of lines, resulting in harmony
- Complementary rhythms
- Specific devices, such as imitation and canon

Historically, counterpoint resulted from the singing together of two or more melodic lines, and thus preceded formal harmonic systems. Nevertheless, the combination of several independent melodic lines will result in harmonies. It will be interesting to examine some contrapuntal music from past centuries and to note techniques developed by earlier composers.

Many of the fourteenth-century composers used fascinating contrapuntal devices in the motets which they composed as part of their duties for the Christian Church. Guillaume de Machaut (1300–1377) used the technique of *isorhythm* in several of his motets. *S'il estoit nulz*

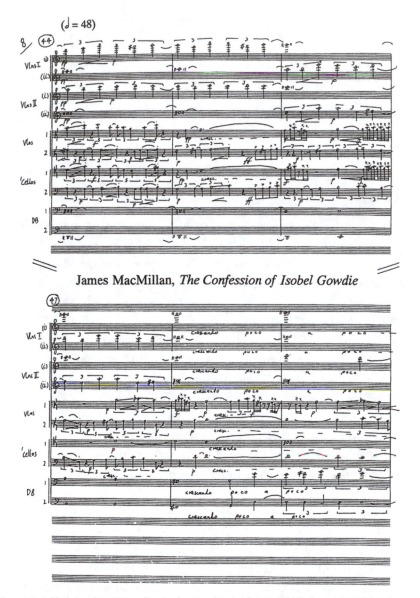

James MacMillan, *The Confession of Isobel Gowdie*

Example 4.18 James MacMillan, *The Confession of Isobel Gowdie* (1990). Copyright 1992 by Boosey & Hawkes Music Publishers Ltd. Reproduced by permission of Boosey & Hawkes Music Publishers Ltd.

Example 4.18 (continued) James MacMillan, *The Confession of Isobel Gowdie* (1990). Copyright 1992 by Boosey & Hawkes Music Publishers Ltd. Reproduced by permission of Boosey & Hawkes Music Publishers Ltd.

is a three-part motet based on the Latin plainsong *Et Gaudebit Cor Vestrum* (see Davison and Apel [1974], no. 44). In fact, it is a multitextual and bilingual motet, the two upper voices singing two different poems in French (*S'il estoit nulz* and *S'amour tous amans joir*), and the bottom voice singing the plainsong in Latin. The plainsong is heard in the tenor (meaning "holding") voice, which is actually the bass of the trio. The plainsong is sung in long notes, and notated in 3/2. Above, the two alto voices (sung by men) have faster-moving counterpoint, notated in 6/8. Thus, three bars of 6/8 fit into one bar of 3/2.

An *isorhythm* is a rhythm that is repeated throughout a section, or, in this case, the entire movement. It is similar to an *ostinato*, although only the rhythm is repeated, not the pitch. The repeated rhythm is called a *talea*. The talea in *S'il estoit nulz* is notated in Example 4.19a.

Usually, the plainchants that underpinned many of the motets of this era were taken from the repertory of Gregorian chant, a kind of self-reference. However, a notable exception was the use of the fifteenth-century French secular song *L'Homme Armé* (*The Armed Man*). This popular song was used as a *cantus firmus* between the fifteenth and seventeenth centuries, and even later, in the twentieth century (see Example 4.19b).

Guillaume Dufay (c. 1400–1474) uses it in his four-voice *Missa L'Homme Armé* (Davison and Apel [1974], no. 66). In the *Kyrie*, the first phrase of *L'Homme Armé* can be traced entering in the tenor voice in bars 5–8. The second phrase occurs in the same voice, bars 16–20. Above and below, the two alto voices and the bass weave contrapuntal lines of extraordinary rhythmic virtuosity.

The *Agnus Dei III* is a remarkable example of the contrapuntal complexity achieved by the *avant garde* of the fifteenth century. A clue to the "puzzle" of the movement is placed at the head: *"Canon: Cancer eat plenus et redeat medius"* (*"Let the crab proceed full and return half"*). On inspection, it can be seen that the *L'Homme Armé* melody can be traced as follows:

• The first phrase in retrograde (bars 9–1) is heard in long notes in the tenor, bars 1–10 of the *Agnus Dei*
• The second phrase in retrograde (bars 20–10) is heard in long notes in the tenor, bars 13–24
• The third phrase in retrograde (bars 29–21) is heard in long notes in the tenor, bars 28–38

Guillaume de Machaut

Example 4.19a Guillaume de Machaut, *S'il estoit nulz* (14th century).

L'homme armé

Example 4.19b Anonymous, *L'Homme Armé* (15th century).

From bar 39 to the end of the movement, the *L'Homme Armé* melody can be heard in its entirety, in its original form, and in notes of half the value. Thus, the final third of the piece has the effect of accumulating in rhythmic excitement. Around the *cantus firmus* melody, the other three voices sing complex, independent contrapuntal lines.

Josquin des Près (c. 1440–1521) creates a *mensuration canon* in the *Agnus Dei* of his *Missa l'Homme Armé* (Davison and Apel [1974], no.

89). The motto, *"Ex una voce tres" ("From one voice comes three")* indicates how the single line of music should be interpreted:

- The soprano voice sings the entire given melody in triple time.
- The tenor voice sings the first third of the melody in duple time (one note sung in the time of three of the soprano part).
- The bass voice sings the first two-thirds of the melody, also in duple time (two notes in the time of three of the soprano part). Thus, the bass uses durations that are half the value of the tenor part.

In addition, the original melody is transposed. The soprano and bass voices sing the line an octave apart in the tonic, while the tenor has a version transposed to the dominant. The movement is in the Dorian mode.

Turning to the twentieth century, Peter Maxwell Davies, during his student days, was fascinated by his study of early music. He even composed his own work, *Missa super l'homme armé,* in 1971 for his ensemble, the Fires of London. It is a parodistic music theater piece with several binary opposites: Christ/Antichrist, sacred/secular, and establishment music/antiestablishment. A plurality of styles is used, ranging from fifteenth century motet, to pastiche realization of eighteenth century continuo, to twentieth-century fox trot dance. The fifteenth century popular melody appears in many guises throughout the work. At the very beginning, it can be heard played by the piccolo above the opening flourish. It is heard intoned by the handbells throughout the first section, which itself is a jaunty version of a Renaissance instrumental fantasia.

At letter J, Peter Maxwell Davies adopts the device of a mensuration canon. The fundamental pulse, 3/2, is upheld by the keyboard (at this point, a harmonium), violin, and handbells (which outlines the *L'Homme Armé* theme). Against this, the clarinet plays in 9/4, that is, 3 quarter notes per minim, or a ratio of 9:6 per bar. The cello simultaneously plays in a ratio of 7:6 per bar. Thus, three different speeds are played against each other: 9:7:6. An aspect of triplicity is reflected on many different levels within the work. Here, it is embedded in a contrapuntal technique that emanates from at least as early as the fifteenth century (see Example 4.20).

Peter Maxwell Davies, *Missa super l'homme armé*

B. & H. 20472

Example 4.20 Peter Maxwell Davies, *Missa super l'homme armé* (1971); Letter J. Copyright 1978 by Boosey & Hawkes Music Publishers Ltd. Reproduced by permission of Boosey & Hawkes Music Publishers Ltd.

Peter Maxwell Davies addresses various other rhythmic/contrapuntal "problems" within this work. Negotiating movement from pulsed to non-pulsed music is effected by the gradual introduction of "free" material in one part, followed in turn by others. This can be heard at letter G, *Tempo di foxtrot*. At letter N, following the 7/16 passage, the harmonium plays independently of the other instruments: *con amore*, a half note = mm. 60, against *Tempo di quickstep*, eighth note = mm. 112. The treatment of the old music becomes progressively more outrageous, ending with the pandemonium in the final section.

Canon can be heard in Górecki's Symphony No. 3, *Symphony of Sorrowful Songs* (1976). Movement I, *Lament of the Holy Cross*, is made up of a canon which starts in the lowest range, played by the double basses (see Example 4.21). It ascends through the strings, winding its way slowly and intensely until the central section. Here a soprano sings a fifteenth-century Polish lament, in which Mary begs her dying son to speak to her. Following this, the canon descends through the strings, making an arch-shaped structure: ascending canon/song/descending canon. The canonic *cantus firmus* is based on the Aeolian mode, on E. Nevertheless the relentless tread of the simple canon makes this a powerful movement, with a duration of 27 minutes.

Fugue. In a tribute to J. S. Bach, Stravinsky imitates a baroque fugal exposition at the start of Movement II of his *Symphony of Psalms* (1930; see Example 4.22). Oboe 1 states the five-bar *subject* in C minor, complete with leaps, *staccato* notes, and sixteenth note rests, all of which are helpful to wind players. The *real answer* (that is, the *subject* exactly transposed) is played by flute 1 in the dominant, G minor. Against this, oboe 1 plays the *counter-subject*, a contrastingly smooth, chromatic line, moving in sixteenth notes, with tied notes and syncopation. A two-bar *codetta* is added before the third entry at figure 2 (see Example 4.22). The *codetta* has the effect of delaying the entry of the next part, thus destroying any sense of predictability in the statements of the *subject* and *answer*. At figure 2, flute 3 enters with the *subject*, again in the tonic, but an octave lower than the first entry. The *counter-subject* is played by flute 1, transposed into C minor to fit the third entry in the tonic. Oboe 1 continues with a free part that contrasts rhythmically with the two flutes. The third entry is answered by the fourth, played by oboe 2 in the dominant, again an octave lower than the first *answer*. The *counter-subject* is hinted at in the flute 3 part. All four voices play in counterpoint, bringing the fugal exposition to a close. (For further study of "the art of fugue," see Horsley 1966; Mann 1958; Nalden 1969; and Oldroyd 1977.)

The beauty of Bach's counterpoint lies in the fact that both the vertical and the horizontal aspects were cleverly calculated. All of Bach's contrapuntal lines could be accounted for within the tonal harmonic system, as if laid on a grid. Chromatic harmonies, accented passing notes, and *appoggiaturas* were all part of Bach's formidable technical equipment. Since the collapse of the formal tonal system, composers have a degree of freedom not available to composers of the "Common Practice" era. Nevertheless, the most convincing contrapuntal writing takes account of some logical harmonic outcomes.

Timbre and Texture

Timbre (French) is the name given to a particular sound made by an individual instrument. A texture is made from a combination of different *timbres*, usually involving several instruments or voices or both.

Each individual instrument has its own collection of *timbres*, or sonic colors. Try playing a chord (of your own invention) at the top of a piano. Then play the same chord in the bottom register of the piano. You will notice that the two are hardly recognizable as being the same set of pitch classes. Thus we can observe that the piano has a variety of *timbres*.

Each of the four strings of a violin has its own tone quality. The sweet, top E-string is wildly different from the bottom, sultry G-string. The particular quality of the G-string is often exploited by composers who mark a passage *sul G*. Though the notes concerned could be played on the higher D- and A-strings, the composer specifies the special timbre of the G-string. In his Romantic, pre-twelve-tone string sextet *Verklärte Nacht* (*Transfigured Night*), op. 4 (1917), Schoenberg indicates the use of the G-string (*G Saite*) for violin 1 at letter K, and later for violin 2 together with cello 1. This endows the chromatic melody with a special passion.

Górecki, Symphony No. 3, Movement I

Example 4.21 Henryk Górecki, Symphony No. 3 (1976): Movement I, *Lament of the Holy Cross*. This extract is used by kind permission of Polskie Wydawnictwo Muzyczne S.A., Krakow, Poland. Copyright 1977 Chester Music Ltd.

(continued)

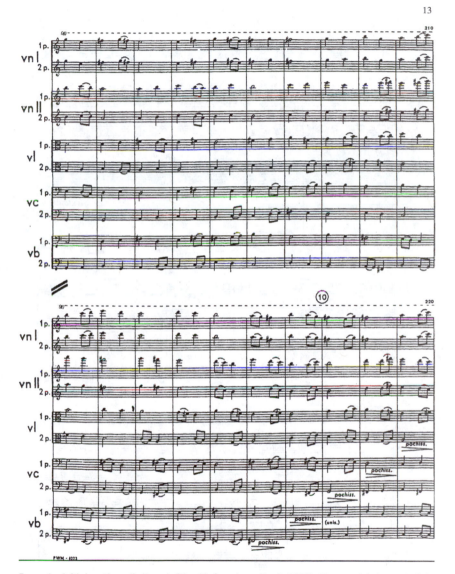

Example 4.21 (continued) Henryk Górecki, Symphony No. 3 (1976): Movement I, *Lament of the Holy Cross*. This extract is used by kind permission of Polskie Wydawnictwo Muzyczne S.A., Krakow, Poland. Copyright 1977 Chester Music Ltd.

Stravinsky, *Symphony of Psalms*

II

B. & H. 16328

Example 4.22 Igor Stravinsky, *Symphony of Psalms* (1930): Movement II. Copyright 1931 by Hawkes & Son (London) Ltd. Revised version: © Copyright 1948 by Hawkes & Son (London) Ltd. United States Copyright renewed. Reproduced by permission of Boosey & Hawkes Music Publishers Ltd.

Similarly, the wind and brass instruments each have their characteristic *timbres*. The low register of the flute is soft and husky compared with its upper register. The special *chalumeau* register of the B-flat clarinet, its lowest octave, has been described as being menacing and dramatic. Conversely, the middle ranges of the F horn and B-flat trumpet are the most often used, and sound less strained than their upper registers. All these characteristics need to be taken into account when painting sonic textures.

One of the main areas of exploration for twentieth-century composers was that of sonic color. Instead of orchestrating melodies with harmonic accompaniments, for example, it was "the sound of the sound" itself which became the main focus of attention. Thus, there was a shift away from applying a formal musical language, such as the tonal system, to whatever were the forces at hand, in favor of creating music for the specific instruments or voices involved. Formerly, a melody could be played by any available instrument. The new æsthetic advocated using specific instruments or voices as the source of the music itself. For example, a sound that was intended to be generated by a trombone could not be substituted by a cello. This æsthetic led to much exploration and experimentation in sonic color by both innovative composers and performers, which, in turn, led to the fastidious notation of the newfound sounds. Dynamics and articulations were indicated for almost every note, in some instances. The resulting music is a kaleidoscope of micro-sonorities.

Pointillism is a term borrowed from the field of painting to describe a particular textural technique. The term was used by late nineteenth-and early twentieth-century French painters, in particular, to describe the building up of a picture by using dots of pure color, rather than mixing colors on a palette. The French painters Manet, Monet, Pissarro, Sisley, and Seurat, together with the Dutch painter Van Gogh, used this technique. Applied to music, this could suggest rapid changes of instrumental color. The German word *klangfarbenmelodien* (sound-color-melodies) indicates a similar idea. Each note of a melodic line could be played by a different instrument, thus creating a succession of sonic colors.

Webern, Concerto, op. 24: Row

Example 4.23a Anton Webern, Concerto, op. 24 (1934): row.

Anton Webern demonstrates this technique in his Concerto, op. 24 (1934), for nine instruments: flute, oboe, clarinet, horn, trumpet, trombone, violin, viola, and piano. There is much triplicity at play in the work: three movements; three groups of three instruments. A glance at the score also reveals that the melodic line is divided into groups of three notes. In the first movement, each three-note group is allotted to a single instrument. Often, the first note of a group is played simultaneously with the third note of the preceding group.

This is a twelve-tone work, the row of which Webern was particularly proud. He constructed a three-note cell, containing the intervals of a m2 and a M3. He transposed this cell three times, and permutated the order of the intervals, to arrive at the twelve-tone row (see Example 4.23a). Each three-note cell is allotted to a different instrument, creating a textural kaleidoscope. Where the cells coincide, Webern is careful to select a transposition which will result in one of the intervals (or their inversions) of the Original Row, that is, m2/M7, M2/m7, P4 (see Example 4.23b).

Webern, Concerto op.24: Mvt. I

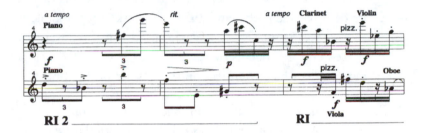

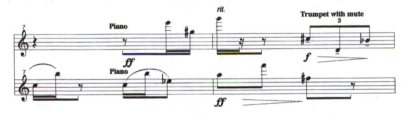

Example 4.23b Anton Webern, Concerto, op. 24 (1934). Copyright Universal Edition A.G. Vienna - reproduced by permission - all rights reserved.

Within the first eight bars of Movement I, the order of the appearances of the row variants is as follows:

O (bars 1–3)
RI 2, that is, RI transposed up a m2 (bars 4–5)
RI (bars 6–7)
O 2, that is, O transposed up a m2 (bars 7–8)

Webern has fun with octave displacement, and places all the notes of this section in the upper pitch register. Each three-note cell has its own characteristic dynamic, here within the loud range: *f* with accented *staccato*; *f legato*; *f* stressed; *f* followed by *diminuendo*; *ff legato*. Different *timbres* are used, including *f pizzicato* for the strings, and muted trumpet. In addition, the rhythm is fluid, with frequent indications of *ritenuto* and *a tempo*. Webern dedicated his concerto to Schoenberg, on the occasion of his 60th birthday — a fitting tribute from pupil to master.

As a conductor, Pierre Boulez is very familiar with the works of Webern. He has adopted, and adapted, Webern's techniques in his own compositions. Boulez is especially fascinated with the micro-detail of sonic *pointillistic* textures. His controversial early work *Le Marteau sans Maître* (*The Hammer without a Master*) is built around poems of René Char. Composed between 1953 and 1955, the work is remarkable not only for its *avant garde* musical language, but also for its fascinating structure. Based on three poems by René Char, the work is developed into nine movements which comment on the settings of the three texts:

1. Before *l'artisant furieux*: flute, vibraphone, guitar, viola
2. Commentary I on *Bourreaux de solitude*: flute, xylorimba, percussion
3. *L'artisant furieux*: voice, flute
4. Commentary II on *Bourreaux de solitude*: xylorimba, vibraphone, percussion, guitar, viola
5. *Bel édifice et les pressentiments*: first version: voice, flute, guitar, viola
6. *Bourreaux de solitude*: voice, flute, xylorimba, vibraphone, percussion, guitar, viola
7. After *l'artisant furieux*: flute, vibraphone, guitar
8. Commentary III on *Bourreaux de solitude*: flute, xylorimba, vibraphone, percussion
9. *Bel édifice et les pressentiments*: double: voice, flute, xylorimba, vibraphone, percussion, guitar, viola

Of the three texts, *l'artisant furieux* has a "before" and an "after"; *Bourreaux de solitude* has three commentaries as well as the setting itself, making four movements in all; and *Bel édifice et les pressentiments* has its setting and a "double." As can be seen, the order of the appearances of the texts and their variants is not straightforward, creating an interwoven structure. In addition, each movement has a different instrumentation, thus ensuring a distinctive sound for each section.

Example 4.24 shows the opening of the last movement, *Bel édifice et les pressentiments*: double, which uses all the instruments and the voice. As with the Webern *Concerto* (see Example 4.23b), every note has its own articulation and independent dynamic. The crosses on the stems of the vocal part indicate *quasi parlando* (as though speaking). The style of writing for the voice is an intentional reference to Schoenberg's *Pierrot Lunaire* (1912), a work with which Boulez was familiar. Like Webern, Boulez creates rhythmic fluidity with *tempo*-altering directions in every bar. With the frequent use of pauses and the indications *libre* (free), *ralenti, encore plus ralenti,* and *assez lent,* together with metronome changes, the *tempo* is constantly in a state of flux. As a result of his own conducting experience, Boulez helpfully adds signals for the conductor in the score.

Before commencing on a new composition, the English composer Rebecca Saunders conducts exhaustive research into the *timbral* possibilities of the instruments for which she is writing. She works with the actual performers, together extending and selecting the range of sounds available beyond the normal. Frequently, her compositions begin with an essay on one sound complex, progressing through a more rhythmic section, and often ending with a surprise. This might involve a music box, four radios (as in *Molly's Song 3: Shades of Crimson*, 1995–1996 [perhaps in a reference to Stockhausen, who used shortwave radios in some of his pieces]), or allowing the piano lid to fall shut, with the damper pedal down. Her scores are frequently prefaced by extensive performance notes that describe the exact playing techniques that are used in the work (see Example 4.25a and Example 4.25b).

Romanian composer Livia Teodorescu has composed several works that explore spectral music—that is, exploiting harmonies created from the upper end of the overtone series. Her Flute Concerto, *Rite for Enchanting the Air* (1998), was written for exploratory flautist Pierre Ives Artaud. It is cast in four movements, one for each member of the flute family: alto flute in G, piccolo, flute in C, and bass flute. The first entry of the soloist, playing alto flute, is a sonic invention in the lower register, involving microtones, and laid over low, *glissando* drones played by *divisi* double basses, celli, and tuba. This texture is completed with rhythmic puffs of air from flutes, clarinets, and brass, together with

Example 4.24 Pierre Boulez, *Le Marteau san Maître* (1953–1955): Movement 9. Copyright 1954 by Universal Edition A.G. Vienna. Reproduced by permission. All rights reserved.

Rebecca Saunders. Performance notes for guitar

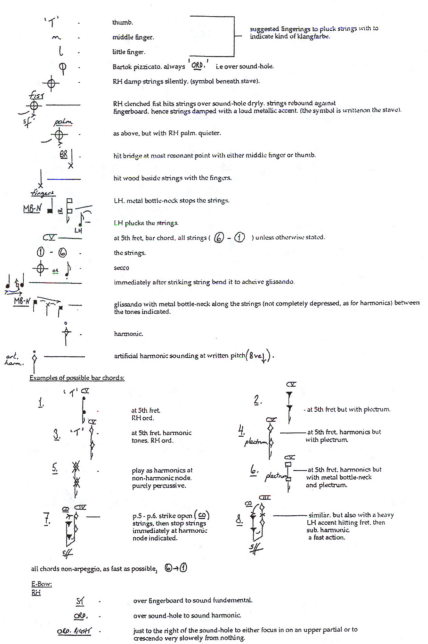

Example 4.25a Rebecca Saunders, *Molly's Song 3: Shades of Crimson* (1995–1996): performance notes for guitar.

Rebecca Saunders, *Molly's Song 3*

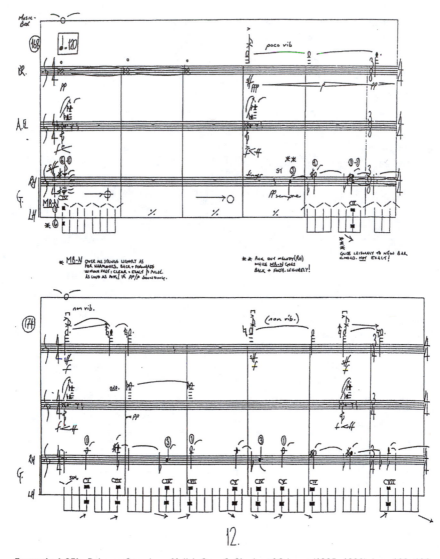

Example 4.25b Rebecca Saunders, *Molly's Song 3: Shades of Crimson* (1995–1996): bars 168–190. Edition Peters No. 7505. © 1997 by Hinrichsen Edition, Peters Edition Limited, London. Reproduced by permission of the publishers.   (continued)

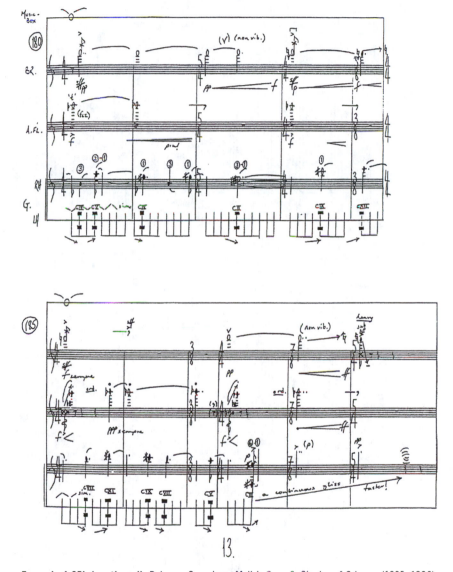

Example 4.25b (continued) Rebecca Saunders, *Molly's Song 3: Shades of Crimson* (1995–1996): bars 168–190. Edition Peters No. 7505. © 1997 by Hinrichsen Edition, Peters Edition Limited, London. Reproduced by permission of the publishers.

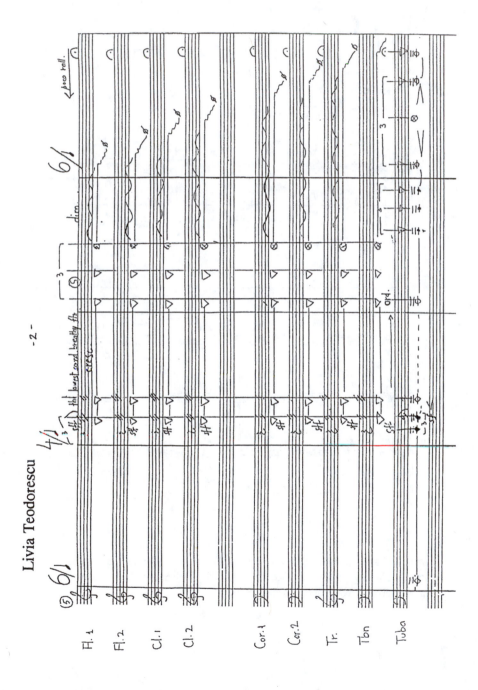

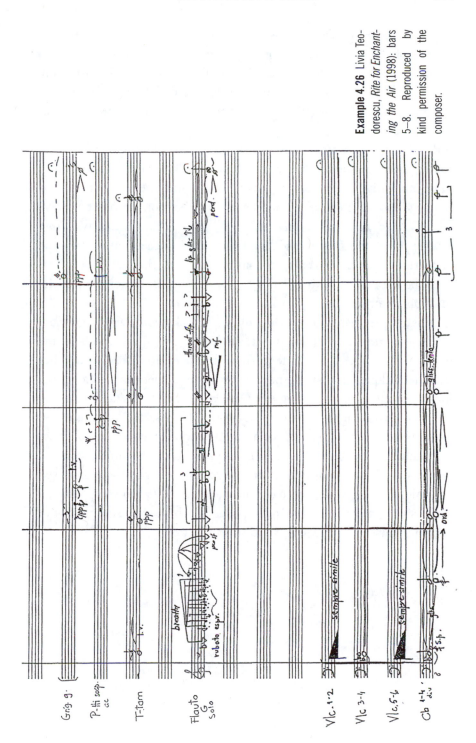

Example 4.26 Livia Teodorescu, *Rite for Enchanting the Air* (1998): bars 5–8. Reproduced by kind permission of the composer.

softly shimmering metal percussion (see Example 4.26). The orchestral texture of the first movement makes a gradual and continuous climb from the lowest register to the highest throughout its seven-minute duration. This acts as a backdrop to the limpid flute line. The movement climaxes with tumultuous rhythmic chords from which the second movement emerges.

In conclusion, we see that this fascination with "the sound of the sound" continues into the twenty-first century among some of the most innovative composers. Opposing this trend, the textures utilized by the school of "process" composers tend to be monochromatic. Steve Reich's *Music for Pieces of Wood*, *Clapping Music*, *Four Organs*, *New York Counterpoint*, and *Drumming* are all successful in their use of one type of texture, sometimes lasting for up to an hour. The fascination here is in the hypnotic working out of the process itself, rather than in the multiplicity of sounds.

This chapter has laid out the building blocks with which composers have worked during the twentieth century, with a glance at some music from earlier times. The purpose has been to inform you about these techniques so that you have knowledge of them as well as of the musico-intellectual standards that they represent. As a developing composer, you might like to try out some of these techniques, either as an exercise, or as the basis of a composition. One or more of these techniques might be suitable for the expression of your initial concept for a particular composition. Later in your experience as a composer, you might invent your own techniques, better suited to your personal expressive purposes. As a new composer, you have the exciting task of carrying musical language forward from this point.

5

TECHNICAL EXERCISES

Having an idea for a composition is a good start, but you need technical ability in order to realize your dreams. Conversely, having a good technical command without having anything to say is equally unfulfilling. The perfect combination is a brilliant concept together with a polished technique. This chapter sets out some technical exercises to help you to develop some means of expressing your musical ideas. When considering these exercises, you might find it beneficial to review the corresponding section in Chapter 4.

Exercise 1: Melodies

Compose three melodies for an instrument that you play, using the following scales:

- **Tonal**
- **Modal**
- **A scale of your own invention**

Initially, choose a scale and play it over several times. In doing this, some musical shapes might present themselves. Decide which mood you intend to evoke. Then allow your subconscious to work. Try simply singing the first thing that your voice alights upon. Don't think, but just let it come! You will probably surprise yourself. Next, try to recapture what you sang by playing it on your instrument. Finally comes the task of writing down your musical thoughts. At this stage, I suggest that you use manuscript paper, pencil, and eraser rather than a music software package, because it is best to start with a clean sheet and not have to fit your rhythm into preset bars. Speaking of which, retain any "quirky" rhythms that might have emerged by changing the time signature when appropriate. Test the accuracy of your notation by playing back what you have written, counting carefully.

Another way of beginning is to draw some possible melodic shapes. The classic melodic shape starts low, ascends to the highest point at the climax, at approximately two-thirds of the total duration, then subsides to the starting position.

Other shapes could be suggested. The possibilities are limitless.

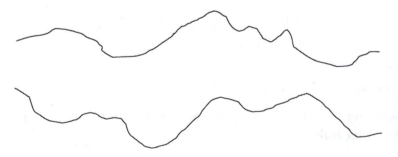

Figure 5.1 Melodic shapes.

You might like to think of titles for your melodies before you begin. This would suggest a mood, or character to fire your imagination. Some possibilities include the following:

Twisted tonality
Modal melancholy
Innocent invention
Icy tentacles
Cheerful tunes
Speedy scales
Perfect pitch
Knotted notes

In reviewing your melodies, you might consider these questions:

- What is the range of your melody? Is it restricted to the range of your voice, or does it utilize the range of your instrument?
- How long is your melody? Does it fall into 4-bar phrases, or are there uneven numbers of bars in some phrases? If you want to make it less predictable, try repeating a short motif, or making a sequence, or transposing a segment.
- Is there any logical thinking within the construction of the melody?
- Does your melody flow?

Taking a further look at Debussy's *Syrinx* for solo flute (Example 4.8), we see that the main motif has a very characterful rhythm and is just two bars long. Bar 1 is repeated in bar 3, while bar 4 leaps down the octave. We are surprised because we think that we are going to hear the same melody again, but Debussy continues with a new triplet idea. Bar 5 begins just like bar 4, but finishes with an upward triplet arpeggio. The opening motif is repeated in bar 9, but down an octave from the original. Bar 10 repeats bar 9 until beat 3, when the original descending scale is answered by an ascending one, which leads to developing material. Bar 13 is reminiscent of the opening motif transposed, although, in fact, it is quite different! Much is made of the secondary triplet idea, by way of simple repetition and augmentation, between bars 14 and 22. The reprise begins in bar 25 by elongating the first note of the initial motif. Bar 26 becomes an exact repeat of the opening bar, followed by a variant of the *acciaccatura* figure, which previously appeared in bars 4, 11, 12, and 14 to 19.

The coda features a summary of all the material used. The opening figure is heard in a smooth triplet rhythm, rather than the original dotted format. The augmented triplets from bar 14 are transposed from E flat onto low D flat, which becomes a pedal note. In the penultimate bar, we hear a quintuplet for the first time (a surprise held to the last). *Syrinx* finishes with an *acciaccatura* onto the low D flat. The piece occupies a range of two octaves plus a m3. Notice that there are rests, or breathing places, between phrases. These are a practical consideration when composing for a wind instrument, but they also literally mark the phrases, which is equally useful for non-wind players. Debussy demonstrates that much can be made out of a small amount of musical material through imaginative use of repetition and variation.

When you're satisfied with your three melodies, play them to a friend. Remember to add tempo indications and dynamic markings.

Exercise 2: Counterpoint

Add a second melody to the three melodies that you have composed for Exercise 1. Choose an instrument played by a member of your class, so that you can perform the results together. Your added melody may, or may not, use the same scale or mode as your first melody. If you choose a different scale or mode, you will be creating bitonality or bimodality.

Essentially, this is an exercise in counterpoint (see Chapter 4). In particular, the main attributes of counterpoint include:

- Taking account of the resulting harmony
- Adding complementary rhythms to make a musical conversation
- Using contrary motion, or inversion
- Trying out specific contrapuntal devices, such as imitation, canon, augmentation, or diminution

If you are composing for a transposing instrument, you might find it easier to work with both instruments initially "in C"; that is, both sounding at the same pitch. Then transpose the part, as appropriate, before playing your work.

As a general principle in adding a countermelody, when the first melody is active, allow the second melody to stay still, or to rest, and vice versa. As in a conversation, when one voice is speaking, the other should listen, and then reply. Allow the countermelody to "breathe" by including rests as part of your musical thinking. Complete your works by adding dynamic markings, and when you are satisfied, perform your duets for the class.

Exercise 3: Harmony

a) **Create harmonic progressions of approximately 10 chords for each type of scale:**
   - **Tonal**
   - **Modal**
   - **A scale of your own invention**

   The chords should be made out of the pitches of each scale or mode.

b) **When you are satisfied with your sequences of chords, add a melody to each harmonic progression.** Try playing your set of chords while improvising a melody around it. This will ensure that your melody will fit the harmony. It is a better way of fitting melody with harmony than by inventing the melody first and then trying to harmonize it.

   Select an available instrument to play the melodic line, and accompany it on a keyboard with your harmonic progression. If necessary, transpose the instrumental part for the performance, although initially you should compose both lines at the same pitch. As before, add tempo and dynamic markings.

   After rehearsal together, perform your melodies with accompaniments for the class.

Exercise 4: Rhythm

a) **Using a number set (for example, your date of birth or your telephone number), construct a rhythm. Choose the note unit (for example, quarter note, eighth note, and so forth).**
   Write out the retrograde.
   Combine the original and retrograde rhythms, one under the other.
   Select suitable time signatures and add bar lines to this duo.
   Example 5.1a shows how to construct a rhythm from a (fictitious) date of birth: 05031982 (5th March, 1982). In this example, the unit is an eighth note. Accents mark the beginning of each number group; the number 0 represents a rest.
   This is followed by its retrograde (Example 5.1b) and, finally, the two rhythms are combined (Example 5.1c).
   Note that you need to decide on only one time signature for the two parts. This will involve renotating one of the parts using the time signature of the other. By adding accents in the original places, the two rhythms become distinct.
   Clap the two rhythms separately, then together, emphasizing the accents.

b) **Notate a gradual accelerando, followed by a rallentando, without using verbal instructions.**

Exercise 5: Group Composition

Compose one verse (per student) of Lewis Carroll's *Jabberwocky* (see Chapter 2). Choose instruments and performers available in the class. Make use of any of the techniques discussed above. Organize a performance of the complete poem.

Exercise 6: Variation Techniques and Pitch Class Operations

a) **Create a note cell of 5 pitch classes.**
   Using only this cell in transposition, inversion, retrogradation, permutation, and octave displacement, compose a short piece for solo oboe (duration: c. 1 minute).

Rhythm Exercise Example 1

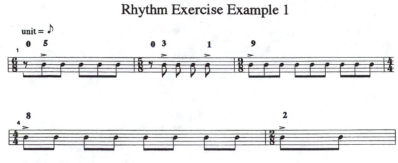

Example 5.1a Rhythm exercise 1.

Retrograde

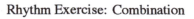

Example 5.1b Retrograde.

Rhythm Exercise: Combination

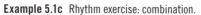
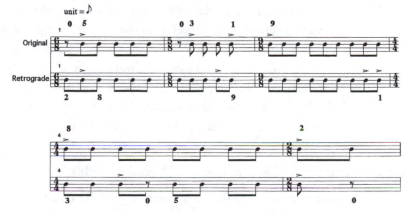

Example 5.1c Rhythm exercise: combination.

Pitch Class operations

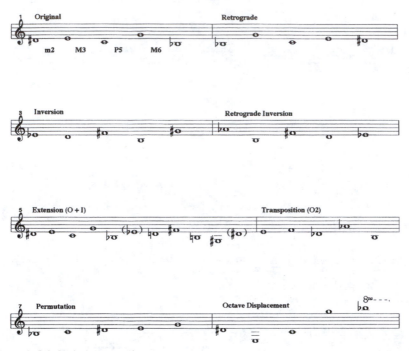

Example 5.2 Pitch class operations.

Create your 5-note cell, taking into account the aural effect of your selected pitch classes. The term "permutation" indicates that the pitch classes appear in a different order from the original (see Example 5.2).

Note the use of enharmonic changes. The inversion is worked out by going in the opposite direction from the original by the same amount; that is, by the same interval. In the transposition, the original note cell is moved up by a m2. You should work out all 48 transpositions available to you (12 transpositions × 4 variants: O, I, R, RI). The extension demonstrates how you might join one variant onto another, to create a stream of related pitch classes.

Exercise 7: Harmonic Construction and Harmonic Fields

a) Using tonally based chords, harmonize middle D in 10 different ways.

5-note chord

Example 5.3 Five-note chord.

> Ensure that you notate middle D! This note can be the top, bottom, or middle note of a harmony. You can use chords in any inversion. Remember to include some added note harmonies.

b) Construct a 5-note chord.
Demonstrate the method of construction.
Transpose it once.
Invert it (5 possible inversions.)

In Example 5.3, the intervallic construction of the chord, reading from the bottom up, is P4, M3, D4/M3, M2. By permutating these intervals, you can construct many other related chords. The inversions are made by placing the lowest note on the top. Though the same pitch classes are involved, the effect of the chord alters with each new position.

> c) Create a harmonic progression of 6 "found" chords suitable for an elegy.
>
> In this exercise, you have the freedom to experiment in order to create your own harmonic sequence. Take into account the register in which you place the chords. They often sound quite different when placed in the bass range, compared with the middle register.

Exercise 8: Advanced Rhythmic Procedures

a) Using your date of birth numbers, or telephone number, create a rhythm (0= a rest).

b) **Notate it in two different ways, using two different units (for example, a sixteenth note for the first version and a dotted eighth note for the second).**
c) **Bar both versions, selecting suitable time signatures.**
d) **To each add a second rhythm that is a variant of the first (for example, retrogradation, augmentation, diminution).**

In Example 5.1a, the chosen unit was an eighth note. The same rhythm notated with a unit of a dotted eighth note is shown in Exercise 5.4a.

Adding the original rhythm, with an eighth note as the unit, results in the addition of a diminished version. Because the rhythms are not of equal lengths, one will finish before the other. You can be ingenious in continuing the shorter rhythm to fit the duration of the longer rhythm. In a compositional situation, overlapping rhythms of varying lengths is a means of extending a passage (see Example 5.4b).

Exercise 9: Textural Flow and Transformations

Utilizing your durational system, orchestrate middle D for: flute, oboe, clarinet, bassoon, horn, trumpet, trombone, percussion, violin 1, violin 2, viola, cello, and double bass.

This is an exercise in orchestration. Middle D is a pitch that can be played by all the instruments. By using only one pitch, you are obliged to concentrate on your rhythm and the timbre of the instruments. Middle D is low on the flute, but high on the double bass. The flute in its bottom register is soft and can easily be overpowered by other instruments, so you need to take care how you use it. Not all the percussion instruments are capable of playing middle D, so you need to choose one or two that can. Combining instrumental *timbres* will produce texture. An imaginative combination might involve *pizzicato* violas accenting the start of a note that is sustained by a *tremolo* vibraphone.

In attempting this exercise, you need to set up a few pages of manuscript paper in orchestral layout. There are several good books on orchestration that you might like to consult in preparation for this exercise, including Walter Piston's *Orchestration* (see the Bibliography). An orchestral score is laid out in families of instruments, beginning at

Advanced Rhythm

Example 5.4a Advanced rhythm.

Advanced Rhythms Combined

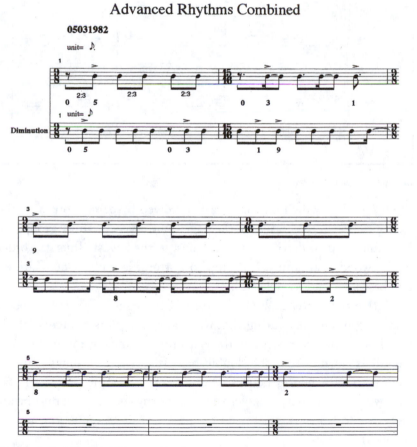

Example 5.4b Advanced rhythms combined.

Score notated at sounding pitch

Example 5.5 Orchestral layout.

the top with woodwinds, then brass, followed by percussion, with the string section at the bottom of the page. Within each family group, the instruments are ordered from the highest to the lowest. Thus, the order of the woodwind family, from top to bottom, is flute, oboe, clarinet, and bassoon (see Example 5.5).

Notice the sentence at the bottom of the page, "Score notated at sounding pitch," indicating that the transposing instruments (clarinet, horn, and trumpet) are all written at sounding pitch. Despite this, it is normal that the double bass is written an octave higher than it sounds, hence the clef. Were you to use a piccolo, the notation would be an octave lower than sounding, using the appropriate clef. In addition, you will need to specify which percussion instruments you are using.

The notes of your rhythm can be scattered among the families of orchestral instruments (see Chapter 4 for ideas on *pointillism* and *klangfarbenmelodien*). Depending on the length of your rhythm, you might choose to make two or three rounds of it, in order to maximize your orchestral ingenuity. It is essential to indicate expression and dynamic markings, since the color of the sounds is of the essence here. Take note of the various instrumental sounds available, such as *con sordino*, *sul ponticello*, flutter tongue, and so forth, as well as the effects of "hairpin" *crescendo* and *decrescendo*. Use your knowledge and memory of instrumental and orchestral sounds.

Exercise 10: Layering

Using your orchestration of middle D as layer 1, add layer 2, making use of pitch material from your pitch class operations (Exercise 6).

Make a copy of your solution to Exercise 9. This contains layer 1, which is made up of middle D, sounded in your invented rhythm. To this, you are going to add a second layer that uses pitch material from your selected 5-note cell from Exercise 6. These pitches will act as a foil to the "drone" created by the constant sounding of middle D. It is suggested that your 5-note cell does not include the pitch D, because this pitch is already sounding. Find a transposition of your 5-note cell that avoids the pitch D.

The rhythm of layer 2 can be freely invented around the rhythm of layer 1. Use the instruments that are not involved in playing layer 1 at any particular moment.

Having worked through these exercises, you will be better equipped to realize your musical ideas. You might devise your own techniques that match, or surpass, the intellectual challenges posed by them. There can be no doubt that a combination of imaginative concept and rigorous technique will produce music that will be appreciated.

6

EXPLORING INSTRUMENTS

In the musical world, the twentieth century was characterized by research into new ways of playing traditional instruments. Virtuoso performers collaborated with pioneering composers, together discovering a range of new sounds elicited from conventional instruments. These new ways of playing became known as *extended instrumental techniques*.

The best way of finding out about instrumental idiosyncrasies is to work with the performers. In addition, demonstrations given by professional players of particular instruments or instrumental groups might be arranged. However, this may not always be feasible, so this chapter will address some interesting new techniques.

Keyboard Instruments

Many composers of different nationalities, such as Béla Bartók, John Cage, George Crumb, György Kurtág, Michael Finnissy, Sofia Gubaidulina, and György Ligeti, have explored the three acoustic keyboard instruments: the piano, the harpsichord, and the organ.

Piano

One of Béla Bartók's interests was teaching young musicians the fundamentals of music, so he developed a series of graded studies for young pianists, aptly entitled *Mikrokosmos,* the world of music expressed in miniature. Between 1932 and 1939, he composed 153 short piano pieces, partly inspired by the fact that his young son started taking piano lessons in 1933. These were published as the six volumes of *Mikrokosmos.*

No. 102 in Book IV, *Harmonics,* demonstrates the use of overtones obtained from a piano. A note, or group of notes, is held down silently. Against this, notes are played aloud. When these sounded notes are part of the harmonic series of the held notes, they will ring on. This intriguing effect is made without the aid of the sustaining pedal. Try out this effect for yourself. Note the difference obtained by playing notes higher, then lower, than the silently held notes. Borrowing from the notation used for violin harmonics, the silently depressed notes are written with diamond shaped note heads (see Example 6.1).

Other pieces in *Mikrokosmos* playfully demonstrate compositional technique as well as piano technique. No. 105 from Book IV, *Playsong (with two pentatonic scales),* has a key signature of E major for the left hand, but no key signature for the right hand! The two pentatonic scales have the pitch B as the common note, and the entire piece operates within the range of an octave. No. 110, also from Book IV, *Clashing Sounds,* lives up to its title, with P5s and m3s sounding a m2 apart.

At about the same time that Bartók was composing these pieces, John Cage took a post as accompanist and teacher at the Cornish School of the Arts, in Seattle, Washington. There he met dancer-choreographer Merce Cunningham. They became lifelong friends and collaborated on many dance scores involving the piano and assorted unusual percussion instruments. On one particular occasion in 1938, they were to perform in a hall that proved too small to accommodate all the dancers, piano, and percussion instruments. So, "necessity being the mother of invention," Cage experimented with playing the "inside" of the piano. Using materials that were at hand, he inserted a variety of screws, bolts, and pieces of felt between the piano strings. This had the effect of transforming the sound of the piano into a true percussion instrument. The technique became known as *prepared piano*, suggesting, as the name indicates, that the piano has to be prepared in some way in advance of the performance.

Later, Cage composed *Sonatas and Interludes* (1946–1948), an hourlong series of 19 pieces which uses the prepared piano. He became interested in Indian philosophy and music, which he learned by studying the work of Gita Sarabhai, Ananda K. Coomaraswamy, and Meister Eckhart. The *Sonatas and Interludes* aim to portray the eight "permanent emotions" found in Indian æsthetics: eroticism, heroism, odiousness, anger, mirth, fear, sorrow, and wonder.

The frontispiece of *Sonatas and Interludes* is a detailed table of how the piano should be prepared. Not every note is prepared, some retaining the normal piano sound. The preparation is very exact, and exacting; it can take up to two hours to make all the preparations. Some strings require more than one type of material, the lower strings, in particular, needing two or three, including eraser, screw, and rubber; screw and nuts; plastic strips; and long bolt, furniture bolt, medium bolt, and small bolt. These have to be placed at the exact measurement from the dampers along the string, as described in the table (see Example 6.2a). The resulting sonic transformation is stunning. Sonata No. III requires the least preparation, if you would like to try one out (see Example 6.2b).

Less taxing than Cage's type of preparation, yet effective in transforming the piano sound, is to stroke, or strike, the piano strings with the hand. Try this effect with, and without, using the sustaining pedal. A string *glissando* can be obtained this way. Placing paper or cloth directly on the strings creates a jangling or muffled sound. Equally as effective is plucking the strings, by either using the fingernails or the fingertips (which makes a difference to the *timbre*). The strings can also be played with light sticks. A problem occurs when specific notes need to be played in this way. It is necessary to mark the strings in some way,

Example 6.1 Béla Bartók, *Mikrokosmos* (1932–1939), Book 4, No. 102: *Harmonics*. Copyright 1940 by Hawkes & Son (London) Ltd.   (continued)

Example 6.1 (continued) Béla Bartók, *Mikrokosmos* (1932–1939), Book 4, No. 102: *Harmonics.*
Copyright 1940 by Hawkes & Son (London) Ltd.

John Cage

* MEASURE FROM BRIDGE.

Example 6.2a John Cage, piano preparation for *Sonatas and Interludes* (1946–1948). Edition Peters No. 675 © 1960 by Henmar Press Inc., New York. Reproduced by permission of Peters Edition Limited, London.

John Cage

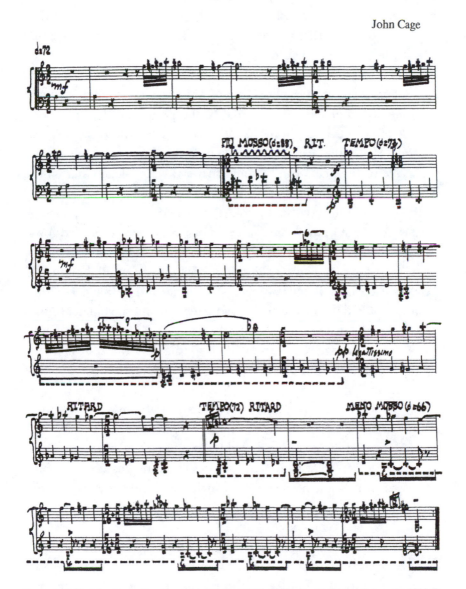

Example 6.2b John Cage, *Sonatas and Interludes* (1946–1948): No. III. Edition Peters No. 6755 ©
1960 by Henmar Press Inc., New York. Reproduced by permission of Peters Edition Limited, London.

so the performer can accurately play the proper notes. However, marking them by using fluid paper or paper stickers can upset the delicate weighting of the mechanism. Perhaps the least invasive method is to mark the specific string with colored chalks, which must be carefully erased after the performance.

Some scores call for playing on the strings of the piano as well as at the keyboard, in the normal manner. In this case, the composer should work out the choreography required of the performer, to ensure that there is sufficient time within the piece to stand up and to sit down, as required. Using the sustaining pedal while standing and reaching into the inside of the piano can be somewhat awkward, depending on the height of the pianist.

In a direct reference to Bartók, the American composer George Crumb composed four large-scale sets of piano works, entitled *Makrokosmos I, II, III, IV* (1972–1979). Volume III, *Music for a Summer Evening*, is for two pianists and two percussionists, while Volume IV, *Celestial Mechanics*, is for two pianos. Volumes I (1972) and II (1973) are for amplified piano, the amplification enhancing the quieter sounds from inside the instrument as well as creating an electronic aura. These volumes contain twelve pieces based on the signs of the zodiac. Structurally, the twelve signs of the zodiac are arranged into three groups of four pieces.

Every fourth piece is a "symbol," notated in a nonstandard format, such as a circle or spiral (see Example 6.3). Gemini, the astrological sign of the twins, is represented by two circles of music separated by a pause of seven seconds. The second circle makes use of silently depressed chords, the harmonics of which are sounded by playing *glissandi* with the fingertips on the strings of the piano. It suggests the *doppelgänger* of the first circle.

Each piece has two, or sometimes three, titles or subtitles; for example, *Ghost-Nocturne: for the Druids of Stonehenge (Night-Spell I) Virgo* are the titles for No. 5 of Volume II. This movement involves the placing of two glass tumblers on the strings of the piano. These are used to create "ghostly" effects by making a *glissando* with the tumblers, while playing trills at the keyboard. Representing the calls of the ancient druids, this movement also asks the pianist to sing into the piano, so that

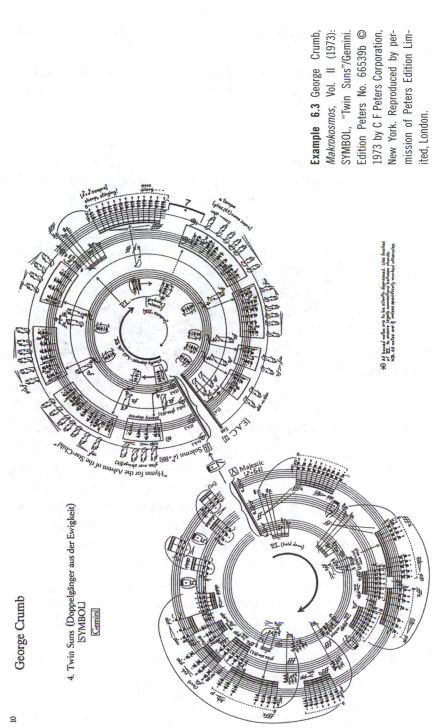

the strings pick up the vibrations. All the instructions are meticulously notated on the score.

Also in the spirit of Bartók's *Mikrokosmos* is Hungarian composer György Kurtág's *Játékok (Games)*. In the preface to the score, published in 1979, Kurtág states,

> The idea for composing "Games" was suggested by children playing spontaneously, children for whom the piano still means a toy…. Thus this series does not provide a tutor, nor does it stand as a collection of pieces. It is a possibility for experimenting and not for learning "to play the piano.

The two volumes contain a mixture of improvisational signs and suggestions intermingled with short, conventionally notated pieces. Several of these are in homage to other composers, including Bartók (Volume 1, p. 7). Another, "playing with overtones" (Volume 1, p. ix), involves changing hands on the silently held note, then playing staccato notes of the harmonic series above and below. Indeed, the two volumes are an irresistible invitation to "play at the piano."

At the other end of the notational spectrum is Michael Finnissy's *English Country-Tunes* (1977/1982–1985). The score appears to be a notated version of a highly complex improvisation. Yet there is something in common with Kurtág's "Games," in that the music sounds improvised. An adventurous improviser can produce fists full of notes, complex rhythms, and dramatic gestures, but setting this into notation can produce a daunting score. Finnissy has not shirked from this task, and the resulting work is virtuosic in terms of its compositional and performance demands. Eschewing the possibilities of playing inside the piano, this work is to be performed in the normal manner, on the keyboard. Though the eight movements of the work bear titles suggesting English folk tunes—for example, "I'll give my love a garland," "The seeds of love," "My bonny boy" — none actually exist in the work. The title is a cover for more subversive, dark, sexual connotations.

With a duration of 45 minutes, *English Country-Tunes* expresses the gamut of emotions, from "unsettled (violent and reckless)," "wistful," "tranquil," "gently," "forceful and boisterous," "vehement" to "almost motionless." As Example 6.4 demonstrates, the notation, here on three

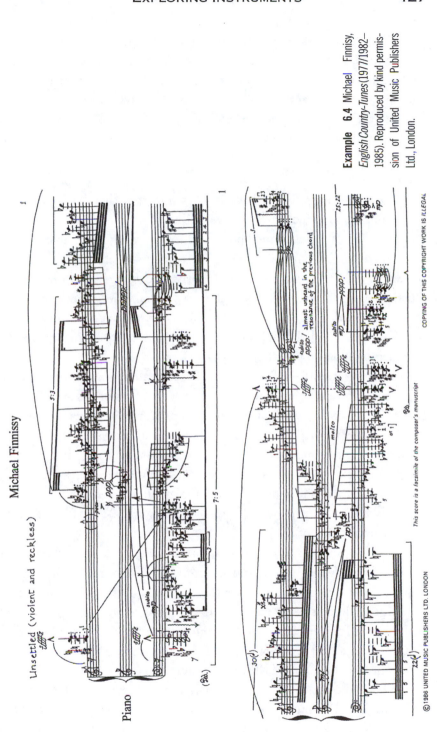

Example 6.4 Michael Finnissy, *English Country-Tunes* (1977/1982– 1985). Reproduced by kind permission of United Music Publishers Ltd., London.

staves, is full of intricate detail and extreme dynamic markings, ranging from *ppppp!* to *sffffz* within a very short space of time. The entire keyboard is covered in a welter of sound. Principal notes are decorated with flurries of grace notes; nests of irregular rhythms create a fluid rhythm (there is no time signature); and hands full of chords skim over the keys at breathtaking velocity. This is music for virtuoso pianists.

Organ

The organ and harpsichord have in common that they both predate the piano. Some manufacturers have built two or more manuals (keyboards), and both adopt a method of adding octaves in order to change the registration. Common to both instruments is the possibility of adding to or subtracting from the 8' norm: the 16' (32' is available on most organs) and/or the 4', 2', and 1' stops. The measurements, in feet, refer to the length of organ pipes, and for convenience, the nomenclature has been adopted for use with the harpsichord. Historically, most organists would also play the harpsichord.

Something to bear in mind is that organs differ from one another. There are different types of action, different numbers of manuals (from two to four), and a range of different stops available. Thus, composing for a specific organ can result in few performances. A solution is to leave open the important detail of registration, relying on the performer to make the choices according to the available stops. General guidelines may be indicated, such as "Great," flutes, reeds, and trumpets, as well as the octave envisaged, by specifying 32', 16', 8', 4', 2', 1', or any combination of these.

Sofia Gubaidulina's *In croce* (1979) for cello and organ uses the symbolism of the cross as a structural feature. The work begins with a high organ solo on two manuals, using the 8', 4', and 2' stops in combination. The melody is centered on E, flickering around F sharp and E, with F and G flat entwining in the countermelody. The E turns out to be the dominant of A major, as the melody outlines the pitches of A major chord in bars 7 and 8. The cello enters at bar 20 on a low E pedal, which is then colored with sighing quarter tones, *tremolo*, and sudden *crescendi*. The duet progresses via a variety of irrational rhythms, the organ melody descending an octave while the cello part rises.

In the central section at Figure 24, a *fff* cadenza for both instruments erupts. The cello plays notated pitch material with rhythmic freedom against improvised clusters for the organ. At Figure 27, the center point of the work, the cello reaches a high F sharp, where it plays a transposed version of the opening organ theme. Against this, the organ accompanies with diatonic minor chords placed a m2 apart, for example, Em for RH plus E flat m for LH. Example 6.5 demonstrates the mixture of graphic and conventional notation that Gubaidulina uses in the score.

From Figure 36, the organ part gradually descends to the depths, the 32' stop lowering the chromatically descending pedal line by two octaves, from Figure 41. Meanwhile, the cello line gradually ascends, arriving at high E (Figure 48) where it plays a reminiscence of the opening organ theme, again in the tonic. Interrupted by shimmering harmonic Es and harmonic *glissandi*, the cello melody is accompanied by a low cluster on the organ. Thus, through the course of the work, the two instruments have exchanged places, the organ beginning high and ending low; the cello, vice versa, symbolically representing the form of a crucifix:, *in croce*.

Composed earlier than *In croce* is György Ligeti's *Volumina* (1961–1962, revised 1966) for solo organ. Consisting entirely of clusters, the work takes its sound world from electronic music. The clusters are played with the arms and palms of the hands as well as with the feet. There is continuous sound for the entire 16-minute duration of the work. The soundscape is sculptured rather in the manner of electroacoustic music in which blocks of sound are fluidly shaped. The work opens with a wall of sound created by depressing all the black and white keys of one manual (by using both arms), covering a range of nearly five octaves. Simultaneously, both feet cover a range of one octave. (Incidentally, on occasion, this has blown a fuse, resulting in the sabotage of the performance!) By carefully releasing first the black keys, followed by the gradual release of the white keys, leaving the feet still in place, the cluster slowly evolves over a two-minute period. In addition to this arms-and-feet technique, use is made of the mechanical swell to effect a sudden, or gradual, *crescendo* or *diminuendo*. The work proceeds in this manner. The sculptured sound blocks are varied at times with rapid *staccato* clusters, *ad lib*, and

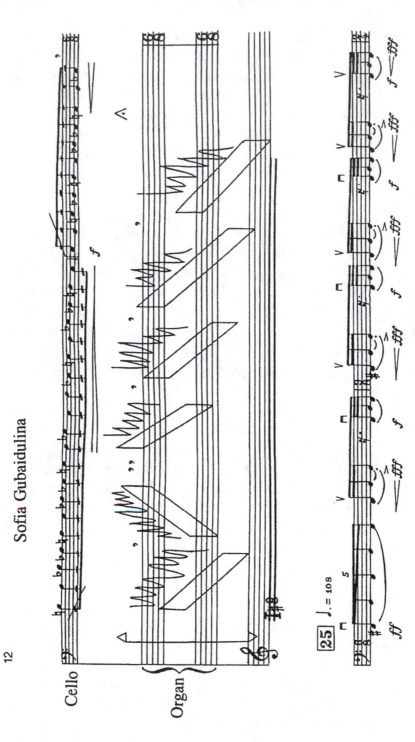

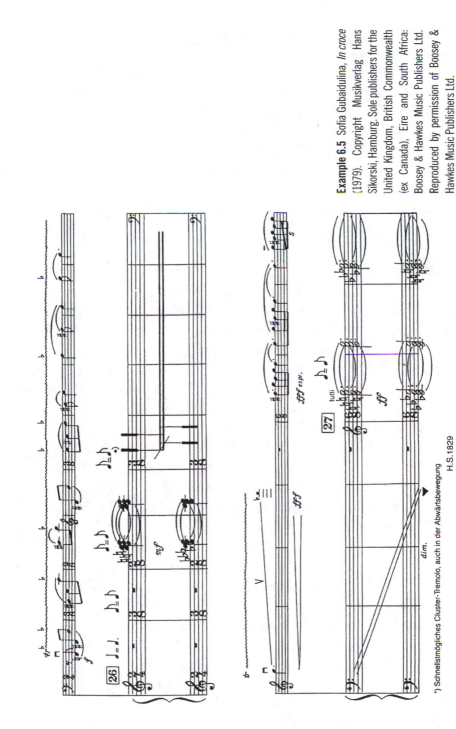

Example 6.5 Sofia Gubaidulina, *In croce* (1979). Copyright Musikverlag Hans Sikorski, Hamburg. Sole publishers for the United Kingdom, British Commonwealth (ex Canada), Eire and South Africa: Boosey & Hawkes Music Publishers Ltd. Reproduced by permission of Boosey & Hawkes Music Publishers Ltd.

*) Schnellstmögliches Cluster-Tremolo, auch in der Abwärtsbewegung

H.S.1829

with internal movement within the pitch ranges of the clusters. The score is graphic, indicating ranges rather than specific pitches, and durations (indicated by numbers) rather than individual rhythms.

Ligeti's *Volumina* marked an entirely new way of approaching composing for the organ. In common with much experimental music of the late twentieth century, the piece addresses the problem of how to write musical thought that is possible to improvise but for which traditional notation is inadequate, and the practicalities of how to realize performances by other musicians. For *Volumina*, one or two assistants are required to operate the stops in places where the organist's arms and feet are fully occupied.

Harpsichord

Ligeti continued his exploration of keyboard instruments, turning his attention to the harpsichord in 1968. Dedicated to harpsichordist Frau Antoinette M. Vischer, *Continuum* is a work of astonishing speed. It requires a two-manual harpsichord, because it opens with the left hand playing *tremolo* G–B flat on the lower manual, simultaneously with B flat–G played *tremolo* at the same pitch in the right hand on the upper manual. This narrow band of *tremolo* sound gradually enlarges its pitch content via the addition of one note at a time. The first extra note to be added is F, rendering a three-note group in the RH playing against the original two-note group in the LH. This has the effect of appearing to change the tempo, though in fact, there is no time signature. A flat, followed by F, are the next notes to be added to the LH, followed soon after by A natural in the RH.

This process of addition continues to the maximum point, at which a group of eight notes in one hand plays against an eight-note group of similar pitches, in the same octave, in the other hand. The shape of each eight-note cell is in contrary motion, and overlaps in such a way that the bottom and top notes do not coincide. The added notes remain within the five finger span of the hand, and are placed in the center of the pitch range. The flow is interrupted by a flickering BM *tremolo*. After this, the process continues, this time gradually enlarging the pitch range by moving outwards on the keyboards, and eventually adding the 16' and 4' stops to the original 8' (normal) so that the sound shoots up and down an octave. Another interruption follows in which the RH plays a high trill, using the 4' stop only. This becomes a m3 (high B–D), a transposition of the opening interval. The LH rejoins, playing the high C sharp between the B and D. The process again continues at this high altitude, with the fingers treading on each other's notes, until, eventually, they alight on a unison note (F flat). Remember that these are played on separate manuals. The F flats are played very rapidly, suddenly stopping, "as though torn off"—one of Ligeti's favorite endings (see Example 6.6).

In *Continuum*, Ligeti uses minimalist techniques, particularly the effect of apparently changing speed through the addition or subtraction of a note to, or from, the five-finger groups. In addition, the outer shape of the band of sound expands and contracts, as well as suddenly jumping register. Inside the band of sound, the notes twitter, outlining changing scales and *arpeggio* patterns. Ligeti here has created a virtuoso, extremely fast-moving continuum of sound for harpsichord.

Stringed Instruments

There were relatively few new playing techniques for stringed instruments developed during the twentieth century. This could be because many of the famous nineteenth century concerti (e.g., the Mendelssohn violin concerto, and the Saint-Saëns, Dvořák, and Elgar cello concerti) fully exploited the technical possibilities of the violin, viola, and cello. The nineteenth century virtuoso Paganini was also responsible for extending violin techniques.

Perhaps more use was made in the twentieth century of massed string harmonics than hitherto (see, for example, Stravinsky, *L'Oiseau de Feu*, 1909–1910). A few other techniques, such as *col legno* (play with the wood of the bow), *sul tasto* (bow over the fingerboard), and "play behind the bridge," became more commonly used than previously. Walter Piston's *Orchestration*, Chapters 1–5 gives a very good summary of the most usual string playing techniques.

George Crumb's *Vox Balaenae* (*Voice of the Whale*) *for Three Masked Players* (1972) was composed for amplified flute, amplified cello, and amplified piano. As with Crumb's *Makrokosmos I* and *II*, the amplification is to make audible the quiet sounds from the instruments, and to

György Ligeti Continuum

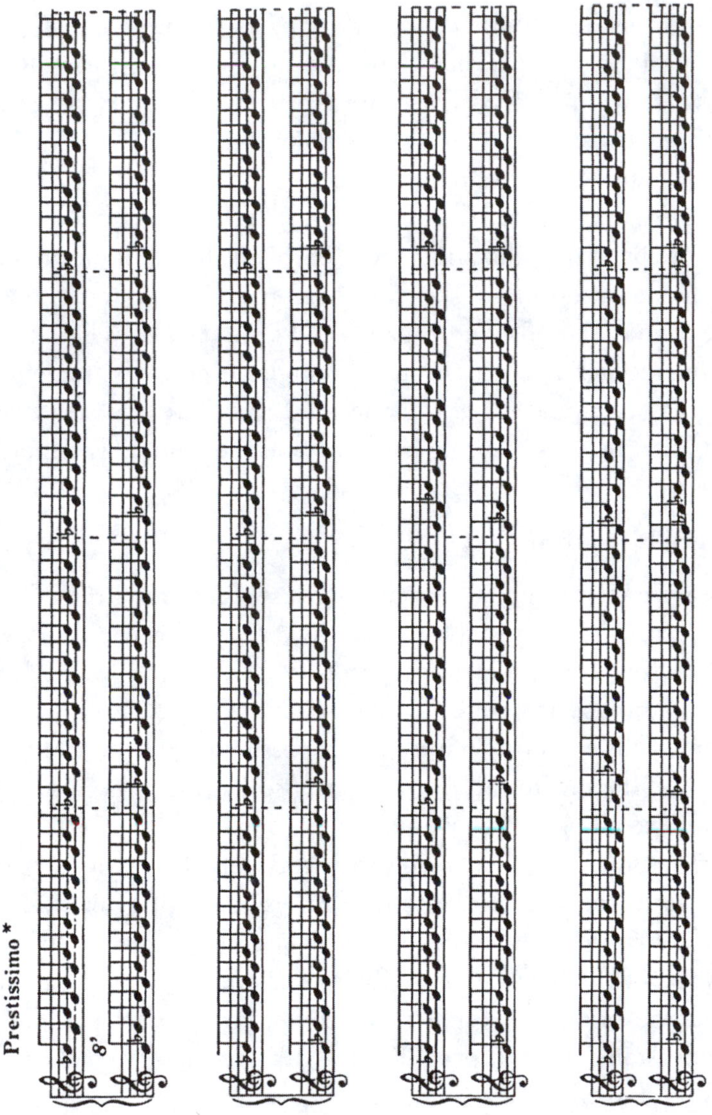

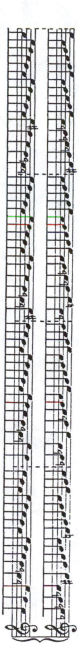

*Prestissimo = extrem schnell, so daß die Einzeltöne kaum mehr wahrzunehmen sind, sondern zu einem Kontinuum verschmelzen. Sehr gleichmäßig, ohne jede Artikulation spielen. Das richtige Tempo wurde erreicht, wenn das Stück (ohne die Schluß-Pause) weniger als vier Minuten dauert. Die vertikalen punktierten Striche sind keine Taktstriche (Takt bzw. Metrum gibt es hier nicht), sondern dienen nur zur Orientierung.

© B. Schott's Söhne, Mainz, 1970

*Prestissimo — extremely fast, so that the individual tones can hardly be perceived, but rather merge into a continuum. Play very evenly, without articulation of any sort. The correct tempo has been reached when the piece lasts less than 4 minutes (not counting the long fermata at the end). The vertical broken lines are not bar lines — there is neither beat nor metre in this piece — but serve merely as a means of orientation.

Example 6.6 György Ligeti, *Continuum* (1968).

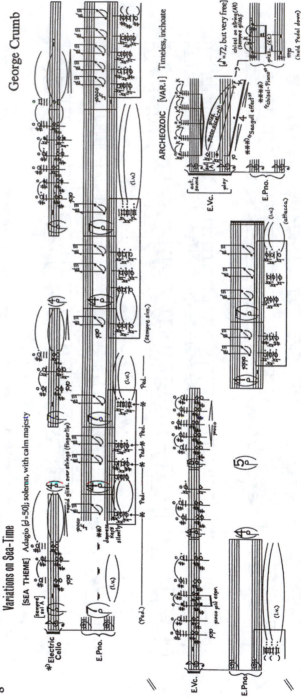

Variations on Sea-Time

George Crumb

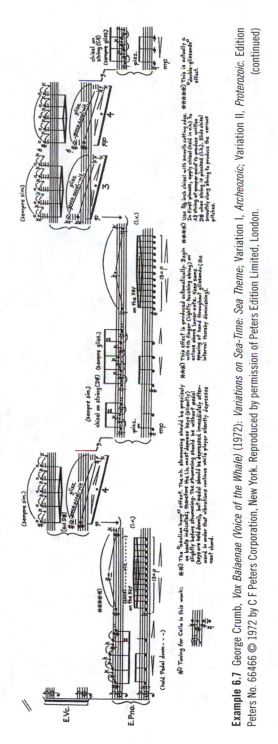

Example 6.7 George Crumb, *Vox Balaenae (Voice of the Whale)* (1972): *Variations on Sea-Time: Sea Theme;* Variation I, *Archeozoic;* Variation II, *Proterozoic.* Edition Peters No. 66466 © 1972 by C F Peters Corporation, New York. Reproduced by permission of Peters Edition Limited, London.

(continued)

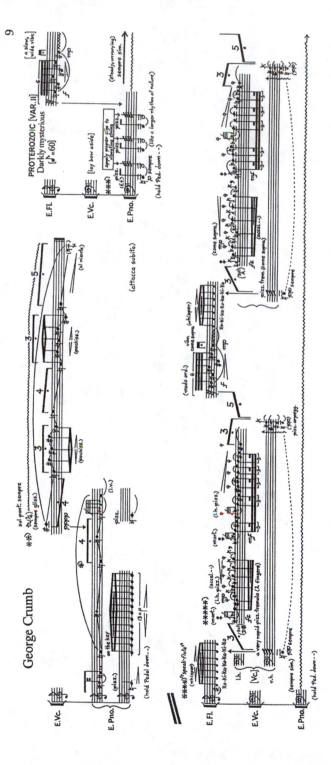

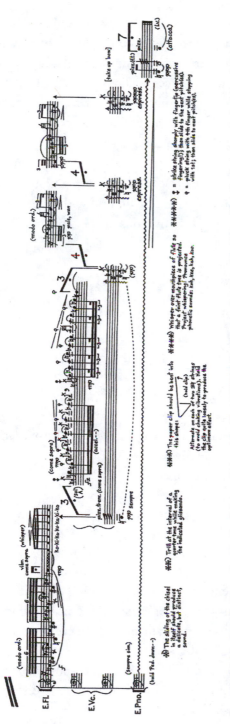

Example 6.7 (continued) George Crumb, *Vox Balaenae (Voice of the Whale)* (1972): *Variations on Sea-Time: Sea Theme*; Variation I, *Archeozoic*; Variation II, *Proterozoic*. Edition Peters No. 66466 © 1972 by C F Peters Corporation, New York. Reproduced by permission of Peters Edition Limited, London.

add an electronic aura. The movement, *Variations on Sea-Time*, has the *Sea Theme* played in harmonics by the cello, accompanied by wave-like *glissandi* on the strings of the piano, resonating over silently depressed chords. Variation 1, *Archeozoic*, introduces a cello sound, which is known as the "seagull effect." On the A-string, a stopped high A, together with a harmonic A sounding an octave higher, make a descending *glissando*. What is heard is exactly like the cry of a seagull.

Crumb's handwritten scores are always meticulously drawn, with detailed instructions (see Example 6.7). The music tends to move more slowly than the notation would suggest. Structurally, the eight movements form a cycle that addresses the divisions of geological time:

> *Vocalise (… for the beginning of time)*
> *Variations on Sea-Time: Sea Theme*
> > *Archeozoic (Variation I)*
> > *Proterozoic (Variation II)*
> > *Paleozoic (Variation III)*
> > *Mesozoic (Variation IV)*
> > *Cenozoic (Variation V)*
> *Sea-Nocturne (… for the end of time)*

Perhaps the stringed instrument that has received the least attention is the double bass. Bertram Turetzky's book *The Contemporary Contrabass* corrects this situation (see Bibliography).

Woodwind

Extended playing techniques developed during the twentieth century apply more to the woodwinds than to any other group of instruments. All four woodwind instruments—flute, oboe, clarinet, and bassoon—have been subjected to much experimentation. In addition, more use has been made of the "subsidiary" instruments within each family. The flutes include the piccolo, "C" flute, alto, and bass; the oboe adds the cor anglais; the clarinets include the E flat, the B flat, and the bass; and the bassoon adds the contrabassoon. Not all players of the standard instrument also play the subsidiary instrument, however.

Figure 6.8

A number of books have been written that explain the new techniques. Bruno Bartolozzi's *New Sounds for Woodwind* opens up vistas of possibilities not previously envisaged. Monophonics, multiphonics, microtonal fingerings, alternative fingerings, trills and *tremolandi*, and various speeds of vibrato for each instrument are all demonstrated in detail, along with fingering charts and a 7" LP. Unfortunately, his fingerings do not produce the suggested results on all makes of instruments. Nevertheless, it is worth consulting this book for the new ways of playing that it introduces.

In general, the flute, oboe, and clarinet have received more attention than the bassoon.

Flutes

Variation II, *Proterozoic*, from Crumb's *Vox Balaenae* (see Example 6.7) calls for a "C" flute that has an extension to low B (a semitone lower than normal). As can be seen, the flautist is required to whisper syllables into the flute, producing a "speak-flute." Vibrato is specified as "slow, wide." The flute line is constantly active, playing rapid note groups decorated with *acciaccatura*.

Books that explain the new techniques specifically for the flute include Thomas Howell, *The Avant-Garde Flute: A Handbook for Composers and Flutists*; Robert Dick, *The Other Flute: A Performance Manual of Contemporary Techniques*; and Pierre-Yves Artaud, *Present Day Flutes*. Pierre-Yves Artaud is the impressive soloist in Romanian Livia Teodorescu's sensuous flute concerto, *Rite for Enchanting the Air* (1998; see Example 4.26).

Oboe

The German oboist, Heinz Holliger, and British oboist, Chris Redgate, have both explored and extended the range of *timbral* possibilities for the oboe. Holliger, who is also a fine composer, has edited the following book that contains illuminating comments: *Studien zum Spielen Neuer Musik* (*Studies for Playing Avant Garde Music*). Another useful book to consult for new oboe playing techniques is Peter Veal and Claus-Steffen Mahnkopf, *The Techniques of Oboe Playing*.

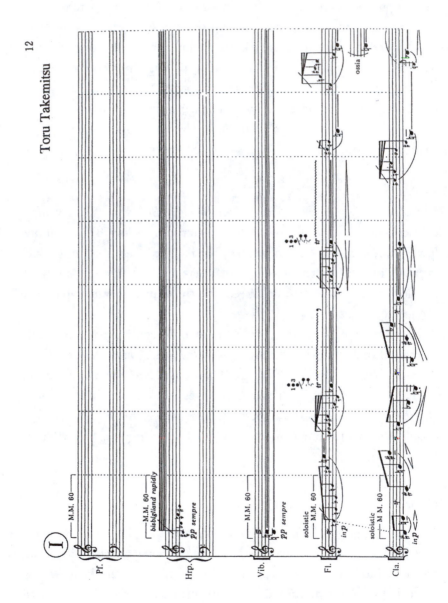

Toru Takemitsu

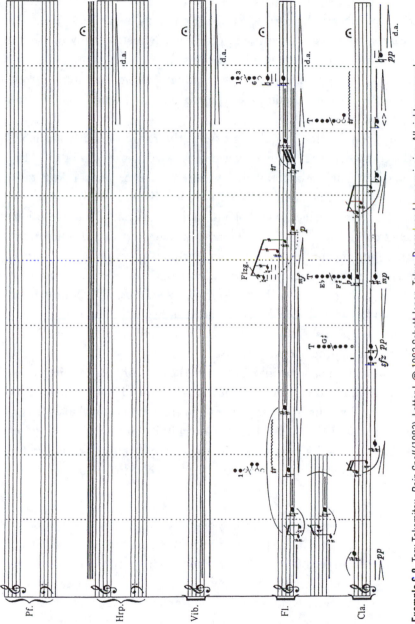

Example 6.8 Toru Takemitsu, *Rain Spell* (1983): Letter I. © 1983 Schott Japan, Tokyo.

Clarinets

As with the flute, the clarinet was the subject of much development during the twentieth century. Phillip Rehfeldt's book *New Directions for Clarinet* discusses a multitude of special "effects," many of which can be applied to all the wind and brass instruments: flutter tongue, pitch bending, *glissando*, key vibrato, throat *tremolo*, slap tongue, key slaps, key rattles, hand pops, mouthpiece alone, air sounds, and circular breathing.

These new playing techniques extend the range of sound available to the composer. They form a palette of *timbres* that should be used for greater expressive enhancement. Japanese composer Toru Takemitsu's *Rain Spell* (1983) is a delicate work for a small ensemble consisting of flute/alto flute, clarinet, harp, piano, and vibraphone. Example 6.8 is taken from Letter I and demonstrates a duet between the flute and clarinet, accompanied by a microtonal harmony played by a *bisbigliando* (whispering) harp and *tremolando* vibraphone. The flute and clarinet play flurries of grace notes, flutter tongue, *tremolando*, and multiphonics trilled and sustained. The dotted bar lines indicate the space of one second. The music is written in time-space notation, events being placed within or across the bar lines in a free rhythm.

The bass clarinet came into its own at the start of the twentieth century. It adds a lower octave to the range of the B flat clarinet. Particularly noteworthy is its use in the penultimate scene of Alban Berg's opera *Wozzeck* (1917–1922). There, playing in its bottom octave, it joins with bassoons and a contrabassoon to represent the murky waters of the mist-shrouded river in which the antihero has drowned himself.

Brass

Brass instruments—horn, trumpet, trombone, and tuba—excel in *sfp* and *crescendo* effects. Many of the extended playing techniques developed for the woodwind instruments apply equally well to the brass section: flutter tongue, pitch bending, *glissando* (for trombone), key slaps, key rattles, hand pops, mouthpiece alone, air sounds, and circular breathing. All these techniques are used in modern music for the brass band. A variety of mutes for each of the instruments is also available and these alter the *timbre* considerably. In addition, it is possible to play with the harmonic series. The microtuning of the overtones above the seventh harmonic is particularly rich when played by the lower instruments.

Hanna Kulenty's *Air* (1991), commissioned by the Dutch *Orkest de Volharding*, makes use of the harmonic series on various changing fundamentals. These, in fact, form the structure of the piece. Example 6.9 shows a passage built on fundamental F, played by the bass trombone, piano, and tenor saxophone (bar 135 onwards). The F chord (F, A, C, E quarter-tone flat, G) is sounded by the two trombones, horn, and alto saxophone. This chord is sustained, but articulated by a small "hairpin" *crescendo–decrescendo* at each bar line, giving a pulsing effect. Above this chord, the three muted trumpets play fast canonic scales in microtonal clusters. This figuration has been taken over from a trio of horn, clarinet, and flute (bars 130–134).

Percussion

The percussion family is the one that has expanded the most during the twentieth century. Almost anything that can be struck or stroked has been added to the traditional drums, timpani, and gongs. There have been concerts of percussion music in which the entire performance space has been covered with hundreds of instruments. Devoted percussion players have collected native instruments from around the world to add to the already enormous variety of color. It is easy for the composer to become bewildered and overwhelmed by the sheer number of percussion instruments now available. However, remember that most orchestras will not own the more exotic instruments and will restrict their collections to those required to perform the standard orchestral repertory.

Percussion instruments are classified according to the material of which they are made: wood, skin, or metal. Within each of these three categories is a subcategory of tuned or indefinite pitch; and within these two categories is another subcategory of relative pitch: high, middle, and low. A few examples:

- Bongos are skinned instruments of indefinite pitch. Usually, they come in pairs that, relatively, are pitched high and low.

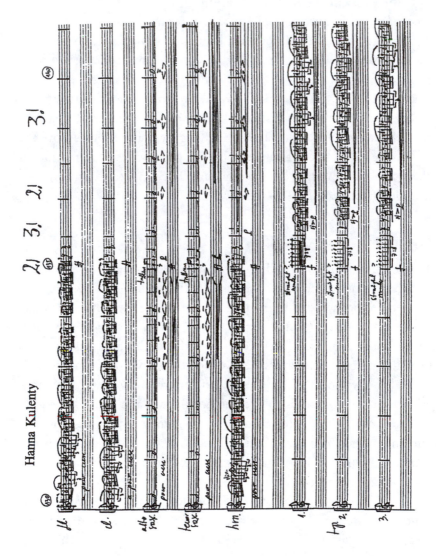

Hanna Kulenty

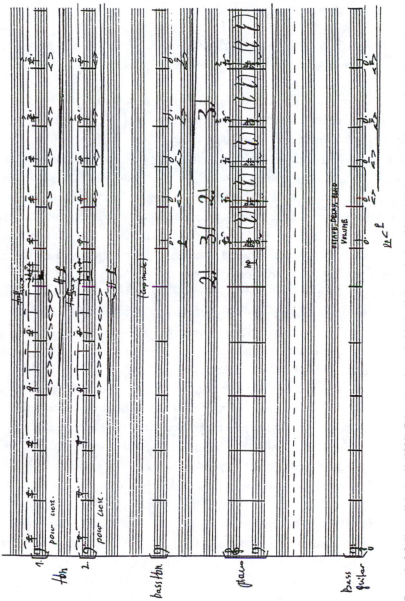

Example 6.9 Hanna Kulenty, *Air* (1991). This extract is used with the kind permission of Polski Wydawnictwo Muzyczne S. A., Kraków, Poland.

- Cymbals are metal instruments of indefinite pitch. They come in various sizes, thus giving a range of high, middle, and low relative pitches.
- Temple blocks are wooden instruments of indefinite pitch which normally come in groups of five of varying sizes, giving a relative range of high, medium-high, middle, medium-low, and low.

The above are ancient instruments, originally found in the oldest civilizations of the world. More recently invented instruments include the timpani, which are tuned skin instruments, built in four different sizes, giving a range from middle C down to two octaves lower. A pedal mechanism, operated with the foot, has been added to the timpani in order to effect exact tunings more easily. Striking the timpani, then depressing the pedal, can create a *glissando* effect.

Among the newer inventions are the keyed instruments: marimba, xylophone, vibraphone, and glockenspiel. Of these, the lower instruments, the marimba and xylophone, are made of wood, and the upper instruments, the vibraphone and glockenspiel, are made of metal. All four of these instruments are pitched and laid out like a piano keyboard. They are played with sticks, the most comfortable number being two in each hand. Sometimes, the keys are bowed with a cello or double bass bow, making rather a celestial sound.

In addition to the bewildering number of instruments is the variety of sticks with which to play them. Materials for the stick heads include wood, felt, wool, metal, wire, rubber, and plastic—all of which, of course, affect the *timbre*. The details of these can be indicated in the score.

Exotic instruments which have been used in twentieth-century scores include a wind machine (Vaughan Williams, *Sinfonia Antarctica*; see Example 4.16a and Example 4.16b), "lion's roar" (Edgard Varèse, *Ionisation*, 1929–1931), motor horns (George Gershwin, *American in Paris*, 1928), flexatone (Mauricio Kagel, *Match*, 1964), and "thunder sheets" (Richard Strauss, *Alpine Symphony*, 1911–1915).

In his excellent book, *Contemporary Percussion*, Reginald Smith Brindle explains important factors such as the layout of the percussion group, the various notation systems in use, and drumming techniques. Following these chapters are sections on each individual instrument, illustrated with photographs and a 7" LP. Despite the comprehensiveness of this book, there is no substitute for a demonstration with a percussion player.

Inexperienced composers sometimes find "adding the percussion" to their work to be quite difficult. The approach must be to think of the percussion instruments as part of the soundscape from the outset, rather than an element to be added at the end of the compositional process. The main problem lies with the percussion instruments of indefinite pitch: how will they blend with the pitched instruments? Experience suggests that, quite often, they "take on" the pitches of the surrounding instruments. Triangles blend with high woodwind; splashes of cymbals mingle with brass. This may be an aural illusion, but it allays the fears that the percussion of indefinite pitch will "stick out like a sore thumb." Among pitched percussion, the vibraphone enhances the sound of the flute.

For the learning composer, it might be best to restrict the number of percussion instruments that you use at first, later adding those with which you are familiar. In selecting which percussion instruments to use, first choose the material: wood, metal, or skin. Then decide whether you need tuned percussion or instruments of indefinite pitch. Finally, select the *tessitura*: high, middle, or low. Working in a systematic way like this will be less overwhelming and you will avoid making random choices.

Example 6.10 lists the most frequently used percussion instruments under the headings of Wood, Skin, Metal, and "Other," followed by "Tuned" and "Indefinite Pitch."

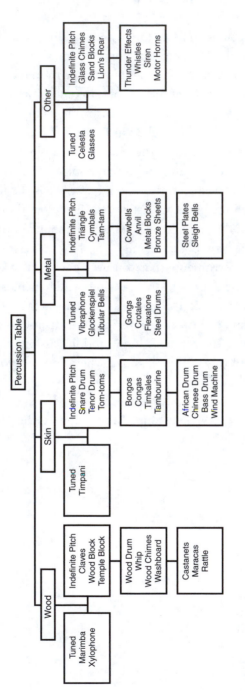

Example 6.10 Percussion table.

7

COMPOSING FOR
TRADITIONAL ENSEMBLES

Composing for a traditional ensemble is a challenging task because there are numerous well-known works already in the repertory. However, this should be a source of instruction rather than a possible comparison to be feared. Traditional ensembles include string quartet, wind quintet, brass group, percussion ensemble, and mixed instrumental ensemble. In this chapter, music from some of these groups is discussed, highlighting potential points of interest to a developing composer, as well as issues of how to utilize invented musical materials and how to expand them to produce an extended piece of music.

As indicated previously, you should start by having an idea of what you hope to achieve in your composition. This might be a structural idea or a particular expressive notion. It is likely that this choice will determine the mood or atmosphere, the structure, and some of the tempi. You should be clear about which musical language you intend to adopt. As for the musical material itself, the classic recipe recommends a combination of *unity* and *variety*. There should be a unifying factor linking the musical materials themselves, but they should in some way be varied. In the end, it is the quality of the invented musical material that will engage the attention of the listeners and performers.

From a practical point of view, you need to know the ranges and capabilities of each instrument for which you are writing. I recommended Walter Piston's *Orchestration*, which explains each instrument together with playing techniques, giving musical examples from the Romantic and early twentieth-century repertory. Make every effort to attend a concert given by a professional ensemble, to experience the excitement of the live sound and the intimate communication between the players and the audience. In addition, listen to some of the many good recordings of ensembles so that you reinforce the memory of the actual sound, which, as you will notice, differs from a synthesized version.

String Quartet

The string quartet has existed since the eighteenth century, with master works in the medium by Joseph Haydn, Wolfgang Amadeus Mozart, Ludwig van Beethoven, and many others. Composers of the twentieth century who have continued the developing tradition of string quartet writing include Anton Webern, Claude Debussy, Maurice Ravel, Béla Bartók, Elizabeth Maconchy, Benjamin Britten, Michael Tippett, Dmitri Shostakovich, Elliott Carter, Witold Lutoslawski, Krzysztof Penderecki, and Brian Ferneyhough, among several others.

The string quartet is a particularly sonorous and homogenous ensemble since all the instruments are of the same family. The two violins, viola, and cello that together make up the ensemble cover a range of over five octaves. It is important to know, and to take into account, the open strings of each instrument, because the fingers, and therefore much of the music, operate around these (see Example 7.1a).

You will notice that the violin shares some open strings with the viola. The strings marked in Example 7.1a, G, D, and A, are at the same pitch. The highest open string on the violin is E, whereas the lowest string of the viola is the C below middle C. The cello strings share the same names as the viola, but are tuned an octave lower. Walter Piston's *Orchestration*, Chapters 1–4, discusses in detail the characteristics of all the stringed instruments. Two important string techniques are sometimes confusing to non-string players: harmonics and double-stopping.

Harmonics

Harmonics have a very attractive, high, almost whistling quality. The topic of harmonics is quite complicated, but put simply, there are two types: natural and artificial. Natural harmonics are played by lightly touching the open strings at the halfway point along the string. The resulting sound is one octave higher than the open string itself (see Example 7.1b).

Artificial harmonics can account for all the other notes. They are played by stopping a string, then lightly touching a P4 higher. The resulting sound is two octaves higher than the stopped note (see Example 7.1c). The stopped note is notated normally, while the lightly touched note is written above it as a diamond shape. Sometimes, it is possible to indicate the resulting sound in brackets, but often, this lies so high that it is well above the range of the ledger lines. In this case, it is omitted. Both types of harmonic are indicated by a small *o* above the note.

It follows that there is a lower limit to the range of artificial harmonics that can be obtained. The lowest note that can be stopped is a semitone above the bottom open string, thus: A flat for the violin; D flat for the viola; and D flat for the cello. The lowest artificial harmonic obtainable sounds two octaves above these stopped notes.

When composing using harmonics, bear in mind that it is not easy to leap very quickly from one artificial harmonic to another. This type of music belongs to the realms of the virtuoso soloist, and thus is not so effective in chamber music. If in doubt, consult a string player.

Double-Stopping

Much of the music for strings is monodic, that is, one note is played at a time. However, it is feasible to play two notes as a dyad (double-stop),

Open strings

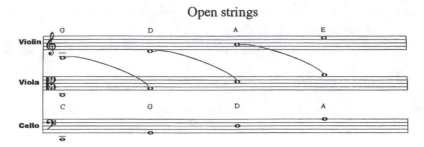

Example 7.1a Open strings.

Natural harmonics

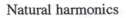
actual sounds

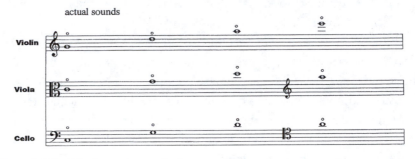

Example 7.1b String harmonics—natural.

Artificial harmonics

Example 7.1c String harmonics—artificial.

three notes as a triad (triple-stop), and four notes as a quadriad (quadruple-stop). Obviously, only one note can be played at a time on any individual string, so the other notes must be played on adjacent strings. When using the bottom string, take care not to demand a second note that is less than a P5 higher, because both notes would have to be played on the same string: an impossibility! It is helpful if one or more of the strings can be an open string, because these resonate more than stopped strings. Always be aware of the hand shape that you are demanding when writing double-, triple-, or quadruple-stops. Some collections of simultaneous notes might lie so awkwardly that they are too uncomfortable to play. Once again, consult a string player if in doubt.

The Alto Clef

Most musicians do not have cause to learn to read the alto clef, used by the viola. However, it is recommended for composers to write for the viola directly into the alto clef (rather than using the treble clef and then transferring to the alto clef afterwards). If this is a problem, try reading, then playing on your own instrument, the viola parts from any string quartet score. You will quickly become fluent in reading and writing in the alto clef. Remember that the middle line of the stave (encircled by the clef itself) is middle C.

The String Quartet Repertory

Let us examine a few string quartets with a view to acquiring some knowledge of the large repertory for this ensemble, and to gathering some ideas for your own work. It is important to be acquainted with the tradition of such a well-established medium before embarking on a new composition.

Haydn and Mozart set the standard for string quartet writing, employing what has become the normal arrangement of melody played by violin I, accompanied by harmonies played by violin II, viola, and cello. However, they utilized other texture types. The minuet and trio movements of Mozart's String Quartet No. 21, "Prussian No.1," K.575 *in D Major* (1798), illustrate a variety of textures within a tonal work (see Example 7.2). The B section of the binary-form minuet begins with a passage played by all four instruments in octaves (bars 30–37). Here,

E. E. 1125

Example 7.2 Wolfgang Amadeus Mozart, String Quartet No. 21, K. 575 in D Major (1789): Minuet and Trio.

(continued)

Example 7.2 (continued) Wolfgang Amadeus Mozart, String Quartet No. 21, K. 575 in D Major (1789): Minuet and Trio.

though tonal, the music is unusually chromatic, so Mozart chooses not to employ the normal texture of melody and accompaniment. The harmony is implied horizontally, rather than vertically. The melodic line dives and swoops in intervals of D7, A4, and m7 connected by m2, with dramatic dynamic markings of forte-piano. Notice that the two violins play in unison, the viola an octave lower, and the cello another octave lower.

This is immediately followed by a passage of single-note *arpeggios* (bars 37–44). The first *arpeggio* outlines an *ascending* chord of a diminished seventh on G sharp (G sharp, B, D, F), the notes of which are divided between the instruments (bars 37–40). This is answered by a *descending arpeggio* that outlines a chord of the dominant ninth in D (A, C sharp, E, G, B flat), which, similarly, is divided between the instruments (bars 40–44). Interestingly, at bar 41, the dominant note, A, is played by the cello, viola, and violin II. Violin I then enters with a high B flat, the most dissonant note of the dominant ninth chord, creating the maximum intervallic clash.

From bar 44 until the end of the minuet, the music echoes the first section of the binary form. Normal textures appear, in which violin I plays a prominent role, supported by the lower instruments playing the tonal harmonic foundation (bars 44–60). Here, we can observe another texture type involving the pairing of the two lower instruments against the two upper instruments. The viola and cello take the lead with a sequential sixteenth-note figure played in thirds. This is answered by the two violins playing a four-note phrase in octaves (bars 60–69). The minuet finishes with a traditional coda in which all four instruments state a perfect cadence, emphasized by being iterated three times, each one being slightly different. It is a mark of a great composer that the smallest detail receives care and attention, making telling differences where others would be satisfied with exact repetitions.

Normally, the four instruments occupy the hierarchic positions of bass (cello), tenor (viola), alto (violin II), and soprano (violin I). The Mozart trio demonstrates yet another texture type in which the instrumental roles are displaced. Here, the cello plays the melody, high in its range, using the treble clef. The actual bass line is played by the viola, sounding below the cello. The eighth-note accompaniment defining the chords is played by violin 1, also sounding below the cello!

It does not matter which instrument plays the bass line, but it is important to assign that instrument for a phrase or so, thus allowing time for this particular texture to establish itself. Sometimes young composers become confused about where the instruments (the viola and cello in particular) lie in relation to each other. The result of this can be that the bass line inadvertently "hops" between the two. It is worth checking this aspect.

Of interest to a composer of the twenty-first century is the variety of textures used by composers of the classical era. Texture is an aspect of composition that became of particular interest to composers of the twentieth century. Anton Webern's *Fünf Sätze für Streichquartett* (*Five Pieces for String Quartet*), op. 5 (1909), shows an exquisite imagination for string sonority (see Example 7.3). This is a pre-serial work, the style of which indicates how close to Schoenberg's musical thinking the young Webern was. Webern used intervals to construct his musical materials. It could be argued that using the interval as the unit of construction is still a valid way of generating musical materials, less rigid and more productive than the use of a twelve-tone row.

Played with mutes and marked *Sehr langsam* (very slow), the dynamic range for the entire fourth movement lies between *ppp* and *pp*. Opening with two high *tremolando* harmonies played over the fingerboard by the two violins, the principal intervals are introduced. Vertically, the intervals read:

Bar 1: M7 (F–E) and m9 (B–C)
Bar 2: A8 (F–F sharp) or enharmonic m9, and M7 (C–B)

It may be observed that the principal intervals here lie on either side of the octave. Read horizontally, the intervals are:

Bar 1: M3 (E–C) and D5 (F–B)
Bar 2: P5 (F sharp–B) and P4 (F–C)

The first *tremolando* chord is played as a short *pizzicato* chord at the end of bar 2, these three chords thus forming a short palindrome. The

Example 7.3 Anton Webern, *Fünf Sätze für Streichquartett*, op. 5 (1909): Movement IV. Copyright 1922 by Universal Edition A.G. Vienna. Copyright renewed 1949 by Anton Webern's Erben. Reproduced by permission. All rights reserved.

motif played by the violins is heard above a pedal E flat in the cello, joined by E natural–F sharp in the viola. This pedal material creates several intervallic connections with the *tremolando* chords. The pitches played vertically by the violins in bar 2 (F sharp, B, F natural, C) are played horizontally by violin I in bar 3. The succession of intervals is P5, A4, P4. This short linear phrase is transposed in bar 4 for violin II, which begins on the second note, B. Adjoining the two canonic entries is a chord that contains all the principal intervals: A4, P4, D8, M7, m7 (G, C sharp, F sharp, C natural, B); see the start of bar 4. The last pitch of the four-note group is overlapped by the cello entry, again beginning on F sharp, but sounding three octaves lower than the entry of violin I.

Here we see one of Webern's favorite contrapuntal devices, a canon. The overlapping notes between the canonic entries refer to the principal intervals: M7 up (C–B) and D8/M7 down (F–F sharp). Another canon is heard in bars 5–6. The last note of the four-note group played by the cello descends to the lowest open string, C. It becomes another little figure in close canon with violin I, beginning one eighth note earlier and played two octaves higher. Between the cello and violin I, the viola adds an embryonic palindromic figure of F sharp, G, F sharp, echoing the palindrome between the violins in bars 1–2. Read vertically, the intervals in bar 5 are those which were first heard in bar 2: A8, D5, P5, A4, M7, m6/M3, P4. Marking the end of this opening phrase is an upward sixteenth note *arpeggio*, played by violin II alone.

Then follows a three-bar phrase comprising a melody played by violin I accompanied by the three lower instruments (bars 7–9). In examining the accompaniment it can be seen that there are three pedals involved, an echo of the pedal hinted at by the cello and viola in bars 1 and 2. Looking carefully at the cello part in bars 7–9, we see that what is indicated is not a double stop but an artificial harmonic. The diamond-shaped note A indicates where to lightly touch the string: a P4 above the stopped note E. As if by magic, this has the effect of causing the pitch to rise two octaves above the lower note; the pitch actually heard is the E above middle C.

Examining the violin II part next, we see that it sustains the B below middle C, so, in fact, it is sounding below the cello. Here, there is a double pedal containing the interval of a P4, (B–E). Above this, the viola plays a triplet figure made up of three pitches, each a M3 apart, D–B flat–G flat. Repeated exactly, five times, this little figure peters out by the substitution of notes with rests (bar 9). Thus, the accompaniment comprises an interesting texture, with violin II as the bass, cello as the tenor, and viola as the alto. The sweet melody played high above by violin I is derived from Movement I (see bar 20). Like the first phrase, the second also finishes with an upward *arpeggio* (bar 10). This time, it is played by the viola in a triplet rhythm, rather than sixteenth notes, and transposed onto F (A4 lower than the previous pitch). The concluding phrase, bars 11–13, refers to the end of the first phrase, bars 5–6. The original palindromic viola figure, F sharp–G–F sharp, is now played by violin I, very high up, in harmonics (bars 11–12). The sound is heard two octaves higher than the written stopped notes. The canonic figure heard between violin I and the cello in bar 5 is now curtailed in bars 11–12; it is played in octaves by violin II and viola, with the cello entering one crotchet later.

The canon in the upper register is interrupted by a low *pizzicato* chord. This refers to the *tremolando* chord at the start of bar 2. The intervals of that chord (P4, A8, A4, P5, M7) are transposed down a D7, onto G sharp, and placed in the lower register. We may remember that the first *tremolando* violin chord appeared as a *pizzicato* chord at the end of bar 2. However, the second *tremolando* chord has not made an appearance as a *pizzicato* chord until bar 12, a technique that can be likened to juxtaposing mosaic pieces in different permutations. The movement concludes with the third appearance of the familiar upward *arpeggio* figure. This time, it is transposed onto G sharp (A4 higher than the previous pitch), with an altered rhythm including a quintuplet sixteenth note pattern, and played, as on first hearing, by violin II. As if flying into inaudibility, the final flourish makes a *decrescendo* from *ppp*.

Typical of the minute detail of Webern's work, everything in this short movement is referenced in altered form: balancing high against low; changing instrumentation; playing the same material in a different manner. Webern's initial selection of intervals generates the flow of pitch material and informs the construction of the harmonies. The sound of this movement is of a fleeting, fluttering, and flying music that is scarcely audible to human hearing: a masterpiece in miniature.

Of Béla Bartók's six famous string quartets, the *Marcia* (Movement II) of No. 6 (1939) is well worth studying (see Example 7.4). Each of the four movements of this quartet begins with an introductory passage that is based on the same theme (a sad, chromatic melody in compound time), which acts as a unifying feature. At the start of Movement II, this theme is played by the cello, beginning on its A string and gradually descending to its lowest note, bottom C. This melody is accompanied by a countermelody played in octaves by all three upper instruments. The viola and violin II play *tremolando*, while violin I plays *legato normale*.

The *Marcia* itself is in ternary form:

A1: Bars 17–79
B: Bars 80–121
A2: Bars 122–191

A1 contains four musical elements:

Bars 17–25: a march-like motive in a dotted rhythm, in 4/4 time
Bars 25–32: a two-note motive separated by rests
Bars 42–49: a canonic figure containing a trill
Bars 58–76: a melody, based on P4, played first by violin II, then passed to violin I

The transition to the central B section (bars 76–79) contains a hint of the dotted "martial" theme, played by the viola, landing on a sustained G sharp. This is surrounded by *staccato* chords of B, played by the other three instruments.

The G sharp held by the viola is taken over by the solo cello playing A flat one octave higher (bar 80). For the next three bars, the cello effects an *accelerando*, notated by adding ever increasing numbers of notes between each beat: 2, 3, 4, then 5. This gesture ends with an upward *glissando* onto a natural A harmonic. In this high register, the cello sings out a melody that is built around intervals of m3 and m2. This melody is accompanied by the two violins playing *tremolando* harmonies. They start by playing the same two notes in "box and cox" fashion (C–E flat and E flat–C). Below the violins and cello, the viola plays four-part *pizzicato* chords,

Bartók

Example 7.4 Béla Bartók, String Quartet No. 6 (1939): *Marcia* (Movement II). © Copyright 1941 by Hawkes & Sons (London) Ltd. Reproduced by permission of Boosey & Hawkes Music Publishers Ltd.

(continued)

Example 7.4 (continued) Béla Bartók, String Quartet No. 6 (1939): *Marcia* (Movement II). © Copyright 1941 by Hawkes & Sons (London) Ltd. Reproduced by permission of Boosey & Hawkes Music Publishers Ltd.

reminiscent of a folk instrument. The chords are to be performed by stroking the strings across in both directions, indicated by the arrows pointing up and down. The rhythm of the chords echoes the *accelerando* gesture of the cello in bars 80–82. The texture here is similar to that of the Mozart trio (see Example 7.2), with the principal theme being given to the cello, and the viola playing the bass line. At bar 99, violin I continues the melody, which forms a canon with the cello entry at bar 104. The transition, beginning at bar 115, to the recapitulation consists of an "ironed-out" version of the dotted "martial" theme, being turned into a four-note sixteenth note figure. This is piled up from bottom to top, so that it eventually appears simultaneously in four keys: Am (cello), F sharp m (viola), Dm (violin II), and Bm (violin I).

The A2 recapitulation follows the events of A1 in the same order, but with everything altered in some respect. The first motive (the dotted "martial" theme) was first presented by the cello and violin I playing two octaves apart, and outlining the chord of F sharp M. In the space between, violin II and the viola answered in canon, playing one octave apart. In the recapitulation, beginning in bar 122, the cello and violin II play the same F sharp M dotted theme, but this time in double stops, fully articulating each major chord in parallel four-part harmony. Thus, we hear a succession of parallel major chords: F sharp M, A sharp M, C sharp M, BM, etc. (Helpfully, the strings required to play the double stops are indicated in the violin II part. Using Roman numerals, the strings are numbered from the top: E = I, A = II, D = III, G = IV.) The answer is made by the viola playing in octave double stops, above which floats violin I playing the dotted theme in harmonics. Could Bartók have had in mind a soldier whistling a jaunty tune?

Bartók used aspects of the tonal system in a new way. In this respect, he had an influence on many composers of different nationalities, including the English composer Elizabeth Maconchy. Her thirteen string quartets delineate a lifetime of creative output. She described her approach to writing for the string quartet:

> [F]or those to whom music is an intellectual art, a balanced and rea-
> soned statement of ideas, an impassioned argument, an intense but
> disciplined expression of emotion — the string quartet is perhaps
> the most satisfying medium of all. (4)

Maconchy's String Quartet No. 3 (1938) is a one-movement work lasting over ten minutes (see Example 7.5). The structure of the entire work may be regarded as being in sonata form. It is made from two musical ideas that are stated in the exposition. Subject 1 occupies bars 1–18 and comprises several interesting elements. Harmonically, this passage alternates between CM/m and E flat m, two pitch centers that lie a minor third apart, E flat being the mediant minor of Cm. Rhythmically, the bars alternate between 4/4 (CM/m) and 5/8 (E flat m), echoing the duality of the harmonic scheme. In the 4/4 bars, the rhythm of the melody establishes the pattern: a dotted quarter note followed by an eighth note. The 5/8 bars each reiterate a rhythm of five eighth notes. Melodically, the line moves by intervals of a m2 and its inversion, M7.

Violin I begins by fluctuating between E (the major third of the chord of CM) and D sharp (enharmonically the minor third of Cm), in the rhythm of dotted quarter followed by an eighth (bar 1). The D sharp eighth note becomes the enharmonic root of E flat m (bar 2), moving in the rhythmic group of five eighth notes. Bars 1 and 2 are repeated in bars 3 and 4, ending with the melody leaping up by a m9 (last note of the 5/8 group). Violin II (bars 5 and 6) has a transposed version of the violin I line from bars 1 and 2. The transposition is onto the dominant, G, of the CM/m chord. The F sharp becomes the enharmonic minor third of E flat m in bar 6. Bars 3 and 4 are repeated in bars 7 and 8. These elements continue to be in play until the end of this passage.

A new rhythm is heard in bars 11 and 12 consisting of a quarter note triplet figure, played in octaves by the viola and cello. This figure is repeated three times, each time starting on a different degree of the CM/m chord: G, the dominant; E, the mediant; and C, the root. This triplet figure causes bar 12 to remain as a 4/4 bar, whereas, had the alternating pattern been adhered to, it should have been a 5/8 bar. To compensate, the group of five eighth notes is played in the time of four. Thus, this quintuplet group (bar 12) moves a little quicker than the eighth notes in the 5/8 bars. This interruption to the established pattern of alternating 4/4 and 5/8 bars prevents rhythmic predictability.

Also worth noting are the interlocking double stops. Violin II, viola, and cello all play double- and sometimes triple-stops. Bars 1, 3, and 5

A. L. & Co. Ltd. 3906

Example 7.5 Elizabeth Maconchy, String Quartet No. 3 (1938). © 1938 Copyright permission granted by Alfred Lengnick & Co. Obtainable from FM Distribution Ltd., Burnt Mill, Elizabeth Way, Harlow CM.20 2HX, UK. Tel: +44 (0) 1279 828 989, fax: +44 (0) 1279 828 990, email: information@ fmdistribution.com, sales@fmdistribution.com, www.alfredlengnick.co.uk (continued)

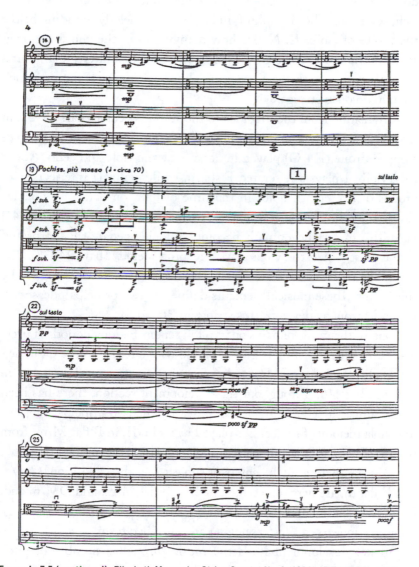

Example 7.5 (continued) Elizabeth Maconchy, String Quartet No. 3 (1938). © 1938 Copyright permission granted by Alfred Lengnick & Co. Obtainable from FM Distribution Ltd., Burnt Mill, Elizabeth Way, Harlow CM.20 2HX, UK. Tel: +44 (0) 1279 828 989, fax: +44 (0) 1279 828 990, email: information@fmdistribution.com, sales@fmdistribution.com, www.alfredlengnick.co.uk

have the viola octave double-stop (C + C) overlapping with the octave double-stop of violin 2 (G + G). This has a binding effect on what is a rich, seven-part chord. Violin I, in fact, has the melody sounding below the top G of violin II. Notice how many notes of the chord are open strings. The open string Cs and Gs will resonate and create a natural *timbral* contrast with the alternating chords of "dark" E flat m, which contain no open strings.

A transition from the first idea to the second occupies bars 19–21, in which there are hints of both. Subject 2 begins in bar 21 with a double-stopped drone (F + G) played in octaves by the viola and cello. Above this, violin I plays a reiterated F sharp, while violin II interjects with groups of five eighth notes in the time of four, on octave G double-stops. The quintuplet figure cuts across beats two and three of the 4/4 bars. This material eventually becomes a double pedal of F sharps and Gs, against which the viola plays a leaping melody (bars 24–35). The leaps take the viola by turns above, then below, the pedals sounded by the violins. These musical elements define the two principal ideas with which Maconchy develops this string quartet.

Tonally, the music remains on its pitch centers for long periods of time. The development section begins at bar 38 with a return to the C "tonic," eventually moving to EM/m at bar 57, where it stays until it alights on B flat at bar 116. Throughout the development section, there has been much "impassioned argument," all based on the two principal subjects. The viola melody of subject 2 is played by violin II, in B flat M/m, from bar 151. This acts as a transition to a recapitulation beginning at bar 160. The two conflicting pitch centers of subject 1 in the exposition, CM/m and E flat m, are here represented by Bm, B flat M/m, and DM/m and, later, by D flat M and Em (the same relationship as at the beginning). Subject 2 appears in a faster-moving and curtailed form.

Further development leads the music through a number of pitch centers before finally arriving back "home" on C for the coda, *poco largamente*. The triplet quarter note motif is heard in triple- and quadruple-stopped *pizzicato* chords, making a rich sonority. On the final page, the 5/8 bars become 5/4 bars, alternating with the 4/4 bars, and thus effecting a *ritardando*. Violin I has a long *glissando* from D sharp descending to E. This is at first the enharmonic mediant of Cm, moving to CM; then, the enharmonic root of E flat m moving to the mediant of CM. Finally, the *glissando* idea transfers to the viola, sinking to a satisfying low E, the mediant of CM.

Clearly, the musical language of this work is based on tonality. Diatonic chords abound, but their function is not that of the hierarchical tonal system. This represents a new way of working with old materials. Maconchy courts accessibility by using familiar musical objects in an unusual manner. Here is a work that demonstrates wonderfully the value of economy in the use of musical materials. Not a note is out of place. Every figure can be traced to its origin. Certainly, it adheres to the classic principles of unity and variety.

Continuing the theme of unity and variety, though in a very different style, is Witold Lutoslawski's String Quartet of 1964. Lutoslawski addresses in this work the issue of how to notate a score for music that is not rhythmically synchronized. Structurally, the quartet comprises a series of "mobiles," often notated with one mobile per page of the score (see Example 7.6).

The work begins with an *Introductory Movement*. Mobile 1 is for solo violin I, playing *con sordino*, in which the principal intervals of m2 and A4 (and their inversions or octave displacements) are heard. These act as the unifying factor in the construction of the linear material for this movement. Mobile 2 (Figure 1 in the score) is for the three lower instruments, also playing *con sordino*. Here, the music is notated in individual boxes for each instrument. Once the instrument has entered, the music within the boxes is to be played rhythmically independently of the others. The cello begins by playing middle C followed by B a quarter-tone sharp, i.e., sounding slightly lower than middle C. The entries of the viola, followed by violin II, are precisely indicated. Similarly, they enter with the middle C and B quarter-tone sharp motif, each with a different rhythm. All three instruments then play melodies based on the interval of A4: G sharp–D for the cello; A–D sharp for the viola; and E–B flat for violin II. Thus, the harmonic field for this section is controlled.

Mobile 3 (Figure 2) is again for the solo violin I. This passage permutates a group of four pitch classes: G, C, B, F sharp. Ending on a repeated C, violin II and the viola then add the notes of a chromatic

Example 7.6 Witold Lutoslawski, String Quartet (1964). This extract is used with the kind permission of Polski Wydawnictwo Muzyczne S.A., Kraków, Poland. Copyright © 1967 Chester Music Ltd.

(continued)

scale, with various octave displacements: C, C sharp, D, E flat, E natural, F, F sharp, G, G sharp, A. There follows the next boxed passage, this time for the three upper instruments. Violin I begins, with entries for violin II and the viola marked. Each instrument has its own different four-note group, which is permutated.

The cello interrupts with a motif that is to become important: repeated Cs played *forte* in an octave double-stop. This marks Mobile 4 (Figure 4) in which all the instruments join with the repeated Cs

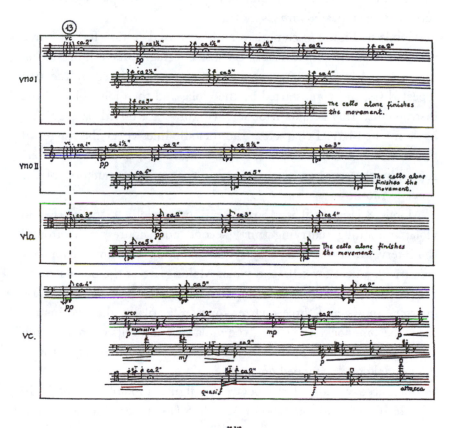

Example 7.6 (continued) Witold Lutoslawski, String Quartet (1964). This extract is used with the kind permission of Polski Wydawnictwo Muzyczne S.A., Kraków, Poland. Copyright © 1967 Chester Music Ltd.

played in octave double-stops. Mobile 5 (Figure 5) represents another way of notating a texture that is rhythmically unsynchronized. Each instrument has a different time signature: 9/8 for violin 1; 2/2 (or 8/8) for violin 2; 3/4 (or 6/8) for the viola; 5/8 for the cello. Each bar (indicated by a dotted line) is to be performed in the time of a metronomic speed of 40 bars per minute. Thus, each slow pulse is divided into 9, 8, 6, and 5 beats. Of great interest is the way in which the texture is at times dense, then thins and appears to slow down. This passage starts with all the instruments playing complete bars, creating a fast-moving, *pizzicato* texture. As the number of notes per bar is reduced, so the texture becomes thinner and slower moving. This passage is interrupted by the repeated *arco* Cs motif.

Mobile 6 (Figure 6) comprises another boxed section for the three upper instruments. Their materials consist of fragmentary figures using the principal intervals. Again, the section is interrupted by the two repeated Cs, this time started by the viola, and then joined by all the instruments. This heralds Mobile 7 (Figure 7), a boxed passage that has a marked lyrical character. The melodic lines cover the ranges of the instruments with leaps, rhythmic figuration, and *tremoli*, interrupted by the repeated octave Cs, this time in a permutation of the previous motif.

Mobile 8 (Figure 8) is a boxed section for violin I, violin II, and viola, containing scurrying thirty-second note figures, built around the interval of a m2. The C octave interruption announces Mobile 9 (Figure 9), a duet for cello and viola. Making use of the open strings, D and A for the cello, and G for the viola, the entwining figures use quarter-, semi-, and three-quarter tones. Eventually, the two instruments become locked together, the viola sustaining its open G string a tone lower than the open A string of the cello, both entangled with microtonal double-stopped notes.

A reduced version of the octave Cs figure announces Mobile 10 (Figure 10), which is an echo of Mobile 5 (Figure 5). The same multiple time signatures are used, resulting in shifting texture densities. This time, the texture is played *arco* and starts in sustained harmonics. The pitches change, according to rhythmic patternings: after 18 eighth notes for violin I and violin II; after 15 eighth notes for the viola; and after 14 eighth notes for the cello. At the same time, the pitch register gradually descends, moving from harmonics to *loco normale*. The texture alternates between sustained, slowly changing harmonies, and dense, fast-moving bars. Finally, this passage is interrupted by the longest outburst of the forte octave Cs.

The last Mobile of this movement (Figure 13) consists of independently played *pizzicato* chords, ending with the cello playing a reminiscence of the opening violin I solo, based on the interval of a m2, with octave displacements. Movement II, *Main Movement*, follows. Though in some ways an experimental work, particularly regarding its method of notation, the principles of unity and variety are clearly evident within the composition.

Listening

Find the scores and recordings of as many of the following twentieth century string quartets as you can, and enjoy listening to them. Here are some suggestions: the dates in brackets indicate the span of years of composition.

Debussy	String Quartet in G (1893)
Ravel	String Quartet in F (1904)
Schoenberg	String Quartets 1–4 (1905–1936)
Webern	*Five Pieces for String Quartet*, op. 5 (1909); String Quartets op. 20 and 28 (1938)
Bartók	String Quartets 1–6 (1909–1939)
Berg	Lyric Suite (String Quartet No. 2) (1925–26)
Britten	String Quartets 1–3 (1930–1975/77)
Crawford Seeger	String Quartet 1 (1931)
Maconchy	String Quartets 1–13 (1933–1982/85)
Tippett	String Quartets 1–4 (1934–1977)
Lutyens	String Quartets 1–6 (1938–1952)
Bacewicz	String Quartets 1–7 (1938–1965)
Shostakovich	String Quartets 1–15 (1938–1974)
Carter	String Quartets 1–5 (1951–1995)
Penderecki	String Quartets 1–2 (1960–1968)
Jolas	String Quartets 1–2 (1966)
Lutoslawski	String Quartet (1964)
Crumb	*Black Angels* (1970)
Gubaidulina	String Quartets 1–3 (1971–1987)
Ferneyhough	String Quartets 1–3 (1976–1987)
Glass	*Company* (1983)

Wind Quintets

Although a well-established ensemble type, and with a history stretching as far back as the classical era, the repertory for the wind quintet is not as large as that of the string quartet. The wind quintet is certainly not a homogenous ensemble, unlike the string quartet. Consisting of a pipe instrument (the flute), two double-reed instruments (the oboe and the bassoon), a single-reed instrument (the clarinet), and a brass instrument (the horn), the wind quintet's common denominator is the fact that all the instruments are blown. Each instrument has a different *timbre*, so the composer's concern is how well they will blend. In fact, an experienced, professional wind quintet spends time balancing and blending their individual playing, which must minimize the composer's worries.

Two of the instruments are transposing: the clarinet and the horn. When initially composing, it is suggested that you write at sounding pitch, so that it is clear how the pitches relate one to another. The chief danger in doing this is that inexperienced composers tend to write too high for the horn. The most comfortable sounding range for the horn lies between the C below middle C and the C above middle C. Once again, Walter Piston's *Orchestration* is recommended for details of the instrumental ranges, normal playing techniques, and examples from the symphonic repertory.

In addition to the standard configuration of the wind quintet, there are auxiliary instruments available. The flute can double on piccolo and/or alto flute; the oboe can double on cor anglais; the clarinet can double on bass clarinet; and the bassoon can double on contrabassoon. This extends both the range and the color of the already vibrant ensemble. The normal range of a "standard" wind quintet covers five octaves, upwards from the lowest note of the bassoon (B flat below cello C) to a high flute B flat. The auxiliary instruments extend the range further, by an octave in each direction (contrabassoon to piccolo). Thus, the pitch range is large, and the textural combinations are many. These can vary from solo passages for each of the individual instruments, through duets, trios, and quartets, to the full quintet. Given that all the players need breathing space, it is good practice to allow at least one player at a time to be taking a rest. Following these guidelines, the textures will naturally evolve.

If taking advantage of the availability of the auxiliary instruments, it is necessary to allow players the appropriate time to put down one instrument and to pick up the other. The time needed might be quite lengthy, especially in the case of the clarinet to bass clarinet and bassoon to contrabassoon, because these are large instruments and are placed on special stands beside the performers.

Now we will take a look at wind quintets by Carl Nielsen, Arnold Schoenberg, Ruth Crawford Seeger, and György Ligeti. Carl Nielsen's wind quintet of 1922 belongs to the neoclassical era of the early twentieth century. It is a tonal work, with the instruments transposed in the score. Movement III, the final movement, begins with a *Præludium* leading to a theme and variations. Auxiliary instruments are used, including the cor anglais in F and clarinet in A, thus making demands on score readers! The *Præludium*, marked *Adagio*, is in Cm, and contains three cadenzas in turn for the flute, cor anglais, and "A" clarinet. This section heralds the theme, played by all the instruments in triple time and cloaked in a diatonic harmonization. The key structure moves from AM for the first phrase to F sharp m (the relative minor) for the second phrase, returning to AM for the third and final phrase. The character of the theme is that of a "simple" folksong.

Variation I is a duo for the horn and bassoon, still in the tonic of AM, with syncopated hocketing that alternates between duple and triple time. The key scheme of AM–F sharp m–AM is retained. Variation II is a display piece for the flute. The other instruments add a syncopated accompaniment. The central section, in the relative minor, is distinguished by a trill figure for all the instruments (see Example 7.7).

In Variation III, a dotted version of the theme is heard, played by the oboe, *meno mosso*, and surrounded by chromatic counterpoint. A change of *tempo* to *più vivo* marks Variation IV. All the instruments play double or triple tonguing, in rhythmic unison, making a lively contrast with the preceding variations. The "A" clarinet is displayed in a cadenza in Variation V. The full range of the clarinet is used in a highly decorated version of the theme. The bassoon adds a couplet figure between phrases and plays the final segment of the theme, in the bass.

The first change of mode is heard in Variation VI, which is in Am. The central phrase is in FM, the flattened submediant major. A haunting minor version of the theme is presented, mostly in three parts until the final phrase, in which all the instruments participate. Remaining

Nielsen

Example 7.7 Carl Nielson, Quintet (1922): Movement III, Variation II.   (continued)

in Am, the bassoon plays a solo for Variation VII. The theme is decorated with perpetual motion triplet figuration. The central phrase is in
CM, the relative major. A canon between the oboe and A clarinet is
the feature of Variation VIII. This is heard above a double pedal of
tonic and dominant, played throughout the variation by the horn and
bassoon.

Reflecting the bassoon solo of Variation VII, the horn has a solo in
Variation IX. The theme is recast in 4/4 time, with a dotted rhythm.
The "echoes" marking the ends of each phrase are particularly effective.
For the first time, the key is changed to FM, with the central phrase
in Am, the mediant. Excitement increases in Variation X, in which
the theme is played by the bassoon in duple time, accompanied by the

Example 7.7 (continued) Carl Nielson, Quintet (1922): Movement III, Variation II.

upper instruments playing in 6/8. Thus, here there is a simultaneous combination of simple and compound times.

The final Variation XI, is marked *tempo di Marcia*, and, indeed, the theme is presented in a martial style, being in 4/4 with dotted and triplet rhythms. Acting as a summary of several of the motives heard in the preceding variations; all the instruments participate in rousing lines, sometimes in octaves. The variation ends with fragments of the theme played in decreasing dynamics, from *ff* to *ppp*. These finish on the dominant of A in order to herald the final statement of the theme. This is presented in a homophonic, 4/4 version, in the tonic of AM, having the character of a benedictory chorale.

In composing a set of variations, it is a good idea to establish the character, speed, and mood for each. In this Nielsen quintet, there are eleven variations, each with its own identity. The key scheme is:

Variations 1–5 are in the tonic, AM
Variations 6–8 are in the tonic minor, Am
Variation 9 is in FM
Variations 10–11 return to the tonic, AM

The set of variations is framed by statements of the theme, the opening version being in triple time, and the final version being in quadruple time.

The theme itself is not always explicit in a particular variation, but rather, there is a shadow, or ghost, of the theme. This is particularly true of Variations V, VII, and IX, which are for solo clarinet, solo bassoon, and then solo horn, respectively. Aspects of a theme that can be varied include:

- Speed
- Modality/tonality
- Mood
- Rhythm
- Meter
- Character
- Instrumentation

In common with many composers, Nielsen has arranged his set of variations so that there is an overall cumulative effect. This can be achieved by an acceleration in tempo for the final variations, or, at least, by increasing the number of notes per pulse, which has the effect of adding to the excitement.

Schoenberg's Wind Quintet (1924) is an early twelve-tone work. Movement I is cast in sonata form. The opening is discussed in Chapter 4 (see Example 4.12b).

Ruth Crawford Seeger's *Suite for Wind Quintet* (1952) was the last work that she composed before her death in 1953. Cast in three movements, it demonstrates Crawford Seeger's modernist aesthetic and her individual use of serial technique. Movement I is based on a seven-note row, which is repeated as an *ostinato* throughout. First heard in the bassoon part, its inversion continues in the oboe part (from bar 38), returning to the bassoon with a transposed version of the original (bar 61). Above, the other instruments duplicate the various notes of the row at the unison or octave, then sustain these notes to form countermelodies and harmonies. Example 7.8a shows bars 1–9, beginning with the row in the bassoon part. The row itself is gradually transformed through octave displacement of selected pitches, and rhythmically by omitting the rests.

Movement III is constructed from a different row (see Example 7.8b). The fundamental cell consists of a four-note pattern containing the intervals M2, m2, M2. By working these intervals in a variety of ascending and descending contours, a unified melodic line may be obtained. Crawford Seeger transposes the four-note group such that it forms a twelve-tone row. The interval between the four-note groups is a M3.

By permutating the pattern of intervals, particularly in the third group, and by systematically omitting one note at a time within each round, the row evolves. For example, Movement III begins with thirteen statements of the row, played by the bassoon and doubled three octaves higher by the flute. The line gradually ascends from low D to over two octaves higher. The first statement includes all twelve notes of the row; the second statement omits the first note, D; the third statement omits the second note, E; the fourth statement omits the third note, F; and so on. This procedure can be traced throughout bars 1–17. In addition, the rhythm is freely composed. Sometimes, segments are displaced by an octave, and some notes are repeated. This process is repeated four times, in alternating passages within this movement, which takes the form of a rondo. Crawford Seeger's technique of

Ruth Crawford Seeger

Example 7.8a Ruth Crawford Seeger, *Suite for Wind Quintet* (1952): Movement I, bars 1–9.

Example 7.8b Ruth Crawford Seeger, *Suite for Wind Quintet* (1952): Movement III, row.

Example 7.8c Ruth Crawford Seeger, *Suite for Wind Quintet* (1952): Movement III, bars 1–17. Reproduced by kind permission of the Family of Ruth Crawford Seeger. (continued)

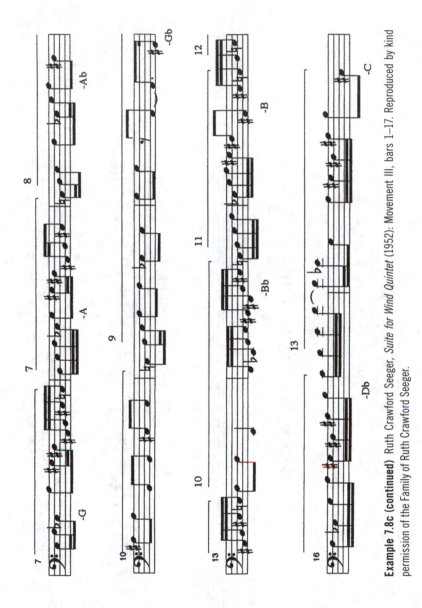

Example 7.8c (continued) Ruth Crawford Seeger, *Suite for Wind Quintet* (1952): Movement III, bars 1–17. Reproduced by kind permission of the Family of Ruth Crawford Seeger.

manipulating intervals is more akin to the working methods of early Webern than to the twelve-tone method of Schoenberg. Joseph Straus includes a Forte analysis of Seeger's *Suite for Wind Quintet* in his and Arnold Whittal's book, *The Music of Ruth Crawford Seeger.*

György Ligeti's *Ten Pieces for Wind Quintet* (1968) exhibits a more gestural approach. In some respects, the ten pieces of the title almost appear to be sketches for a larger work. From this point of view, they are interesting to study, because they invite alternative treatments. The score is notated with transposed parts (clarinet in B flat and horn in F).

Some of the pieces are linked by texture or by technique. Pieces 1, 3, and 9 employ sustained harmonies that gradually change by the movement of one note at a time. All five instruments are involved in creating the texture. Each instrument moves on a different part of the pulse: one instrument moves on part of a triplet; another on part of a quadruplet; and another on part of a quintuplet. In Piece 3, the inner speed becomes more rapid towards the middle section, then decreases at the end. Piece 9 is a trio for the three upper instruments, piccolo, oboe, and clarinet. All three instruments begin together at the same pitch, a high E flat. Not until half way through this piece (bar 8) do the instruments diverge. Ascending cluster chords are created, which slowly mutate until high A flat is reached.

Pieces 2 and 7 both sport *staccato* chords separated by long silences placed so that the listener does not know when to expect the next sound. Piece 2 turns out to be a display for the clarinet. Scalic sixteenth note fragments at the start become descending runs punctuated by *staccato* chords and odd silences. This is balanced by ascending runs, finishing with frantic wide leaps. Piece 7 begins similarly with *staccato sff* chords that punctuate the surrounding silence. From some of the chords emerge unexpected sustained notes. Six *sfff staccato* cluster chords played by all five instruments mark the center of this piece (bar 23). The last short section (bars 38–44) is a contrapuntal texture in which each instrument subdivides the pulse into different divisions (see Example 7.9).

Pieces 4, 8, and 9 are linked in that they are trios, contrasting with the other pieces that involve the complete quintet. Piece 4, marked *prestissimo leggiero e virtuoso*, creates a "jagged" texture in which the

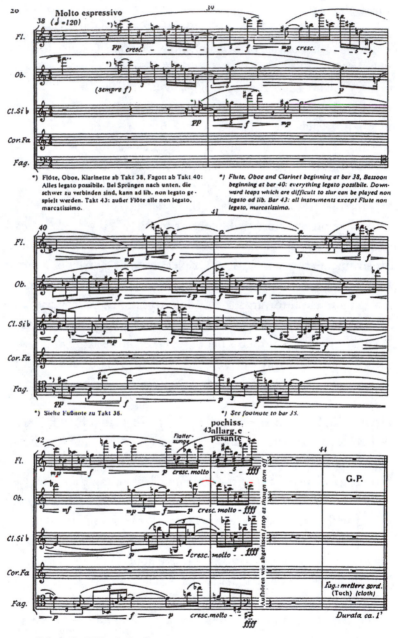

*) Flöte, Oboe, Klarinette ab Takt 38, Fagott ab Takt 40: Alles legato possibile. Bei Sprüngen nach unten, die schwer zu verbinden sind, kann ad lib. non legato ge- spielt werden. Takt 43: außer Flöte alle non legato, marcatissimo.

*) Flute, Oboe and Clarinet beginning at bar 38, Bassoon beginning at bar 40: everything legato possibile. Down- ward leaps which are difficult to slur can be played non legato ad lib. Bar 43: all instruments except Flute non legato, marcatissimo.

*) Siehe Fußnote zu Takt 38.

*) See footnote to bar 38.

Ligeti, Wind Quintet

Example 7.9 György Ligeti, *Ten Pieces for Wind Quintet* (1968): Pieces 7 and 8. © 1969 Schott Musik International GmbH, Mainz. © renewed 1997. Reproduced by permission. All rights reserved. (continued)

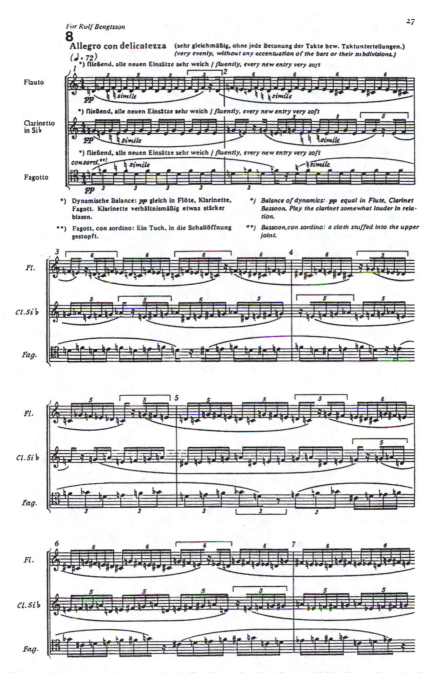

Example 7.9 (continued) György Ligeti, *Ten Pieces for Wind Quintet* (1968): Pieces 7 and 8. ©
1969 Schott Musik International GmbH, Mainz. © renewed 1997. Reproduced by permission. All
rights reserved.

flute, clarinet, and bassoon play leaping lines that cover the extremes of the high range. Similarly, Piece 8 begins with the same instruments playing in the middle range. Each plays pitches middle D and F simultaneously but with different rhythmic patterns: quintuplets for the flute, quadruplets for the clarinet, and triplets for the bassoon. This is a rhythmic technique that is used in Pieces 1, 3, and 9 also. Piece 8 eventually turns into a quintet, containing reminiscences of elements from the other pieces (see Example 7.9).

The two central pieces, Piece 5 and Piece 6, both employ a playing technique whereby long notes are articulated with rapid *staccatissimo* repeated pitches. The familiar rhythmic technique of varying subdivisions of the pulse is used in the slowly evolving harmonies. Piece 5 is a quartet in which the oboe is omitted. The oboe rejoins the ensemble for Piece 6 in which it is given a cadenza role. Uniquely in this work, this piece ends with breath sounds alone, articulated by the *staccatissimo* technique. Several of the pieces finish with silent bars, marked "stop as though torn off," a trademark Ligeti ending.

Mixed Ensemble

The mixed ensemble is so called because it includes instruments from the different families: woodwind, brass, strings, and percussion. Unusually, there is no standard mixed ensemble; there are as many different combinations as there are works. In general, however, it can safely be stated that usually there is only one player per part; that is, there is no string section, as in an orchestra. Leading contemporary music ensembles in Europe, such as the London Sinfonietta, the German *Ensemble Modern*, *Klangforum Wien*, and *Ensemble InterContemporain* in Paris, have set the standard of virtuoso performance and commissioned new works. Three works for various mixed ensembles will be discussed. They are all by British composers: Nicola Lefanu, George Benjamin, and Judith Weir.

Nicola Lefanu's *Deva* (1979) for cello and ensemble is an early work in the composer's *œuvre*. The title is an Indian word meaning "a good spirit," represented by the solo cello. The seven-piece ensemble comprises alto flute, clarinet, bassoon, horn, violin, viola, and double bass. The alto flute lends a husky *timbre* to the ensemble, the majority of instruments occupying the middle/low range of the sound spectrum. The score is notated at sounding pitch and is dedicated to the cellist Christopher van Kampen who gave the first performance with the Nash Ensemble, in London in 1979.

It is always a good idea to attract the attention of the listener from the first sounds, and Lefanu achieves this with the opening cello line. Playing the natural harmonics obtained from the open G-string, the cello plays repeated high Gs, followed by harmonic G and A several times, the phrase ending with the harmonic "flattened" seventh (microtonally flattened F). Thus, Lefanu sets forth her *timbral* palette from the start. The principal pitches are those obtained from the harmonic series available from the open strings. The ensemble comments sparingly on the melodic line of the cello. The cello melody remains in the upper register and becomes highly decorated, introducing chromatic notes, that is, foreign to the set of pitches obtainable from the harmonic series. The melody floats, as does the accompaniment, which creates an aura of harmonic notes that are not synchronized.

Structurally, the cello line makes a gradual descent, returning to the upper register towards the end. The ensemble operates together as a unit. Its function is to interrupt, or to comment upon, the melodic material of the cello, in a series of refrains. These are based on chordal sequences that are sometimes repeated and sometimes transformed. Thus, there are two musical strands at play: one for the solo cello and the other for the accompanying ensemble.

Rhythmically, there is a fluid mixture of free-flowing, unsynchronized sections (notated with dotted bar lines) and metrically barred passages that move naturally from one to the other. The score repays study for the variety of methods of notating the free passages (see Example 7.10).

Taking its inspiration from Turner's painting entitled *Norham Castle: Sunrise* is George Benjamin's work, *At First Light* (1982). Commissioned by the London Sinfonietta, this chamber orchestra gave the first performance, conducted by Simon Rattle, in London in 1982. The work was composed for the normal London Sinfonietta ensemble, comprising flute/alto flute/piccolo, oboe, clarinet/bass

Example 7.10 Nicola Lefanu, *Deva* (1979). Copyright 1978 Chester Music Ltd. (continued)

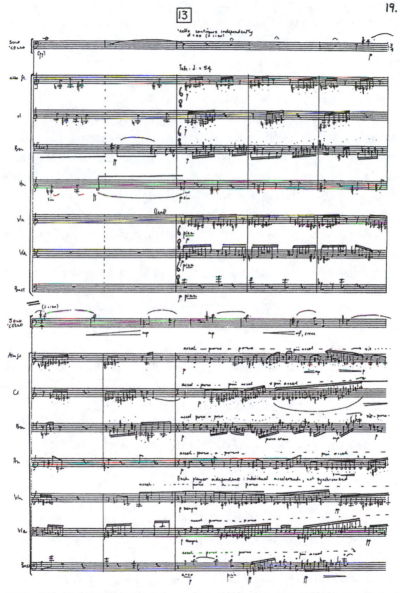

Example 7.10 (continued) Nicola Lefanu, *Deva* (1979). Copyright 1978 Chester Music Ltd.

clarinet, bassoon/double bassoon, horn, trumpet/piccolo trumpet, percussion, piano/celesta, two violins, viola, cello, and double bass. Although there is only one player per part, the percussionist commands a large array of instruments. With a predominance of traditional metal instruments, the percussion battery also includes a newspaper and "ping-pong ball with flat-bottomed drinking glass." Like Lefanu's *Deva*, Benjamin's *At First Light* is an early work, composed when he was 22 years old.

In no sense does the music convey a program. Rather, the impressionist style of Turner's early nineteenth-century painting is captured in Benjamin's coloristic use of the ensemble. His use of *timbre* and texture, fleeting wisps of sound, *glissandi* and harmonics makes for a scintillating soundscape. Every note has its particular method of articulation detailed in the score. The composer here uses sound like a painter uses color: thoughtfully and carefully applied, then standing back and testing the result. In addition, there is a strong sense of individual harmony, coupled with rhythmic fluidity (see Example 7.11).

Judith Weir has always taken an interest in folksong, and in her *œuvre* has made use of folksongs from China, Serbia, and her native Scotland. Her work *Distance and Enchantment* (1988) embeds two folksongs, one from Northern Ireland and the other from Scotland (see Example 7.12). Both songs recount tales of people who disappear.

Composed for the Domus Piano Quartet, a mixed ensemble of violin, viola, cello, and piano, it is particularly interesting to see how Weir treats the melodies. The Ulster melody is stated first, with all four instruments presenting the line at the same pitch. Some instruments sustain their pitches while others move forward, playing the next notes of the song in unison (bars 1–53). This technique is typical of Weir and is akin to that used by Ruth Crawford Seeger in her *Suite for Wind Quintet*. However, unlike the Crawford Seeger work, Judith Weir uses the modal language of folk music.

Weir establishes a conflict, in the first 50 bars, between the Aeolian mode on B, the Phrygian mode on B, the Lydian mode on G, and the tonalities of BM/Bm. The sustained notes make drones, mostly on or around middle B. These sustained notes are occasionally rhythmicized with irrational divisions of the pulse. The mood is melancholic. Pertaining to the character of traditionally performed folksongs, techniques used include the decoration of the melodic line, drones, maintaining the same *tessitura*, and heterophony—the effect heard when several voices sing or play the same tune, but slightly out of time with one another. This is the essence of Weir's technique in the presentation of the folksongs. The piano picks out the notes of the original tune, which are doubled at the unison by individual stringed instruments. Rather than adopting extended instrumental techniques, Weir explores modality to create new harmonic combinations. She makes use of traditional performance techniques.

AT FIRST LIGHT

GEORGE BENJAMIN

Example 7.11 George Benjamin, *At First Light* (1982): Movement I. © 1985 by Faber Music Ltd. Reproduced by kind permission of the publishers.   (continued)

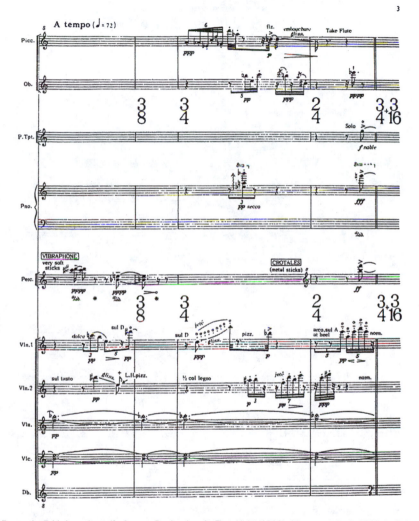

Example 7.11 (continued) George Benjamin, *At First Light* (1982): Movement I. © 1985 by Faber Music Ltd. Reproduced by kind permission of the publishers.

with love to Domus on their tenth birthday

DISTANCE AND ENCHANTMENT

Judith Weir (1988)

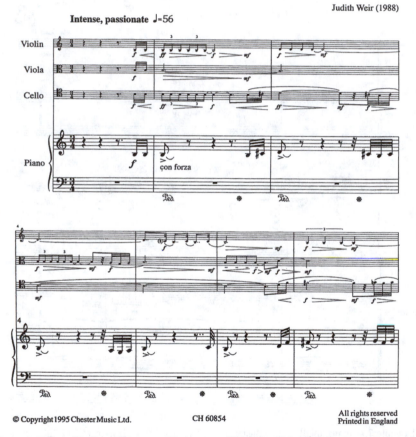

Example 7.12 Judith Weir, *Distance and Enchantment* (1988). Copyright 1995 Chester Music Ltd. (continued)

Example 7.12 (continued) Judith Weir, *Distance and Enchantment* (1988). Copyright 1995 Chester Music Ltd.

8

COMPOSING FOR VOICES

Composing for the human voice requires special care. Singers need to be able to pitch their notes from other voices or instruments around them. Not many singers possess perfect pitch, by which notes can be accurately sung almost "automatically." Most rely on sympathetic writing that enables them to pre-hear their pitches. Composers should take this into account. In addition, there is a difference between composing for amateur and composing for professional singers. Amateur singers will need more assistance with pitching than do professionals, although both appreciate some understanding from composers of their particular performance problems. A good way to test the viability of your writing is to sing the parts yourself, while playing the surrounding music. If you can't pitch the vocal line, how do you expect others to? Claiming that you are not a singer is no excuse! The ability to pitch notes, especially against other harmonies, is a skill common to all musicians and is not unique to trained singers.

In this chapter, we will discuss composing for a solo voice, as well as composing for a choir. In addition, it must be decided whether the work will be accompanied or *a cappella* (literally meaning "as in chapel," but more generally "unaccompanied"). An accompaniment can be used most helpfully to "give" the singers their notes.

Vocal Style

Classical singing developed the style of *bel canto* (beautiful singing), which is most closely associated with the singing of arias or *lieder*. However, the human voice is capable of an enormous range of vocal expression, from extreme guttural responses to the wildest joy. Some twentieth-century composers have sought to liberate the voice from the straightjacket of *bel canto* in order to better express the gamut of human emotions. While many modern composers still use the *bel canto* style, others have used the extended vocal techniques developed by enterprising singers, such as Dorothy Dorow, Mary Thomas, Jane Manning, Cathy Berberian, Roy Hart, and Linda Hirst, to name a few. Therefore, one of the decisions that you need to make concerns the vocal style that you intend to use: *bel canto* or extended techniques. Your choice will depend on the requirements of your chosen text, as well as the preferences of the particular singer.

Prior to starting any work for voice, you must choose a text. However, before you do that, there are aesthetic questions that you might consider.

What Is the Function of the Text?

If you decide to select a text to set to music, then the meaning of the words themselves will determine, for example, the mood, atmosphere, *tempo*, and probably the structure, as well as suggesting some possibilities for word painting.

In the Text Setting, Can You Hear the Words?

To an extent, most of the words of songs can be heard. Nevertheless, the listener is put in the position of straining to hear the words through the music. If the text is of a philosophic or abstruse nature, then the listeners might well give up the struggle to make sense of the words that they're hearing. It might be better simply to read the words as prose or poetry, without the "impediment" of added music. Taking this into account should inform the composer's choice of text.

Is the Voice an Instrument, Like Any Other?

On the other hand, you might come to the conclusion that you'd rather regard the voice as just another instrument. When composing for string quartet, for example, you don't need to have a text on which to "hang" the music. What you compose for an instrumental medium is abstract music, and you may wish to regard a solo voice, or vocal ensemble, in the same light. Abstract music stands for itself; it is not a medium through which another art form is expressed.

Is the Voice Restricted to Singing Words, or Are There Other Sounds That the Voice Can Use?

If this is the case, you might decide to compose for the voice using meaningless sounds, such as "aah," "mmm," "la-la," and so forth, all of which occur in the vocal and choral repertory. In the end, however, these *phonemes* (monosyllabic sounds) are rather boring and elementary when compared with the variety and virtuosity of the sounds which the human voice is capable of uttering. Unless you intend to create your own streams of "meaningless" phonemes, you will probably return to the classic solution of setting a text to music!

Choice of Text

There are some interesting examples of concrete poetry that might appeal to a composer who does not want the task of merely illustrating a poem with music. Several composers, including Luciano Berio and Rebecca Saunders, have plundered the works of James Joyce (*Finnegan's Wake* and *Ulysses*, for example) for such texts. John Cage's *Writings*, *Empty Words*, and *Silence* will yield fruitful results also. The French composer Darius Milhaud resorted to setting a catalogue of agricultural machinery for voice and ensemble, in a piece entitled *Machines agricoles* (1919).

No matter whether your choice of text is traditional or experimental, poetry or prose, in general, the fewer the number of words, the better. If you choose a text that is very verbose, the tendency will be to set the words syllabically, without allowing the time and space needed for the listener to grasp the meaning. Fewer words will encourage the repetition of phrase or line, and the use of *melisma* (several notes sung to one syllable) to enhance the expression. Japanese haiku are a fruitful source of short but stimulating and imaginative poems. Haiku have a particular structure of three lines, which contain a pattern of syllables: 5, 7, 5. There are many that have been translated into other languages, including English. Here is an example by the great Japanese poet Basho (1644–1694):

Mirror-pond of stars …
Suddenly a summer shower
Dimples the water.

[Translator unknown]

Some texts lend themselves to musical setting more than others. Texts that mention sonic objects, such as bells, water, storms, sirens, and so on, invite word painting. An extramusical sound given a musical representation can provide the material for the entire song. On the other hand, the composer should resist the temptation to give musical expression to every minute event mentioned in the text. Taking a broad brushstroke approach is better.

Copyright

One aspect of text selection is very important: it is *imperative* to obtain the permission of the copyright holder of the text prior to public performance. This is easier than it sounds. It is usually simply a question of contacting the publisher of the text to seek this permission. The publisher's address will appear inside the book. Publishers and writers are normally willing to give their permission for the performance of their work, without incurring a payment. This is because the royalties due to the writer as a result of a public performance should be collected and distributed by a performing rights society. Remember that it is *illegal* to perform or to publish copyrighted material without the consent of the copyright holder. Failure to obtain this permission could result in legal action against you. In most countries, copyright protection extends to 70 years after the death of the writer (including composers).

Accompaniment

The function of the accompaniment can be to do the following:

- Establish the mood of the song
- Provide the pitches for the singers
- Perform instrumental introduction, interludes, and a postlude

An accompaniment can provide an introduction that can suggest the atmosphere, as well as hinting at the pitch material for the singers. The accompaniment can also provide interludes between blocks of text, so that there is *timbral* contrast. A postlude acts as a coda, "framing" the sung text with an instrumental texture.

Structure

The text itself might suggest a structure for the setting. If not, the composer needs to consider how to structure the piece. Rarely is the chosen text set to music in a straightforward way, in the manner of storytelling. Usually, the text is divided into sections according to its meaning. Alternatively, a musical structure might be imposed upon the text.

A narrative poem cast in a number of verses, with a regular rhyming scheme, such as a folksong, is termed *strophic*. Potentially, though traditional, this form can be musically unrewarding because it invites predictable repetition. A traditional folksong sets the verses to the same music, regardless of the development of the story. A typical folktale type begins with the happy lovers and ends with the demise of one, or both, of them. How inappropriate is it in this circumstance to use the same music throughout? Another form is termed *through composed*, in which the text and music develop freely, as the name suggests. This form enables the composer to clothe the text with suitable musical expression.

Pre-Compositional Work

Having selected an inspiring text, it is a good idea to *speak* the words aloud before you begin to set them to music. This will allow you to roughly measure how much time is needed to enunciate the words. Taking an example from the Basho haiku (see above), the last line, "Dimples the water," requires considerable tongue dexterity to actually say the words: "(Di)mples the" employs lips, tongue, and teeth in quick succession. The conclusion for the composer must be to allow time within the music for the singer to execute such tongue twisters.

Speaking the text aloud will also suggest an appropriate rhythm for your setting. It would appear that some melodists invent the melody first and then cram the syllables around the notes of the tune! While this approach might ensure that the melody itself will be memorable, it may work against the natural stress of the words. An alternative approach is to allow the rhythm of the words to suggest the outline of the melody. The result will be that the words will always fit the tune, the text and melody being rhythmically interlinked. Word stress is also a factor to be considered. Emphasized syllables are normally accented within the music. Some young composers like to accent the written text before beginning to invent the music. Singing the lines as you compose should ensure that your text and vocal lines fit each other.

Works for Discussion and Study

Solo Voice

A trained singer will have a vocal range of at least two octaves. However, each voice is unique, both in its exact range and special color. When composing for a particular singer, it is wise first to ascertain the singer's range and most comfortable *tessitura*.

Benjamin Britten's vocal works are highly "singable" and repay study. He had a gift for composing for the voice and wrote vocal and choral works for children, as well as for trained and untrained voices. During the 1940s, he made arrangements of folksongs from various countries, for voice and piano. They were written for the tenor Peter Peers, accompanied by Britten himself at the piano, for performance at their numerous recitals.

The Ash Grove is a well-known Welsh folksong containing two verses. In verse 1, a lover is wandering "amid the dark shades of the lonely Ash grove," recalling how he had met his love there. In verse 2, the Ash grove remains the same, with the blackbird "warbling his note from the tree" and "still trembles the moonbeam on streamlet and fountain." However, everything has changed because his love now "sleeps 'neath the green turf down by the Ash grove."

This is a strophic folksong, that is, the melody remains the same for both verses. Yet Britten uses the piano accompaniment to convey the change in mood between the two verses. The four-bar introduction hints at the melody to come, and is placed in the high register. The hands play in parallel tenths using only notes from the F Major scale, this material lasting throughout verse 1. Could this striking music represent the line "the bluebells were ringing"? A piano interlude separates the two verses, in which the accompaniment music effects a descent to the lower register, in preparation for the "black" mood of verse 2. The melody is a repeat of the familiar folksong, still in F Major. The piano harmonizes this bitonally, passing through the keys of Gm, B flat m, Cm, Dm, and Am before eventually returning to F Major for "Ye echoes." Thus, the final two lines of the poem become an echo of the music for verse 1: high register, F Major, decorated parallel tenths this time. The song ends with a postlude that is a harmonized version of the introduction.

So the accompaniment is used to convey the difference in mood between the verses, even though the folksong melody remains the same. Britten selects just one sonic idea, from the several word-painting opportunities mentioned, on which to base the accompaniment figure: that of bluebells ringing (see Example 8.1).

The Trees They Grow So High is another British folksong, from the county of Somerset. Again, it is a strophic narrative, in six verses with a refrain. Britten treats the melody itself like an ostinato, around which the accompaniment music grows. Taking this idea from the words of the refrain, "Whilst my bonny boy is young he's a-growing," the music

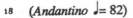

Example 8.1 Benjamin Britten, folksong arrangement: "The Ashgrove," verse 2. Copyright 1943 by Boosey & Co. Ltd. Reproduced by permission of Boosey & Hawkes Music Publishers Ltd.   (continued)

Example 8.1 (continued) Benjamin Britten, folksong arrangement: "The Ashgrove," verse 2. Copyright 1943 by Boosey & Co. Ltd. Reproduced by permission of Boosey & Hawkes Music Publishers Ltd.

accumulates. Unusually, the song starts without an instrumental introduction. Verse 1 and the refrain are sung unaccompanied. In verse 2, the
piano enters, playing just one part in the right hand as a countermelody
to the folksong. For verse 3, the left hand enters, so at this point there
are three parts. The structural device of adding one part for each verse
is continued until the climax in verse 5, in which there is a maximum of
six parts. Here, the bass descends by steps over fourteen bars, becoming
a syncopated pedal. The other added parts rapidly disappear, leaving the
voice alone for the final refrain, an echo of the opening.

In this arrangement, Britten imposes his own structure on a strophic
folksong, taking his cue from the principal idea underlying the narrative, that of "growing." These two arrangements are miniature gems.

Towards the end of his life, Igor Stravinsky composed a number of
works using the serial technique. One such collection was *Three Songs
from William Shakespeare* (1953) for voice, flute, clarinet, and viola. The
first, *Musick to heare*, is a setting of Shakespeare's Sonnet No. 8. With its
reference to "musick" it is a natural choice for a composer. Stravinsky's
setting is based on two note rows, one of four pitch classes, the other of
five pitch classes. The principal note row (of four pitch classes) is cun-
ningly rotated to produce a number of ambiguities (see Example 8.2a).

The flute plays the opening statement of the row. As can be seen, the
four pitch classes of O1 (B, G, A, B flat) are inverted and transposed,
becoming I10 (A flat, C, B flat, A natural). Thus, the last two pitch
classes of each of these four-note cells are the retrograde of one another
(A, B flat). O1 is then repeated. Starting with the note B (enharmonically C flat), the flute continues with another inversion, I1 (C flat,
E flat, D flat, C natural). This introduction finishes with a transposed
statement of the original, O4 (D, B flat, C, D flat). Once again, the
last two pitches of this pair are the retrograde of each other (D flat,
C). There are nine different pitch classes involved here, rather than the
familiar twelve.

The flute line is accompanied by the clarinet and viola, between them
playing row 2. Once the octave displacements have been disentangled,
it emerges that row 2 is nothing but the first five notes of CM scale
(C, D, E, F, G)!

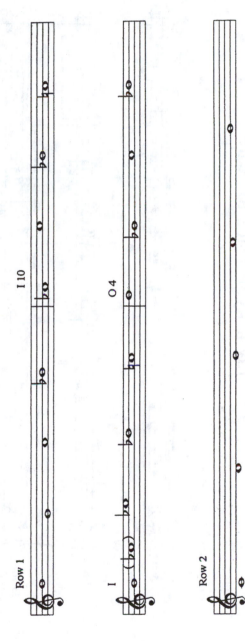

Igor Stravinsky, *Musick to heare*: Rows

Example 8.2a Igor Stravinsky, *Musick to heare* (1953): rows.

Stravinsky, Musick to heare

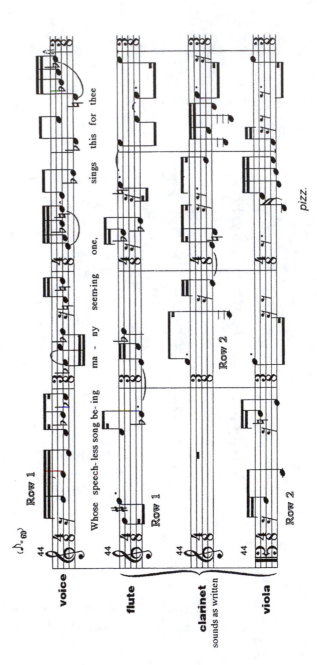

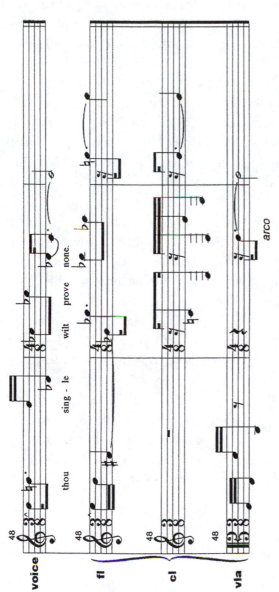

Example 8.2b Igor Stravinsky, *Musick to heare* (1953): bar 44 — end. Copyright 1954 by Hawkes & Son (London) Ltd. US Copyright renewed. Reproduced by permission of Boosey & Hawkes Music Publishers Ltd.

When the voice enters, in bar 9, her pitches are those of O1, followed by I10, just as heard in the introductory flute statement. In fact, the vocal line throughout this song uses only the pitch material of row 1. Likewise, row 1, played by the instruments in various transpositions and octave displacements, accompanies the vocal line. These are so arranged that the ends of the phrases are marked by the interval of P5. This occurs first at the end of the instrumental introduction: C + G at bar 8, then again at bars 13 and 21. At bar 34, the P5 is B + F sharp and at bar 43, G + D. The song finishes with C + G, a return to the tonic. Meanwhile, row 2 is heard only once more, in the final section, beginning at bar 44. Here, the texture is at its fullest, being created from a contrapuntal web of rows 1 and 2 (see Example 8.2b).

Although this is a song that uses serial techniques in the construction of the pitch cells, the vocal line is eminently singable. There is a certain amount of repetition of note and cell, with only occasional large leaps. However, it is a work that is probably best suited to a trained singer.

On the other hand, Luigi Dallapiccola's *Goethe-Lieder*, also written in 1953, is best suited to a soprano with perfect pitch. The wide leaps, "awkward" intervals, and lack of repetition are vocally demanding. Here, an Italian composer sets a text in German by the famous poet Goethe (1749–1832). The poem contains seven verses taken from *West-östlichen Divan*. Each verse becomes an independent song in Dallapiccola's setting, thus creating a song cycle. It is written for soprano and three clarinets (E flat, B flat, and bass), and has an interesting textural superstructure imposed by the composer:

Song 1:	voice	E flat clarinet	B flat clarinet	Bass clarinet
Song 2:	voice	E flat clarinet	—	—
Song 3:	voice	E flat clarinet	B flat clarinet	—
Song 4:	voice	E flat clarinet	B flat clarinet	Bass clarinet
Song 5:	voice	—	B flat clarinet	Bass clarinet
Song 6:	voice	—	—	Bass clarinet
Song 7:	voice	E flat clarinet	B flat clarinet	Bass clarinet

The first, central, and last songs (1, 4, 7) are for the whole ensemble. Each clarinet in turn has a duo with the voice. Then, there are two trios: Song 3 (voice with E flat and B flat clarinets) and Song 5 (voice, B flat, and bass clarinets). Each clarinet plays in five songs, though not quite all the possible permutations are accounted for. As can be seen, the couplings are systematically ordered.

Song 5 is particularly interesting for its word painting within a twelve-tone style. Here is the poem, with English translation:

Der Spiegel sagt mir: ich bin schön!	The mirror tells me: I am fair!
Ihr sagt: zu altern sei auch mein Geschick.	You all say: to age is also my fate.
Vor Gott muss alles ewig stehn,	Before God everything must stand forever,
In mirliebt ihn für diesen Augenblick.	Love him in me, for this moment.
Goethe	**[Translator unknown]**

In this song, the word *Spiegel* (mirror) is selected for its potent musical representation. Dallapiccola takes the idea of reflection as the inspiration for his word painting. He interprets this notion in both the pitch and rhythm parameters. One twelve-tone row is used throughout the song cycle. The arrangement of the row for Song No. 5 is shown in Example 8.3a.

It can be observed that notes 1, 2, and 3 have the same intervallic relationship as notes 6, 7, and 8, that is, m2 and M2. The interconnections between the variants of the row are fascinating.

The score is notated at sounding pitch (see Example 8.3b). The voice sings the text, using nothing but the notes of the row:

Bars 1–5:   O1, notes 1–12
Bars 6–9:   I2, notes 1–12
Bars 10–11: R3, notes 1, 2, 3 and R6, notes 1, 2, 3
Bars 12–14: I2, notes 1, 2, 3, and O1, notes 6, 7, 8
Bars 14–20: O1, notes 1–12

There is a telling *melisma* on the word *schön* (beautiful). The voice in this song is accompanied by the B flat clarinet and bass clarinet, which play their parts in reflecting the image of the mirror. The B flat clarinet enters in bar 2 with a canonic version of the vocal line. In bar 2, the B flat clarinet plays an inversion of the vocal line of bar 1. Bar 3 of the B flat clarinet part is an inversion of bar 2 of the voice melody. The counterpoint between the voice part and the B flat clarinet part continues in this manner.

Dallapiccola, Goethe-Lieder

Example 8.3a Luigi Dallapiccola, *Goethe-Lieder* (1953), Song 5: row.

Dallapiccola, Goethe-Lieder, Song 5

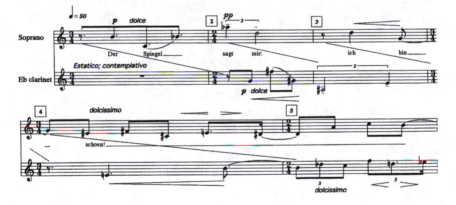

Example 8.3b Luigi Dallapiccola, *Goethe-Lieder* (1953): Song 5.

Not only is the pitch reflected, but the rhythm is distorted as well. (Perhaps it is a distorting mirror!) Notes 1–3 of the vocal line are dotted eighth notes, whereas notes 1–3 of the B flat clarinet are straight eighths (in other words, they are reduced by a third). The vocal triplet in bar 2 is expressed as a quarter note followed by a half note, whereas the B flat clarinet version in bar 3 is retrograded—a half note followed by a

Dallapiccola, Goethe-Lieder, Song 5, Bars 9-14

Example 8.3c Luigi Dallapiccola, *Goethe-Lieder* (1953): Song 5, bars 9–14.

quarter note. The voice rhythm in bar 3, effectively two quarter notes, becomes dotted (i.e., enlarged) in the B flat clarinet version, bar 4. The *melisma* on *schön* (beautiful), bar 4, is expressed as six eighth notes in triple time. The B flat clarinet version becomes triplet eighth notes in duple time (6:4 instead of 6:6). This rhythmic distortion continues.

Pitchwise, the B flat clarinet enters with I9, notes 1–12 (bars 2–6), and continues with O8, notes 1–12 (bars 6–9). At bars 10–11, the B flat clarinet plays RI2, notes 1, 2, 3 followed by RI7, notes 1, 2, 3. Combined with the vocal part here (R3, notes 1, 2, 3 and R6, notes 1, 2, 3), a complete twelve-tone row is created. Similarly, bars 12–14 also contain a twelve-tone row: the voice sings I2, notes 1, 2, 3 and O1, notes 6, 7, 8 against O5, notes 1, 2, 3 followed by I6, notes 6, 7, 8, played by the B flat clarinet.

Meanwhile, the bass clarinet eventually enters in bar 9 with O10, notes 1–12, but rhythmically in notes approximately double the value of the initial vocal statement. This phrase ends in bar 14 (see Example 8.3c).

The final line of the verse begins in bar 14 with the voice singing O1 complete. The clarinets both enter canonically in bar 15.

The B flat clarinet plays I9, notes 1–11, while the bass clarinet plays O1, notes 1–10. Thus, the final chord contains notes 10, 11, and 12 of O1. In this song, Dallapiccola displays a technical mastery that is both intellectually satisfying as well as being expressively appropriate.

Elisabeth Lutyens was one of only a few English composers to adopt the twelve-tone method, which she used in her own way. Her *"and suddenly it's evening"* (1966) is a setting of four poems by the Sicilian poet Salvatore Quasimodo (1901–1968). The title is the last line of the fourth poem. It is set in both the original Italian and an English translation, by Jack Bevan, both versions appearing in the score. It is written for a tenor and chamber ensemble. The ensemble is divided into three groups of instruments:

Coro di strumenti:	two trumpets, two trombones, double bass
Ritornello 1:	harp, celesta, percussion
Ritornello II:	violin, horn, cello

The structure, devised by the composer, has the four poems surrounded by instrumental movements:

1. *Ritornello* 1
   Tenor and *Coro di strumenti*   "On the willow bough"
   Ritornello 1
2. *Ritornello* 2
   Tenor and *Coro di strumenti*   "In the just human time"
   Ritornello 2
3. Introduction: *Coro di strumenti*
   Tenor and *Ritornelli* 1   "Almost a madrigal," verse 1
   Tenor and *Ritornelli* 2   "Almost a madrigal," verse 2
   Coda: *Coro di strumenti*
4. Antiphon 1. *Ritornelli* 1 and 2
   Tenor solo   "And suddenly it's evening"
   Antiphon 2. *Ritornelli* 1 and 2
   Coda: *Coro di strumenti*

As with Dallapiccola's structure, there is an ordered permutation of the available instrumental ensemble, ensuring a changing textural palette. The title poem is set as a short, unaccompanied song for the solo tenor. Verse 2 of "Almost a madrigal" uses *sprechtstimme* (speech-song, a device introduced by Schoenberg in *Pierrot Lunaire*, 1912). The rhythm of the words is precisely notated but the text is spoken, rather than sung.

The tenor solo of Section 4 uses Lutyens' twelve-tone row twice: first as the original, then as the inversion. The double treble clef indicates that the pitches are heard an octave lower than written (see Example 8.4a).

Antiphon II (Example 8.4b) begins with the horn (in F) quietly playing a transposition of O, notes 1–12 (bar 40). The horn is echoed softly by the harp playing O in canon, four beats later and at the same pitch. The violin overlaps the end of the harp phrase, playing I. Occasionally two adjacent notes are played together, forming a dyad. This is echoed by the celesta, similarly playing softly in canon, four beats later and at the same pitch. The cello enters at bar 47, playing the retrograde variant. The echo at the end of this phrase is divided between the celesta and harp (bar 51). In bar 52, the celesta plays a palindromic chordal progression created from ten notes of the row, followed by a dramatic harp *glissando* from the top to the bottom of the instrument. Until this moment, the antiphon has been very quiet, the dynamics ranging from *ppp* to *mp*. This Antiphon is colored by non-pitched percussion that binds the two instrumental groups together. The percussion instruments successively go through the various *timbres*: wood (woodblocks, claves, maracas), metal (cymbals, tam-tam), and finishing with skin (tom-toms). The section ends with tom-toms alone, playing a notated *accelerando*. The scoring is delicate and economical, each note contributing essentially to the texture.

Cathy Berberian's *Stripsody* (1966) was composed in the same year as Elisabeth Lutyens's *and suddenly it's evening*. Better known as a

Lutyens' Twelve-Tone Row

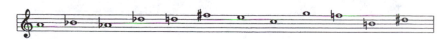

Example 8.4a Elisabeth Lutyens, *and suddenly it's evening*, (1966): row.

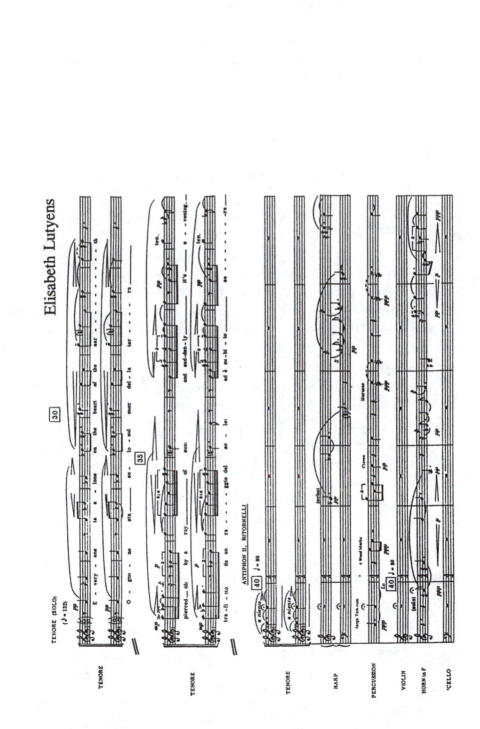

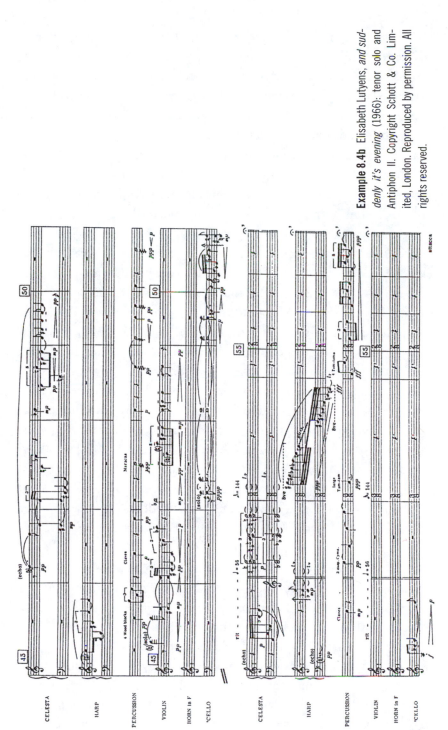

pioneering singer of contemporary music than as a composer, Berberian created this work for her to sing. *Stripsody* is a comic work for solo actress-singer. The text is entirely taken from comic strip cartoons, and mainly consists of the phonemes that appear "silently" on the page. Cathy Berberian turns these dumb utterances (e.g. "gulp," "pant pant," "sniff sniff," and so forth) into vocalizations. The text has these sounds arranged alphabetically; some are ordered into scenes. In performance, the start and finish of each scene is indicated by hand gestures given by the singer. The score contains graphics by Roberto Zamarin, written on a three-line stave, indicating low, middle, and high *tessitura*. The individual scenes are surrounded by opening and closing bar lines.

Stripsody is best experienced as a live performance, where its comic elements can be made more manifest. It is a work in which there are few meaningful words, but it contains an array of onomatopœic vocal sounds. Humor in music is often difficult to convey on a sophisticated level. However, in this work Berberian has used her own knowledge and experience of extended vocal techniques to create genuine music theater for a virtuoso soloist (see Example 8.5).

Continuing the theme of vocal music theater, Peter Maxwell Davies' *Eight Songs for a Mad King* (1969) explores the expression in music of madness. The scenario is taken from the historical evidence surrounding the insanity of the British King George III (1738–1820). His illness caused him to indulge in soliloquies that lasted for hours without ceasing. Confined to his rooms without human company, except for the ministrations of his loyal servants, he took to addressing his pet caged birds. Occasionally, the King had spells of lucidity during which he became aware of his incapacity.

The text for this work was assembled by Randolph Stow and contains sentences known to have been spoken by George III. Peter Maxwell Davies wrote the work for performance by the actor-singer Roy Hart, together with his ensemble, the Fires of London, comprising singer, flute/piccolo, clarinet, percussion, piano/keyboards, violin, and cello.

The vocal range covers an enormous four octaves, and includes: bass *tessitura*, *falsetto*, harmonics, growling, and screeching, as well as normal singing. Lasting over half an hour, the work is a monodrama, the bass/baritone representing the King. The instruments represent the

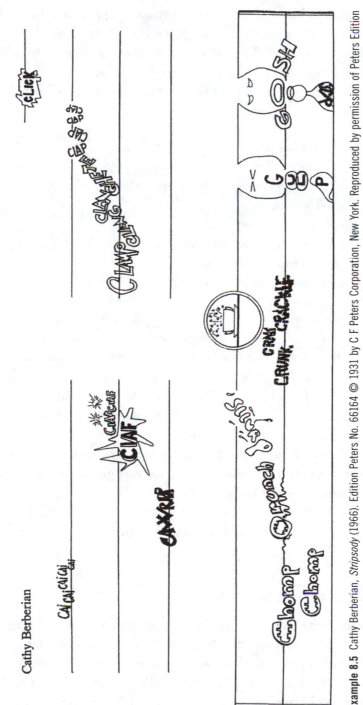

Example 8.5 Cathy Berberian, *Stripsody* (1966). Edition Peters No. 66164 © 1931 by C F Peters Corporation, New York. Reproduced by permission of Peters Edition Limited, London.

King's pet birds and, in a staged version, appear seated in a cage. The King addresses the birds through the bars of the cage. This is pictorially represented in the score of the third song, "The Lady-in-Waiting (Miss Musgrave's Fancy)" (see Example 8.6).

The eight songs of the title are contained in a number of scenes, which delineate the scenario:

King Prussia's Minuet
The Country Walk
The Lady-in-Waiting (Miss Musgrave's Fancy)
The Waterman
The Phantom Queen
The Counterfeit: Recitative and Air ("I love Dr. Heberden")
Country Dance (Scotch Bonnett)
The Review (A Spanish March)

Both the narrative and the music allude to aspects of the King's eighteenth to nineteenth century style of courtly life. His memories of his early years surface from time to time, and find expression in parodies of Handel's *Messiah*, with which the King was familiar (c.f. "Comfort ye" in "Country Dance (Scotch Bonnet)"). The music makes use of pastiches of various eighteenth-century forms; "The Phantom Queen: Hei's ay a Kissing me," for example, passes through an *arietta* for flute and clarinet, an *allemande* for harpsichord, a *courante* for flute and clarinet, and a *rondino* for piano, all of which are grotesquely interrupted by utterances from the King.

The work is a *tour de force* for a male singer, accompanied by a versatile ensemble that can leap across the centuries in terms of musical style and performing techniques.

Composing for Choirs

Many of the same steps used in composing for individual singers need to be taken when writing for a choir. There are many more amateur choirs than professional, those of professional standing being attached to the church (for example, King's College Chapel Choir, Cambridge), to national broadcasting organizations (BBC Singers), or to national

Peter Maxwell Davies , *Eight Songs for a Mad King*

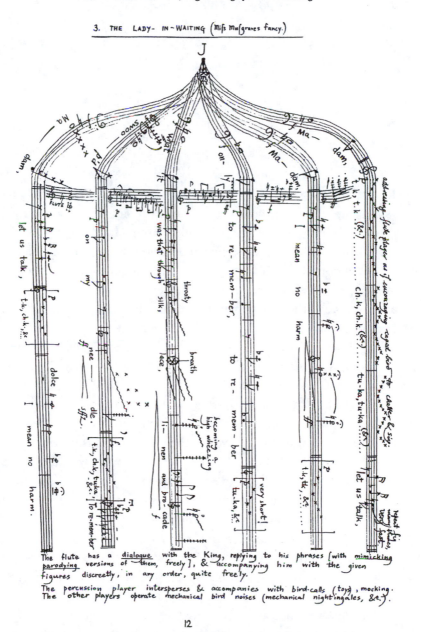

Example 8.6 Peter Maxwell Davies, *Eight Songs for a Mad King* (1969): *Miss Musgrave's Fancy*. Copyright 1971 by Boosey & Hawkes Music Publishers Ltd. Reproduced by permission of Boosey & Hawkes Music Publishers Ltd.

Vocal ranges

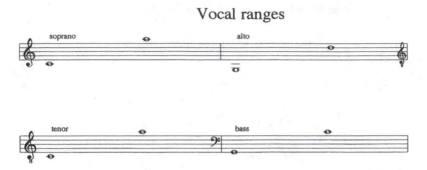

Example 8.7 Vocal ranges.

opera houses (La Scala, Milan). On the other hand, amateur choirs can spring up wherever there is an interest in singing, at a community, town, or city level. (One example is the Huddersfield Choral Society, which has been in existence for over 150 years.) Some amateur choirs are men-only, TTBB (such as the high-standing Welsh choirs), or women only, SSAA, or are made up of different ages of children (youth choirs). All these factors will influence the level of technical and æsthetic difficulty that you demand in your composition.

The average vocal ranges of the standard choral soprano, alto, tenor, and bass are shown in Example 8.7. The particular choir, or the occasion of performance, might determine the choice of text. However, in general when writing for choir, there is more scope for the repetition of words or phrases. Sentences can be divided effectively between the parts. An important factor is whether the choral piece is to be accompanied or to be sung *a cappella*. If the latter, the singers will need to be able to pitch their notes from the other parts, so care must be taken to ensure that resonating notes can clearly be heard. There are certain intervals that amateur singers find difficult to negotiate, especially A4 and M7, so perhaps it is best to avoid these.

The Canadian composer R. Murray Schafer has taken a special interest in encouraging new approaches to word setting. His little book *When Words Sing* is packed full of tried and tested ideas for young singers and composers. In particular, Chapter 13, "Choric Textures," is inspirational in its examples of the visualization of a variety of choral shapes. The score of his work for youth choir, *Epitaph for Moonlight* (1966), is included in the book. It was composed for singers who could not read music notation, so Schafer devised an ingenious method of "drawing" the score. The result is a highly adventurous and sophisticated choral piece in twelve parts.

Schafer's work is almost a prelude to the work of the Greek composer Iannis Xenakis. Xenakis's choral work *Nuits* (*Nights*) (1967–1968) is for twelve solo voices singing *a cappella*, all of which need to be professional singers, preferably with perfect pitch. It was composed for the soloists of the choir of the French broadcasting organization *l'O.R.T.F.*

The inspiration for this work came from Xenakis's experience of witnessing angry crowds at demonstrations in Athens during World War II. Xenakis was a young man during this time, and was a member of the resistance movement. The work is dedicated to "unknown political prisoners, and thousands of forgotten ones whose very names are lost." It deals, in a stochastic manner, with the characteristic sounds made by an angry crowd: the calls, the whistles, the shouts, the combinations of high and low voices, and the tension and climax-building of the crowd chanting together, then falling out of synchronization. Xenakis's original handwritten score is graphic in its visualization of the choric textures.

The twelve parts are divided into three per voice-type: 3S, 3A, 3T, and 3B. The text is invented and consists of phonemes related to German and French pronunciation. Structurally, *Nuits* contains three sections (A, B, C), defining varying texture-types, built into the form A, B, C, A2, B2, A3, and concluding with a coda. Section A (bars 1–70) starts with high voices answered by low, the trios of voice-types in turn calling and then falling silent. The phrases eventually overlap with greater frequency until all twelve voices sing together (bars 57–70), finally converging in unison on middle D. All the lines are singing *glissando*, marked *fff*, and notated with quarter-tones. Although apparently in quadruple time, the bar lines act as a visual guide to the singers rather than indicating accentuation. The texture-type in this section is *glissando* and fluid. The only exception is the trio of tenors who sing a sustained triad: C, C three-quarter-tone sharp, and D sharp (bars 38–46).

Section B, on the other hand, begins rhythmically and gradually passes to a sustained texture. All voices start on middle D (where the previous section ended), then expand upwards and downwards by quarter-tones until the climax at bar 120. Between bars 70 and 95, the half note pulses are subdivided into 2, 3, 4, or 5, then mixed together from bars 85–95. The climactic chord at bar 120 is built from the interval of a third, in various forms, stretching from low G for bass 3 to high B for soprano 1. At this point, all sing in rhythmic unison, finishing the phrase with a unique *staccato* effect and extreme *crescendi* (*pp* to *fff*) repeated four times in rapid succession, finally breaking off into silence.

Section C (bars 128 to 168) contains a mixture of textural elements including whistles, calls, cries, and quasi-speech patterns. In addition, there are sustained unison notes, usually sung by two singers, in which one singer is instructed to "climb as far as necessary for this voice to 'beat' against the other at the frequency indicated by the numbers." Great control and aural finesse is required to achieve this effect accurately. A recapitulation begins at bar 169, with the *glissando* texture of section A heard in varied form. Around the *glissandi* are "clouds on the syllable TSI" (see Example 8.8).

Section B2 starts at bar 205, with all voices singing middle C (transposed from the middle D of the exposition), then suddenly leaping to a *fff* cluster chord in the upper register. Section A3, beginning at bar 214, uses another variation of the *glissando* texture, to which all the voices contribute. The coda (bar 241) contains low sustained notes with quarter-tone harmonies emerging, then disappearing. *Nuits* concludes with a low *tremolando* note, F three-quarter-tone sharp, sung by all three basses, and ending with a short, but emphasized, whisper.

Xenakis's work is dramatic, very original in its soundscape, and, indeed, evokes the frightening experience of being part of an angry crowd. It is a very "visual" score, being an example of the use of "sculptured textures." Needless to say, it requires highly trained, virtuoso singers to perform *Nuits*.

In contrast to Xenakis's vocal work is John Tavener's *Akathist of Thanksgiving* (1988) for solo countertenors, solo tenors, solo basses, choir, organ, and string orchestra. The English composer John Tavener has become a devout member of the Orthodox Christian Church, and this large-scale work was written to celebrate the anniversary, in 1988, of 1000 years of Christianity in Russia (988–1988). It is a setting of the *Akathist of Thanksgiving* written in 1940 by Archpriest Gregory Petrov.

The *akathist* is a hymn of thanksgiving, to be sung at particular celebrations of the Orthodox Church. The usual form of the hymn is in thirteen sections, each containing a *kontakion* and an *ikos*. Tavener selects ten sections for his setting. He makes use of the Orthodox Church modes and style of singing, which moves slowly and mostly by step. Though the demands on the singers are not great, the quality of singing is vital. Intensity, vibrancy of tone, and devotion are essential in order to convey the power of this music.

The closing passages of *Ikos II* are typical of Tavener's style. For *a cappella* choir, the chorus is subdivided into fifteen parts: 4 sopranos, 3 altos, 3 tenors, 2 baritones, 3 basses. Bass 1, the two baritones, and the three altos sustain a drone on the tonic and dominant of B, in the middle range, with a floating high F sharp (the dominant) sung by soprano 4. There are sufficient voices involved in singing the drone to ensure continuity of sound when individuals need to take a breath. Around the bass-heavy drone, basses 2 and 3 intone the descending notes of an Orthodox mode on B. Simultaneously, tenors 2 and 3 intone the ascending form of the same scale (B, C, D sharp, E, F sharp, G, A). These are set heterophonically, so that the voices move apart on different beats and then reunite. The effect is of a notated resonant acoustic in which the lines become blurred. The phrases are repeated three times. Above, sopranos 1, 2, and 3 sing a melody based on the same degrees of the mode, in notes of half the value of the moving tenor and bass parts. The melodic line is treated almost serially, in that it consists entirely of the same set of pitches repeated seven times, in the same order. Singing only the notes of the mode, the three sopranos sing in parallel triads, which, perforce, change from major to minor, to diminished, and to augmented. Thus, clashing harmonies are created where the soprano triads collide with the rotating lines of the tenors, baritones, and basses.

The instruments join in at the end of the *ikos*, contributing to the blurred haze of the modal sonority. Here, Tavener departs from traditional Orthodox liturgical practice, in which only vocal music is the norm. The ritual continues for approximately 80 minutes (see Example 8.9).

Xenakis

B & H 19822

Example 8.8 Iannis Xenakis, *Nuits* (1967–1968).

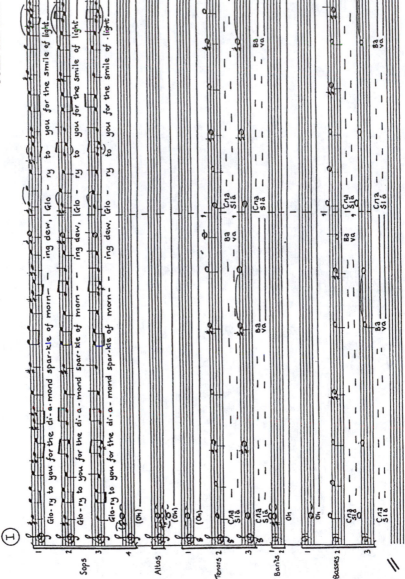

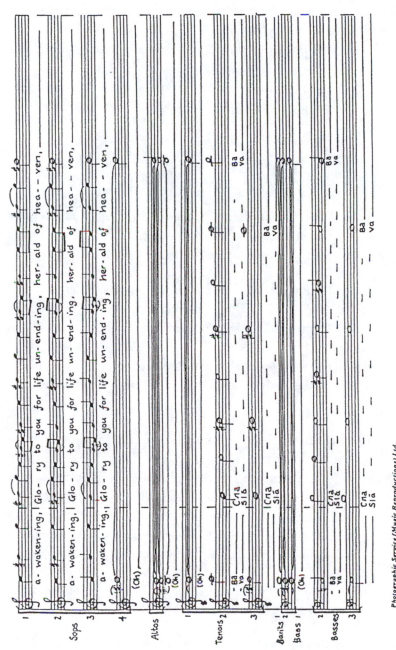

Example 8.9 John Tavener, *Akathist of Thanksgiving* (1988): *Ikos II*. Copyright 1988 Chester Music Ltd.

Text Underlay

Works that employ a text must acknowledge the source by author, title, work, publisher, city of publication, and date. The text used in the work cannot be printed in the program without written permission from the publisher.

While the musical quality of the work is paramount, it *is* important to pay attention to notational details. These are important points:

- Write the text *under* the vocal staff
- Write the dynamic markings *above* the vocal staff (so as not to collide with the text)

The latter detail differs from the convention for instrumental music, in which the dynamic markings are placed under the stave.

There are two ways of underlaying the text:

1. *Traditional*, in which syllables should be treated correctly.
   Monosyllabic words ("the," "there," "through," "tough," for example) are not hyphenated (*not* "throu-gh," "tou-gh," and so forth).
   Multisyllabic words *are* hyphenated, though not according to any specific rules! "Mu-lti-sy-llab-ic" and "mult-i-sy-llab-ic," and so forth, are correct.

A glance at the music examples in this chapter, printed by different publishers, reveals that there is a variety of notational practices with regard to indicating where the syllables fall. Where one syllable occupies more than one note, some publishers indicate this with a slur (see Example 8.1). Dallapiccola's *Goethe-Lieder* notates both a continuous line and a slur (Example 8.3b). Tavener's *Akathist* uses a line (Example 8.9). Perhaps the solution is to select the method that best suits you.

2. *Phonetic*, in which the written sound of the word is placed *under* the note to which it applies.

Examples of this method can be seen in Lutyens's *"and suddenly it's evening"* (Example 8.4b), Maxwell Davies's *Eight Songs for a Mad King*

(Example 8.6), and Xenakis's *Nuits* (Example 8.8). This method is particularly suited to *avant garde* settings of modern texts.

These two methods should not be confused. Do not overlook the expressive impact of *melisma*, used to heighten carefully selected words. A completely syllabic setting can suggest insensitivity to the words.

Writing for the voice usually involves the inclusion of another art form, that of literature. Inspiration for the music can be triggered by the text, the sound of the words, and the meaning expressed. Thus, composing a song or a work for voices is a collaboration between two arts, both of which communicate via sound.

9

Composing for a Monodic Instrument

A monodic instrument is one that normally plays one note at a time. All woodwind and brass instruments are monodic. Stringed instruments also can be considered to be monodic, even though they are capable of playing double-, triple-, and quadruple-stopped chords. However, stringed instruments do not usually play streams of chords, in the way that keyboard instruments do. Thus, pianos, organs, and other keyboard instruments, as well as guitars and harps, are not monodic.

Plurality in Singularity

Writing for a solo monodic instrument is perhaps the most taxing compositional challenge. Ironically, composing for a single instrument is technically more difficult than writing for an ensemble. This is because the task is to create a satisfying work in which only one note at a time is heard. It is not simply about composing a melody without harmony, but rather, giving the impression of melody *and* harmony, even though only one note at a time is played. The solution is to think in terms of layers. Several strands of musical materials are progressing simultaneously, with the instrument hopping between the various lines, picking out a few notes at a time to suggest the development of the individual threads. In fact, what is created is an aural illusion. Melody, harmony, and counterpoint can all be implied. Several functions are to be performed simultaneously by one monodic instrument: plurality in singularity.

For an ideal model of this compositional technique, we can study the works for solo instrument by Johann Sebastian Bach. His suites for solo cello and sonatas and partitas for solo violin are masterpieces of the craft of musical suggestion. The *Prélude* to Suite No. 1 for Violoncello (BWV XXVII.1) offers a perfect illustration (see Example 9.1). In GM, the first four bars demonstrate the layers perfectly. Working in two-beat groups, the notes delineate the following harmonic progression: I, IV, VII, I. The top notes, B, C, C, B, outline the melody, which includes passing notes. Underneath, the bass note G, occurring on beats 1 and 3, is a pedal. Making use of the open strings G and D, the opening is built around the characteristics of the cello.

The movement proceeds similarly, sometimes outlining harmonies by *arpeggio* figures (as above), and sometimes using scales to emphasize modulations. An example occurs in bars 9–10, effecting a modulation to the dominant, DM, via chords V7 (bar 9) and I in DM (bar 10). Bars 11–12 outline VII7–Ib in Am, followed by a harmonic sequence in bars 13–14, outlining VII–I in Em. The harmonic sequence in bars 15–16 has a surprise in the resolution. Returning to the tonic, GM, with V7b in bar 15, the supposed tonic chord in bar 16 turns out to be V7 in CM, with F natural as the melody note. The resolution onto CM occurs in bar 17. The tonic bass note, G, becomes a pedal note lasting through bars 16–19. Above the pedal are chords VII (bar 18) and I (bar 19).

The descending scalic passage takes the music to C sharp, almost the lowest note of the cello, a dramatic harmony note suddenly indicating a modulation to the dominant, DM. Averting this suggestion, the next bar (21) cancels the C sharp with C natural, indicating V7d in GM. However, this note cannot resolve in the conventional tonal manner because this open-string C is the lowest note of the cello! Bach solves the problem by taking the music upwards in a series of rising scales that outline V7 in GM. The top of this ascent is marked by the highest note yet heard, E flat, at the very beginning of bar 24. Apart from representing the melodic climax of the movement so far, it turns the chord V7 into Vm9 in GM, with the added chromatic twists of C sharp and C natural. Five bars are taken up with the dominant chord (bars 21–25), which only briefly resolves onto the tonic in bar 26. The second half of this bar hurtles into an augmented sixth chord (German: B flat, C sharp, G sharp) in DM. This resolves normally onto V7 (bar 27), then I in DM (bar 28). The DM chord immediately becomes the dominant of GM with the return to C natural in the next bar (29). The bass notes of bars 29–31 become a descending melody: D, C, B, A.

From bar 31 until the end of the *Prélude*, Bach takes advantage of the open strings of the cello, using them as pedal notes around which he weaves melodic patterns. The playing technique involves rotating between adjacent strings. In bars 31–36, the top A string is the pivotal pedal note. This changes to the open D string, which acts as a lower dominant pedal note for bars 37–41. A chromatic scale ascends through bars 37 and 38, reaching the highest note of the piece, tonic G, at the start of bar 39. The cadential harmonic progression of Ic, V with suspended 3rd, resolving onto V7, is outlined in bars 39–41. These three bars represent an inversion of the opening linear direction: bottom–top/top–bottom. The final resolution onto a GM tonic is effected by a triple-stop, the only stopped chord in the movement.

Rhythmically, the *Prélude* is a *moto perpetuo*, moving along mostly in sixteenth notes. Structurally, it is fundamentally an ascent, the climactic high note being reached at the end. Though only one note at a time is heard, the melodic, harmonic, and contrapuntal threads are clearly conveyed. In addition, Bach takes into account the build of the

Example 9.1 Johann Sebastian Bach, Suite No. 1 for Violoncello (BWV XXVII.1): Prélude.

(continued)

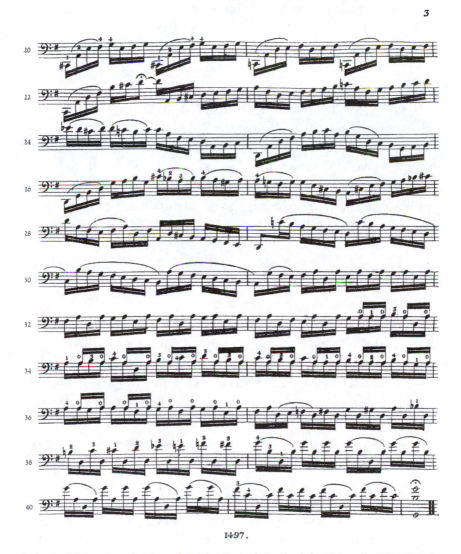

Example 9.1 (continued) Johann Sebastian Bach, Suite No. 1 for Violoncello (BWV XXVII.1): Prélude.

instrument and its traditional playing technique. It is a masterpiece of baroque music from which composers of any era can take lessons.

Béla Bartók was clearly familiar with J.S. Bach's works for unaccompanied instrument and drew on baroque techniques when he composed his Sonata for Solo Violin (1944). It was written for Yehudi Menuhin who gave the first performance that year, in New York. The second movement (of the four) is a *Fuga*, and is as much a *tour de force* for the performer as it was for the composer (see Example 9.2).

This *Fuga* is in four parts, all played by the one instrument. Formally, it follows the fugal schema of exposition, episodes, middle entries, and final section. The exposition starts with the bass "voice" announcing the fugue subject. Rhythmically, the subject contains a number of rests, which not only allow the line to "breathe," but will be useful later in enabling other parts to be heard. Though highly chromatic, the beginning of the subject outlines a Cm/CM tonality. In bars 3 and 4, three-note groups of eighth notes are built from the intervals of m2 + M2, or *vice versa*. The last bar (5) of the subject has these three-note groups turned into M2 + M2, suggesting Whole Tone scales.

The tenor voice enters at the end of bar 5 and continues until bar 10 with the answer: the subject transposed onto the dominant, Gm/M. The countersubject (the counterpoint against the subject) is announced in the bass voice, developing the m2 + M2 cell that was part of the subject (bars 3 and 4). This then transforms into an ascending chromatic scale (bars 8–10). Rhythmically, the countersubject fits into the gaps between the notes of the subject. Omitting a codetta, which sometimes appears in baroque fugues, Bartók brings in the alto voice immediately after the answer has been completed (end of bar 10).

As with the traditional exposition, the third entry of the subject is back on the "tonic." Here, it is the top voice, in C but an octave higher than the opening statement of the subject, and is easily heard. At this point, the violin is playing three simultaneous parts. The highest voice has the subject. The countersubject is played by the alto voice, while the bass line plays a free part. In fact, this line still retains hints of the m2 + M2 cell, and often plays in sixths or thirds with the alto part. This entry continues until bar 15, where the fourth voice, the soprano, enters with another answer, in G an octave higher than the alto entry. So the voices have entered in the traditional order: bass/tonic, tenor/dominant, alto/tonic, soprano/dominant. This final entry marks the climax of the exposition, at which all four voices are sounding. However, this is mostly an illusion, because the parts work in pairs, soprano and alto, tenor and bass. The only two places where all four parts are heard together in quadruple-stopped chords occur in bars 18 and 19. The end of the exposition is marked by a cadence onto Dm (bar 21).

Following the exposition is episode 1, bars 21–37. The episodic material consists of sixteenth note scales alternating with the three-note cell played in sixths. At bar 28, an upper pedal note of C sharp is heard above the m2 + M2 cell played in descending sixths. The ascending scales of bars 21–22 and 26–27 are balanced by descending scales in bars 30–31. Another pedal passage occurs at bars 32–35. At first, the pedal note is an A, which changes octave. It is heard in various formats: first on the bottom string, then as a high double-stopped octave, followed by a harmonic, and finally an open A string together with a stopped A (played on the D string) at the same pitch. The pedal note then changes to B flat, which is given a similar treatment.

Middle entry 1 occurs at the end of bar 37, in which the subject is heard high up, in F sharp. It is indicated with *marcato il tema* and accompanied underneath by sixteenth note *arpeggio* work, taking the score to bar 44. Here, the subject is heard in inverted and augmented form, played by the bass part. The alto part is a reiterated pedal note on the open A string, and the soprano part decorates with sixteenth notes around the open E string. This passage is reminiscent of baroque string writing. At bars 47–48 the soprano part moves into parallel fifths, still in counterpoint with the subject. Episode 2 begins at bar 50, this time with E flat pedal notes. The *Fuga* movement continues with traditional episodes and middle entries until the final section, bars 99–107. Here, the subject is scraped out in four-part parallel chords, which simultaneously outline Cm/M, Gm/M, Am/M and Em/M. The last of these chords becomes a pedal chord, sounding above the final statement of the three-note cell in the bass voice. Bars 104–105 become surprisingly "simple," using only open strings. However, the double-stopped open-string A + E makes a *glissando* upwards to a *ppp* harmonic A + E. The

H. 15594

Example 9.2 Béla Bartók, Sonata for Solo Violin (1944): *Fuga*, bars 1–54. Copyright 1923 by Boosey & Hawkes, Inc. Copyright renewed. Reproduced by permission of Boosey & Hawkes Music Publishers Ltd.

(continued)

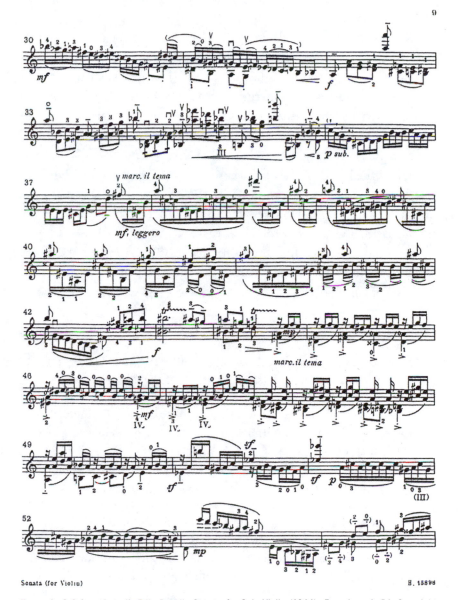

Example 9.2 (continued) Béla Bartók, Sonata for Solo Violin (1944): *Fuga*, bars 1–54. Copyright 1923 by Boosey & Hawkes, Inc. Copyright renewed. Reproduced by permission of Boosey & Hawkes Music Publishers Ltd.

movement finally concludes with the opening gesture, C–E flat, the latter strengthened by being played as a double-stopped E flat on two strings (G and D).

Not only has Bartók written a twentieth-century version of a fugue, but, in doing so, he has exploited violin technique to the fullest. This aspect of having a thorough knowledge of the capacity of the instrument before commencing to write became even more true of composers in the last part of the twentieth century. Working in collaboration with virtuoso performers, Luciano Berio composed a series of pieces for solo instruments, each entitled *Sequenza*. The first, for flute, was written in 1958, and the last, No. XIII for accordion, was completed in 1996. No. VII, for solo oboe, was composed in 1969 for, and dedicated to, the brilliant oboist Heinz Holliger. He demonstrated technical possibilities for Berio and later recorded the work.

Berio has described his compositional starting point for the series in the liner notes to the CD recording of the complete set of *Sequenzas* (Soloists of Ensemble Contemporain, DG457 038-2, 1998, 3 discs):

> The title, *Sequenza*, underlines the fact that the construction of these pieces almost always takes as its point of departure a sequence of harmonic fields, from which spring in all their individuality, the other musical functions. In fact, almost all of the *Sequenzas* have in common the intention of defining and developing through melody an essentially harmonic discourse and, above all when dealing with the monodic instruments (flute, oboe, clarinet, bassoon trumpet, trombone), of suggesting a polyphonic type of listening, based in part on the rapid transition between different characteristics, and their simultaneous iteration … the best solo performers of our own time—modern in intelligence, sensibility and technique—are those who are capable of acting within a wide historical perspective, and of resolving the tensions between the creative demands of past and present, employing their instruments as a means of research and expression. Their virtuosity is not confined to manual dexterity nor to philological specialisation.

Applying his ideas to *Sequenza* No. VII for solo oboe, Berio continues his search for "virtual polyphony." Structurally, this work is laid out on a repeating time frame of 3", 2.7", 2", 2", 2", 2", 1.8", 1.5", 1.3", 1.3",

1", 1", 1". These thirteen durational distances are indicated by dotted lines in the score, and are repeated thirteen times. There is no time signature, the music being placed within each bar in time-space notation. This results in a fluid rhythm, though the brevity of some of the time frames, in which many notes occur, indicates great velocity. Occasionally, and more particularly towards the end of the piece, extra pauses are introduced that disturb the predictability of the durational pattern (see Example 9.3).

In a sense, this particular *Sequenza* is a duet, the piece being accompanied by a drone on the pitch B. This note may be sounded electronically, or by another instrument (such as a viola) playing offstage. At the start of the work, the oboe plays the note B at the same pitch as the drone, reiterating it many times, with at least five different fingerings and articulated with a wide range of dynamics. This creates a subtle *klangfarbenmelodie* on a single pitch. The choice of this particular pitch, B above middle C, has special significance because there are over ninety different possible fingerings on the oboe for this note. The first pitch classes of the first harmonic field appear at the start of round 2 of the time frame. Pitch classes C and B flat (a m2 on either side of the drone, B natural) are introduced. Eventually, D and A are added. In this manner, Berio's harmonic fields can be deduced. The B pitch center eventually gives way to other, shorter, pedal notes: F sharp at the end of round 3, D in round 5, E in round 7, and so on, with the original B making fleeting appearances *en passant*.

As well as employing nonstandard fingerings that subtly color specific pitches, other extended playing techniques are employed. These include the playing of chords and harmonics, effects using over-blowing, *tremolando*, *glissando*, double trills, and trills with microtones. Heinz Holliger has written a helpful page of instructions with examples of fingerings and lip pressures. A virtuosity of instrumental technique, coupled with musical intelligence and sensibility, is required to perform any one of Berio's *Sequenzas*.

The same is true for the works of trombonist-composer Vinko Globokar (who was the collaborator and inspiration for Berio's *Sequenza* for trombone). The title of Globokar's piece for solo trombone, *Res/As/Ex/Ins-pirer* (1973) makes play with several French words associated

Example 9.3 Luciano Berio, *Sequenza* No. VII for solo oboe (1969): rounds 1–8. Copyright 1971 by Universal Edition A.G. Vienna. Reproduced by permission. All rights reserved.   (continued)

with composing and playing the trombone: *respirer, aspirer, expirer,* and *inspirer.* The duration of the work is thirteen minutes, during which time there is continuous sound, despite being written for a brass instrument. Technically, this is achieved via "circular breathing," a skill that can be acquired, albeit very taxing for the performer. Structurally, the work is built on two rhythmic threads.

Thread 1 consists of a two-cell block, which is repeated 10 times in succession, between 2 and 11:

Thread 1:   x2, x3, x4, x5, x6, x7, x8, x9, x10, x11
Thread 2   is based on a Fibonacci series worked in retrograde:
        102(110), 60(68), 38(42), 26, 16, 10, 6, 4, 2

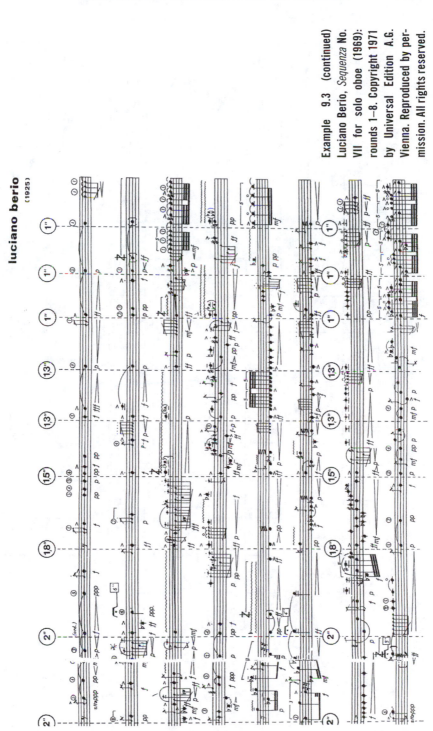

Globokar

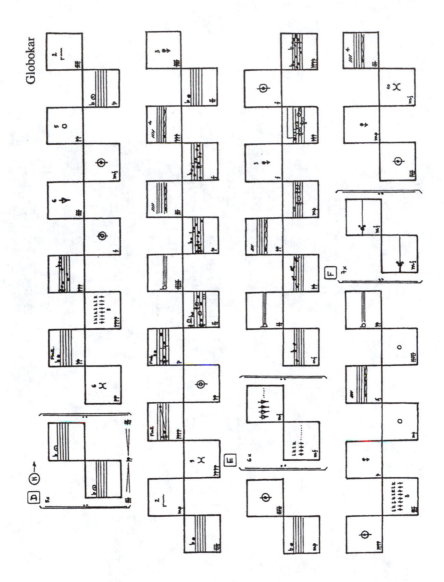

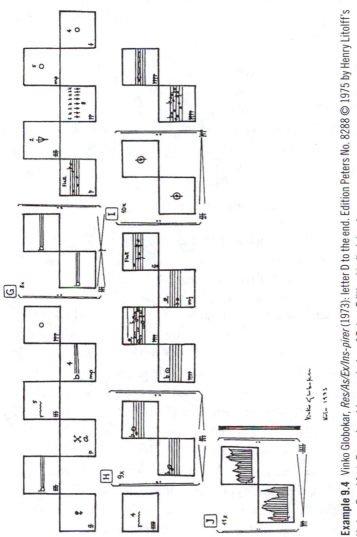

Example 9.4 Vinko Globokar, *Res/As/Ex/Ins-pirer* (1973): letter D to the end. Edition Peters No. 8288 © 1975 by Henry Litolff's Verlag, Frankfurt. Reproduced by permission of Peters Edition Limited, London.

The numbers in brackets are the true Fibonacci numbers, while the unbracketed numbers are those actually used within the piece. The ten blocks of thread 1 alternate with the nine blocks of thread 2. The cells comprise twelve different ways of playing. The music is notated graphically, with a page of performance notes explaining the symbols used. The score starts with:

Letter A: Thread 1 played twice
    Thread 2 follows, with 102 cells
Letter B: Thread 1 played 3 times
    Thread 2 follows, with 60 cells
Letter C: Thread 1 played 4 times
    Thread 2 follows, with 38 cells

The structure continues in this pattern until:

Letter I: Thread 1 played 10 times
    Thread 2 ends with 2 cells
Letter J: Thread 1 played 11 times

Extended instrumental techniques are used, including playing chords that result from singing and playing simultaneously. Lip vibration, rolled "rrrr," tongue-stops and flutter-tongue are all included in the sound palette. The score indicates specific pitches and ways of playing, leaving the performer free to execute the instructions within the cells. Once again, this work demonstrates the principle of plurality within singularity (see Example 9.4).

The Finnish composer Kaija Saariaho has composed numerous works for flute, partly because she is particularly drawn to this instrument and partly as a result of the artistic collaboration that she has developed with the American flautist Camilla Hoitenga. Saariaho's *NoaNoa*, for solo flute and live electronics, was first performed by Hoitenga in Darmstadt in 1992. Jean-Baptiste Barrière supervised the live electronic element.

Saariaho has composed several works that have developed from the materials, or the experience, of previous compositions. *NoaNoa* (1992) emerged from the music of Saariaho's ballet, *Maa*, composed the previous year. The Tahitian word *NoaNoa* means "scent" and was also the title of an engraving by the artist Paul Gauguin, produced during his Tahitian period. Thus, even before the music has begun, there are multiple references. At various points in the music, the flautist enunciates a French text in an intense manner, "through" the flute, as it were:

L'arbe sentait la rose (la rose) très odorant (sentait rose rose sentait rose) s t
r t, s t s t s, t t t t t t.

The rhythm of the text is notated exactly. The text appears here exactly as it does in the score, the brackets indicating the creative way in which principal words are selected for repetition and varying orders. The text eventually collapses into a series of phonemes heard in the previous phrase. This mirrors the compositional technique in which the musical line develops by the repetition of partial phrases, and the interpolation of groups of notes in a nonlinear fashion. There are a number of musical cells in play, each of which recurs several times in different juxtapositions. The cells themselves develop by compositionally playing with the pitches and the rhythms of the note groups.

One cell is heard at the start, consisting of a compound M3, C–E/short–long (see Example 9.5).

A very recognizable motif, this is heard several times within the work, each played with a different articulation (see bars 11–12, 19, 36, 41–42, 54, 61–63, 88–92, 94–96 [retrograde variant], 111–113, 169–175 [the end]). The motif heard in bar 10 is transformed in bars 11, 13–14, and 15–16. The pitches and rhythm of bar 16 reappear exactly in bars 31, 34, and 44, but with different dynamics. The rocking M7 motif, D–C sharp, first heard in bar 17, is rhythmically developed in bars 18–19, 21, and 38, and is transformed into a low m2 *glissando* in bars 46–47. The first phrase of the text is spoken "through" a held middle C, the lowest note on the flute. Sustained throughout seven bars (bars 22–28), the middle C gradually moves from *senza vibrato* to *molto vibrato* to a trill which becomes more energetic and intense as it progresses. This note is rhythmically articulated by the spoken text.

The first of two complete scales appears in bar 29. Scale 1 is heard again in bar 56, extended in bars 60 and 85, and fragmented in bar 82. The second scale appears towards the end of the piece in bar 143, then microtonally varied in bars 144–146, 148–151, and 153, and fragmented

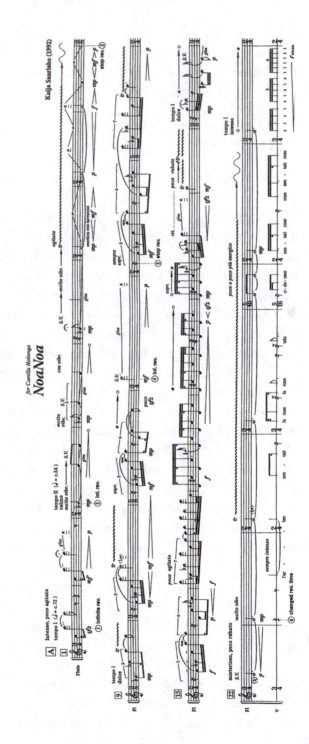

for Camilla Hoitenga
NoaNoa

Kaija Saariaho (1992)

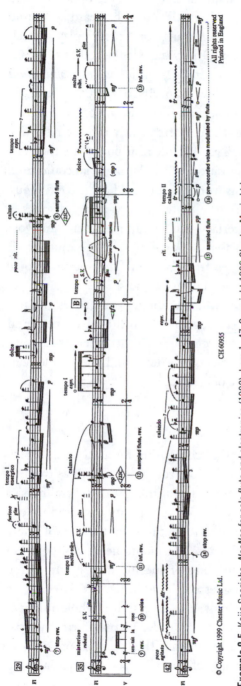

Example 9.5 Kaija Saariaho, *NoaNoa* for solo flute and electronics (1992): bars 1–47. Copyright 1999 Chester Music Ltd.

in bars 154–155, 160–161, and, finally, in bar 167. A multiphonic chord, played *tremolando*, appears in bars 33 and 37, not to be heard again until its echo in bar 156. This is only one of a range of extended playing techniques demanded by the composer. Others include the ability to effect a genuine *glissando*, seamlessly change from *senza vibrato* to *molto vibrato* to trill, perform mictrotones, overblow to specific notes in the harmonic series, speak while playing, and project energetic dynamics.

The musical materials within the cells frequently include rests. Not only is this helpful to the wind player, but the rests punctuate the musical discourse. Though the juxtaposition of cellular material could result in a fractured line, in fact, in this work the musical flow is continuous.

The live electronics amplify the flute with varying degrees of reverberation. Prerecorded material includes sampled flute and voice modulated by the flute. All this is triggered at specific points in the score. The sonic spectrum ranges from normal flute sound through infinite reverberation, to prerecorded filters, to noise.

Saariaho is another composer who thoroughly researches the possibilities of the medium prior to composition. In this case, the plurality within singularity includes the solo flute with its stock of extended playing techniques, the involvement of a text, and the subtle sonic enhancement effected by the use of electronics.

Conclusion

It is clear from these examples that composing for a monodic instrument requires technical virtuosity of the composer as well as from the performer. In the most interesting works of this genre, several musical layers are in play simultaneously. With the capacity of sounding only one note at a time, the monodic instrument is given the task of implying a multiplicity of musical threads. Harmonic fields can be established through the repeated sounding of specific note groups. Thus, melody and harmony can be suggested. In addition, the full range of instrumental *timbres* can be employed as layers. The whole might be enhanced with integrated electronics in order to transform the "natural" sound of the individual instrument. This element provides yet another layer to add to the principle of "plurality within singularity."

10

MOVING AHEAD

You're probably now at the stage of having composed a piece of music and are ready to give it a hearing. Perhaps your college has arranged for a workshop at which you can hear your work sympathetically rehearsed. Or you might have responded to a composition competition or another performance opportunity. There are various practical aspects of presenting your score and set of parts to performers that will encourage goodwill towards you, the developing composer.

Firstly, remember that the score is *not* the music! The score itself is only a representation of the music, in the same way that a script is the dialogue (together with stage directions) for a play or film. How the text, be it musical or verbal, is interpreted depends on the skills of the conductor/producer and musicians/actors. Every written note on the page represents a physical action. While some regard the actual score as a work of art in its own right, in fact it is only a means to an end. So a balance must be struck between spending too little or too much time in the preparation of the materials. It goes without saying that scribbled notes presented on torn-off sheets of manuscript paper will put everyone in a bad mood! On the other hand, even the best handwritten or computer-set score is not, by itself, a guarantee of musical quality. However, a composer who takes the task seriously will ensure reasonable care in the presentation of both the score and the set of parts.

Presentation

While the musical quality of your work is paramount, there is no doubt that visual presentation plays its part in creating an impression, favorable or otherwise. Here are some general guidelines:

- Both handwritten and computer-set scores are equally acceptable.
- Present a *copy* of your work. This may be a photocopy of a neatly handwritten score in black pencil. Check that your original is sufficiently dark to photocopy well. If not, it will be necessary to make an ink score.
- NEVER PART WITH YOUR ORIGINAL SCORE.
- Avoid using ballpoint pens and felt-tip pens for music copying, because they do not give the necessary differentiation between thick (for note-heads and beams) and thin (for tails and bar lines). An italic nib pen is ideal. Professional music copyists use at least two different nibs.

Notation

The notation employed in the score and parts should follow standard editorial practice wherever possible. Do not invent a sign when a conventional one exists. Your music is likely to be performed by players who are very familiar with the traditional system (and are often annoyed when confronted by a composer who apparently does not know the normal, standard practice!). *The Essentials of Music Copying* by Homewood and Matthews is a good resource (see the Bibliography).

On the rare occasion when you wish to use a sound or playing technique for which there is no standard notation, it is legitimate to invent a sign. In this case, a performance note is necessary. Specialized notations should be used for particular genres, for example, jazz chord notation, guitar tablature, and lute tablature.

Paper

Manuscript paper can be obtained from any good music shop, in a range of formats. Twelve-stave manuscript paper is the standard, but other formats are useful for particular genres, for example:

- Voice/instrument + keyboard
- Quartet
- Eighteen-stave
- Ten-stave

Alternatively, individual layouts can be created using a computer music program.

Scores

For scores, either portrait or landscape format can be used, though conductors generally prefer portrait. Scores should be *backed up* (i.e., printed on both sides of the page). Scores should open with:

- A title page containing the title of the work and the name of the composer
- Page 1, listing the instruments/voices needed for a performance. State whether the score is transposed or not. Include the approximate duration.
- Page 2: performance notes and program note

The first page of the score should start with a system that contains a stave for each voice or instrument used, even if not all are performing at the beginning. This page should also repeat the composer's name, title of the work, copyright symbol ©, and date of composition.

Title pages can be created by using a word processor. If creating a handwritten title page, dry lettering is recommended, for neatness. Either way, photocopy the master title page onto the card (or paper) title page *before* it is bound.

- Scores should be bound, using *spiral binding* on the *left*. Colored card sheets for title pages and acetates (Perspex sheets) can be purchased from art materials shops.
- Photocopy your work in either letter or legal size, according to legibility. When asking a copy shop to prepare the copies, be careful to explain that you want the score to be spiral bound *centered* on the *left*. Sometimes, copy shops will bind longer scores at the top, which is not convenient for the performers or conductor.
- Scores that use transposing instruments may be written at sounding pitch, or the parts may be transposed in the score. Generally, it is preferred that modern scores are written at sounding pitch, making reading easier. Either way, it is imperative that you indicate which method you have used, as follows:
  - "Score written at sounding pitch" *or*
  - "Clarinet in E flat"; "Horns in F"; "Trumpets in B flat"; and so forth.

Transposing instruments used in a score that is notated at sounding pitch need to be identified in the preface. Thus E flat clarinet, F horn, B flat trumpet, and so on, indicate which particular instrument is required to perform the work. It is conventional practice that the piccolo part is written down an octave and the double bass part is written up an octave from their actual sounds. This is so that not too many ledger lines need to be used.

- The full name of each instrument should appear on the first page of the score. Subsequently, an abbreviation can be used. (N.B. "vibes" = vibraphone.)
- Number the bars, either in tens throughout the score, or at the start of each system.
- The sign ∕⁄ should not be used in a score (even though there are examples of its use in some published scores). It is used to indicate "Repeat the previous bar." However, a score is a vertical and

forward-moving object, and at all times, it is necessary to be able to read up and down it, without going backwards.

- Perhaps more controversial is the advice to repeat accidentals tied from one bar to the next. The reason is, as above, that it is necessary to be able to read a score vertically without having to retrace tied notes back to their origin (which may even be on a previous page). If ambiguity can be avoided, repeat the accidental.

Parts

Use heavyweight paper for parts to avoid flopping or curling on the music stand. Portrait format is generally preferred. Here are some pointers to keep in mind:

- Ten-stave manuscript paper gives more room than twelve-stave.
- Write largely, clearly, and legibly, with 3 or 4 bars per stave (depending on the number of notes in each bar).
- Mark bar numbers in the score *and* the parts.
- Indicate the *tempo*, dynamics, articulation, and bowing.
- Leave empty staves between passages involving high or low ledger lines, to avoid collisions.
- Write on one side of the page only. The performer can slide the next page across in convenient rest bars, rather than turning the pages.
- Photocopy your originals, ensuring good contrast and legibility.
- Bring your spare set of parts along to the rehearsal, just in case.
- Mark cues in rests bars.

Example 10.1a–c shows three different ways of using rests in a score.

Normally, a long rest may be broken down, at least into 10-bar blocks. A 26-bar rest, for example, equals 10 bars plus 10 bars plus 6 bars. This makes it easier for the performer to work out where he or she should next play. For example, in a rehearsal that has stopped at (for example) bar 17, the performer needs to count 4 bars plus 6 bars before his or her next entry (see Example 10.1b).

Rests: a

Example 10.1a Rests: a.

Rests: b

Example 10.1b Rests: b.

Rests: c

Example 10.1c Rests: c.

Other events should also be marked in all parts, such as pauses, *ritardandi*, changes of time signature, and the relationship between simple and compound units (see Example 10.1c).

- Fill to the end of each staff. Performers are often thrown by bars that are split between 2 staves. A bar line at the end of each staff is reassuring.
- Transposing instruments must have their parts transposed.
- Ensure that your name and the title of the work are written on each part.
- The name of the instrument should also be indicated at the top of the page.
- Fix together the pages of each part—in a folder, for example.

Texts

See Chapter 8 for advice on notating works that use texts.

Program Notes

The inclusion of a short program note assists the reader in placing your work. Some or all of the following points may be addressed in the note:

Context
    Is this your first string quartet?
    Does the work involve Cageian aleatorism?
    Are you using a post-minimalist language?
Circumstances
    For which situation is this piece composed?
Conception
    What is the main idea expressed in the work?
Content
    Describe the structure and some of the techniques used.
Conclusion
    What do you hope to achieve in this composition?

Planning

Allow plenty of time for the composition, copying and photocopying of your scores and parts. Curiously, it seems to take as long to copy and present a score as it does to compose it in the first place.

Self Criticism

The following criteria should be helpful in gauging your own development:

- Quality of musical imagination: the key to being a successful composer. The imagination can be stimulated through contact with interesting new music and æsthetic ideas.

- Individuality of style and expression. You should aim to develop your own style and expression, rather than imitate that of another composer.
- Technical competence and practicality. These come with practice. Writing in a practical way for a particular situation is a sign of good judgment. You might need to adapt your style to suit the occasion.
- Ability to communicate. Music that communicates to the listener will be remembered. Musical communication does not depend upon style, genre, or complexity, but needs to appeal to both the heart and the head.
- Awareness of context. An awareness of the artistic context in which you aspire to work will inform your concepts and make your music intelligible to like-minded musicians.
- Presentation. Immaculate presentation of your scores will make a favorable impression on performers, upon whom you rely.

Performance Opportunities

When you feel ready, you should seek out opportunities for performances of your work. This can involve responding to "Calls for Scores," entering composition competitions, or creating your own performance spaces. The latter can be achieved through collaboration with fellow composers and performers. Creating a composers' collective, together with other developing composers, is a good way of establishing yourself on the new music circuit. For example, Peter Maxwell Davies initiated his performing ensemble, the Fires of London, during the 1970s. He wrote a large number of chamber music works for this ensemble, which earned such a strong reputation that it performed all over the world. Michael Nyman has formed his own band, the Michael Nyman Band, which, similarly, performs worldwide. The Bang on a Can group was formed in New York by composers Michael Gordon, David Lang, and Julia Wolf. They organize a festival of new music, using the same name, as well as perform in the United States and Europe.

There are many composition competitions organized especially for younger composers, that is, those under the age of 30. The purpose of these is to give the younger generation the opportunity of emerging. The prize might be financial, though more importantly, it will involve a performance of the music. This, in turn, could attract the attention of critics, publishers, and promoters. Other composition competitions exist with an age range of up to 40 years, while others have no age limitation at all. Some have regional or national geographical limitations. A good source of information about composition competitions, festivals of new music, short composition courses, new publications, and CDs is Gaudeamus Information, which can be viewed at the Gaudeamus web site: www.gaudeamus.nl.

Many countries are members of the International Society for Contemporary Music (ISCM), an umbrella organization for contemporary music. It was founded in 1922 and now has a membership of over 50 countries. Each member country organizes its own activities, which frequently include a regular festival of new music. These are often high-powered events that are broadcast on national radio stations. Music by emerging composers is usually featured alongside more established composers at these festivals. An annual "World Music Days" is organized to take place in a different country each year. In the United Kingdom, the Society for the Promotion of New Music (SPNM), established in 1943, organizes a program of events that take place throughout the year in various locations. The focus of the SPNM is on emerging composers (of any age), giving them opportunities for performances by experienced professional performers. In addition, imaginative schemes aimed at developing young composers of school age are also organized. These festivals and other new music events offer the chance to hear contemporary music played live, including the thrill of experiencing first performances.

Summer schools that offer composition courses are held in many countries. Often mature composers are employed to coach developing composers. Attending a short course like this can be useful for encouragement, as well as for meeting other composers and performers.

Further study may be undertaken at graduate and postgraduate levels. The place of study should be chosen with care, taking account of the ethos of the particular institution or department of music and what it offers to developing composers. In particular, the teaching reputations of the staff composers are important factors. Enrolling in a course with the expectation that you will be taught by a particular established composer, only to find that he or she is frequently away, may prove to be a great disappointment! Access to collections of writings on music, new music scores, and recordings is vital to your own knowledge and development. The music department should also be able to set up workshops at which you can hear your new works rehearsed. It is by hearing your own work in real time, and with the correct sound, that you will learn the art and craft of composition.

Armed with talent, desire, experience, and knowledge, you are ready to continue the journey of exploration. Honing your technique so that your music succeeds in expressing your original intent becomes the fulfillment of your dreams. Seeking for, and finding, your composing voice is part of your inner search. You will become aware of your own individual mental creative space. Some composers are inspired by the beauty and power of nature; others fly to outer space in their imaginations; while yet others travel backwards to the time of an ancient civilization. Composing is musical communication between people; it is not a solitary activity. Rather, it brings you into contact with musicians at all levels. It can humble you in the presence of great performers. It gives you the opportunity of lifting people's spirits onto another plane. Sometimes, you feel as though you are a conduit for a higher presence, rather than the originator of the initial idea, even though it was you who slaved to notate the music that you could imagine!

The musical future is yours.

Notes

Chapter 1

1. Bruce Boucher. A New Idea of Beauty, The Artfund Quarterly (Winter 2002): 35.

Chapter 2

1. Richard Steinitz on the music of George Crumb, *Musical Times* (October 1978): 844.
2. Jonathan Harvey describing his *Inner Light (3)*, *Musical Times* (July 1975): 125.
3. Xenakis, *Formalised Music*. Bloomington and London, 1971: 8.
4. Paul Griffiths, "Tavener and *Ultimos ritos*," *Musical Times* (June 1974): 468.
5. Thea Musgrave, "A New Viola Concerto," *Musical Times* (August 1973): 790.
6. Music critic of *Chicago Times* (September 2001), on Rouse's *clarinet games*.
7. Music critic of *The Guardian* (London, February 2002), commenting on Magnus Lindberg's *Cantigas*.
8. Music critic of *The Guardian* (London, 2002), describing the première of Magnus Lindberg's *Parada*.
9. Pauline Oliveros, program annotation for *Sound Fishes* (1992).
10. Annie Gosfield on the UK première of her 50-minute work, *EWA7* (1999), 25th Huddersfield

11. Contemporary Music Festival program book (Huddersfield, November 2002): 33.

Bibliography

Books

Artaud, Pierre-Yves. *Present Day Flutes*. Paris: Éditions Billaudot, 1995.

Bartolozzi, Bruno. *New Sounds for Woodwind*. 2nd ed. Translated by Reginald Smith Brindle. London: Oxford University Press, 1982.

Brindl, Reginald Smith. "Contemporary Percussion." London: Oxford University Press, 1977.

Carroll, Lewis. *Through the Looking Glass and What Alice Found There*. Oxford: Oxford University Press. 1971.

Cage, John. *Silence*. London: Calder and Boyars, 1968.

— *Empty Words*. London: Marion Boyars, 1980.

— *X, Writings '79–'82*. New York: Marion Boyars, 1987.

Cope, David. *New Music Composition*. New York: Schirmer, 1977.

Cott, Jonathan, ed. *Stockhausen: Conversations with the Composer*. Cott, London: Robson Books, 1974.

Dallin, Leon. *Techniques of Twentieth Century Composition*. Dallin, Iowa: Wm. C. Brown Co., Publishers, 1974.

Davison, Archibald T., and Willi Apel, eds. *Historical Anthology of Music*. Vol. 1, 12th ed. Cambridge: MA: Harvard University Press, 1974.

Dick, Robert. *The Other Flute: A Performance Manual of Contemporary Techniques*. New York: Oxford University Press, 1975.

Hindemith, Paul. *Craft of Musical Composition. Volume I: Theory*. Translated by Arthur Mendel. London: Schott, 1945.

Holliger, Heinz, ed. *Studien zum Spielen Neuer Musik*. Wiesbaden, Germany: Breitkopf & Härtel, 1973.

Homewood, S., and C. Matthews. *The Essentials of Music Copying*. London: Music Publishers' Association, 1990.

Horsley, Imogen. *Fugue: History and Practice*. London: Collier-Macmillan, 1966.

Howell, Thomas. *The Avant-Garde Flute: A Handbook for Composers and Flutists*. Berkeley: University of California Press, 1974.

Jarman, Douglas, ed. *The Twentieth-Century String Quartet*. Todmorden, United Kingdom: RNCM/Arc Music, 2002.

Lawson, Colin, ed. *Cambridge Companion to the Clarinet*. Cambridge: Cambridge University Press, 1995.

Mann, Alfred. *The Study of Fugue*. London: Faber and Faber, 1958.

Messiaen, Olivier. *Technique of My Musical Language*. 2 vols., 2nd ed. Translated by John Satterfield. Paris: Leduc, 1956: chaps. 1–7.

Nalden, Charles. *Fugal Answer*. Oxford: Oxford University Press, 1969.

Oldroyd, George. *The Technique and Spirit of Fugue*. Oxford: Oxford University Press, 1948.

Pevsner, Nikolaus. *The Sources of Modern Architecture and Design*. London: Thames and Hudson, 1968.

Piston, Walter. *Orchestration*. London: Gollancz, 1979.

Rehfeldt, Phillip. *New Directions for Clarinet*. 3rd ed. Berkeley: University of California Press, 2003.

Rufer, Josef. *Composition with Twelve Notes*. Translated by Humphrey Searle. London: Barrie and Rockliff, 1954.

Schafer, R. Murray. *When Words Sing*. Scarborough, Ontario, Canada: Berandol Music, 1970.

Smith Brindle, Reginald. *Contemporary Percussion*. Oxford: Oxford University Press, 1975.

— *Serial Composition*. Oxford: Oxford University Press, 1977.

— *Musical Composition*. Oxford: Oxford University Press, 1995.

Straus, Joseph. *The Music of Ruth Crawford Seeger*. Cambridge: Cambridge University Press, 1995: 182–205.

Turetzky, Bertram. *The Contemporary Contrabass*. Berkeley: University of California Press, 1974.

Veal, Peter and Claus-Steffen Mahnkopf. *The Techniques of Oboe Playing*. Kassel: Bärenreiter, 1998.

Articles

Saariaho, Kaija. "Timbre and Harmony: Interpolations of Timbral Structures." Pt. 1. *Contemporary Music Review* 2 (1987): 93–133.

Smith, Geoff, and Nicola Walker Smith. "Sonic Architecture in the Music of Margaret Lucy Wilkins." Pts. 1 and 2. *Contemporary Music Review* 11 (1994): 319–324.

Scores

Andriessen, Louis. *Hoketus*. Amsterdam: Donemus, 1977.

Bach, Johann Sebastian. Six Suites for Violoncello. Paris: Janet et Cotelle, 1824.

Bartók, Béla. *Music for Strings, Percussion and Celesta*. Vienna: Universal Edition, Suite No. 1 for Violonoello (BWVXXVIII): Prelude 1937.

— String Quartet No. 6. London: Boosey & Hawkes, 1941.

— Sonata for Solo Violin. London: Boosey & Hawkes, 1947.

— *Mikrokosmos*, revised ed. London: Boosey & Hawkes, 1987.

Benjamin, George. *At First Light*. London: Faber, 1985.

Berberian, Cathy. *Stripsody*. New York: Peters, 1966.

Berg, Alban. *Wozzeck*. Vienna: Universal Edition, 1955.

Berio, Luciano. *Sequenza VII* for solo oboe. London: Universal Edition, 1971.

Boulez, Pierre. *Le Marteau sans Maître*. London: Universal Edition, 1957.

Britten, Benjamin. Folksong Arrangements, Vol. I: *British Isles*. London: Boosey & Hawkes, 1943.

— *Rejoice in the Lamb*. London: Boosey & Hawkes, 1943.

— *Four Sea Interludes from the Opera 'Peter Grimes.'* London: Boosey & Hawkes, 1945.

Cage, John. *Sonatas and Interludes*. New York: Edition Peters, 1960.

Carter, Elliott. String Quartet No. 2, 2nd ed. New York: Associated Music Publishers, 1962.

Crumb, George. *Vox Balaenae*. New York: Edition Peters, 1972.

— *Makrokosmos Vol. II*. New York: Edition Peters, 1973.

Dallapiccola, Luigi. *Goethe-Lieder*. Milan: Zerboni, 1953.

Davies, Peter Maxwell. *Eight Songs for a Mad King*. London: Boosey & Hawkes, 1971.

— *Missa Super L'homme armé*. London: Boosey & Hawkes, 1978.

Debussy, Claude. *Syrinx*. Paris: Jobert, 1927.

Feldman, Morton. *For Frank O'Hara*. London: Universal Edition, 1986.

Finnissy, Michael. *English Country-Tunes*. London: United Music Publishers, 1986.

Globokar, Vinko. *Res/As/Ex/Ins-pirer*. Frankfurt: Litolff/Peters, 1975.

Górecki, Henryk. Symphony No. 3: *Symphony of Sorrowful Songs*. Kraków: PWM, 1977.

Gubaidulina, Sofia. *In croce*. Hamburg: Sikorski, 1980.

— *Seven Words*. Hamburg: Sikorski, 1985.

Hildegard von Bingen. *Ave Generosa*. Christopher Page, ed., *Abbess Hildegard of Bingen*, Oxford: Antico Church Music, 1982.

Kulenty, Hanna. *Air*. Kraków: PWM, 1991.

Kurtág, György. *Játékok*. Budapest: Edition Musica, 1979.

Lefanu, Nicola. *Deva*. Kent, United Kingdom: Novello, 1981.

Ligeti, György. *Ten Pieces for Wind Quintet*. Mainz, Germany: Schott, 1969.

— *Continuum*. Mainz: Schott, 1970.

— *Volumina*. Frankfurt: Edition Peters, 1973.

Lutoslawski, Witold. String Quartet. London: Chester, 1967.

Lutyens, Elisabeth. *and suddenly it's evening*. London: Schott, 1970.

MacMillan, James. *The Confession of Isobel Gowdie*. London: Boosey & Hawkes, 1992.

Maconchy, Elizabeth. String Quartet No. 3. London: Lengnick, 1957.

— *Modes of Limited Transportation*.

Messiaen, Olivier. *Quatuor pour la fin du temps*. Paris: Durand, 1942.

Mozart, Wolfgang Amadeus. String Quartet No. 21, 'Prussian No. 1,' K. 575 in D Major. Zürich: Eulenburg, 1968.

Musgrave, Thea. Horn Concerto. London: Chester Music, 1974.

Nielsen, Carl. Quintet. Oslo: Wilhelm Hansen, 1923/1951.

Nørgård, Per. *The Secret Melody:* Movement I from *Libro per Nobuko*. Copenhagen: Wilhelm Hansen, 1997.

Reich, Steve. *Piano Phase*. London: Universal Edition, 1980.

Saariaho, Kaija. *Verblendungen*. Copenhagen: Edition Wilhelm Hansen, 1984.

— *NoaNoa*. London: Chester, 1999.

Saunders, Rebecca. *Molly's Song 3: Shades of Crimson*. London: Peters Edition, 1997.

Schoenberg, Arnold. *Verklärte Nacht*. Berlin: Verlag Dreililien, 1917.

— Wind Quintet, op. 26. Vienna: Universal Edition, 1952.

Seeger, Ruth Crawford. *Suite for Wind Quintet*. Tetra/Continuo Music Group, Inc., 1952.

Stockhausen, Karlheinz. *MANTRA*. Kürten, West Germany: Stockhausen-Verlag, 1975.

Stravinsky, Igor. *Symphony of Psalms, New Revision*. New York: Boosey & Hawkes, 1948.

— *Three Songs from William Shakespeare*. New York: Boosey & Hawkes, 1953.

Takemitsu, Toru. *Rain Spell*. Japan: Schott, 1983.

Tavener, John. *Akathist of Thanksgiving*. London: Chester, 1988.

Webern, Anton. Concerto, op. 24. Vienna: Universal Edition, 1948.

— *Fünf Sätze für Streichquartett*, op. 5. Vienna: Universal Edition, 1949.

Weir, Judith. *Distance and Enchantment*. London: Chester, 1995.

Williams, Ralph Vaughan. *Sinfonia Antarctica*. Oxford: Oxford University Press, 1953/1968.

Xenakis, Iannis. *Nuits*. Paris: Boosey & Hawkes, 1969.

Discography

Andriessen, Louis. *Hoketus*. The California Ear Unit. NA 019 CD, 1989.

Bach, Johann Sebastian. *Six Suites for Violoncello Solo*. Susan Shephard (cello). MET CD 1034, 1999. 2 discs.

Bartók, Béla. *String Quartet No. 6*. Chilingirian Quartet. CHAN 8660, 1989.

— *Sonata for Solo Violin*. Krysia Osostowicz (violin). Hyperion CDA 66415, 1990.

— *Music for Strings, Percussion and Celesta*. BBC SO, c. Pierre Boulez. Sony SM2K 64100, 1994.

Benjamin, George. *At First Light*. London Sinfonietta, c. George Benjamin. Nimbus NI 5075, 1987.

Berberian, Cathy. *Stripsody*. Cathy Berberian (mezzo-soprano). Virgin Classics VC 90704-2, 1988.

Berg, Alban. *Wozzeck*. Vienna State Opera, c. Dohnányi. Decca 417 348-2, 1988.

Berio, Luciano. *Sequenzas*. László Hadady (oboe). DG457 038-2, 1998. 3 discs.

Birtwistle, Harrison. *The Mask of Orpheus*. BBC Symphony Orchestra, BBC Singers, c. Andrew Davis and Martyn Brabbins and soloists. NMC D050, 1997.

Boulez, Pierre. *Le Marteau sans Maître*, Elisabeth Laurence (alto), Ensemble InterContemporain, dir. Pierre Boulez. CBS MK 42619, 1989.

Britten, Benjamin. *Rejoice in the Lamb*. The Sixteen, c. Harry Christophers, Margaret Phillips, organ. Collins 13432, 1993.

— *Four Sea Interludes from the Opera 'Peter Grimes.'* BBC National Orchestra of Wales, c. David Atherton. BBC MM135, 1994.

Cage, John. *Sonatas and Interludes*. Yuji Takahashi (prepared piano). Denon C37-7673, 1985.

Carter, Elliott. *String Quartet No. 2*. Arditti String Quartet. KTC 1066, 1988.

Crumb, George. *Vox Balaenae*. Aeolian Players. Columbia RM32729, 1974.

— *Makrokosmos Vols. I and II*. Christiane Mathé (solo piano). Koch 3-6409, 1996.

Dallapiccola, Luigi. *Goethe-Lieder*. Emelie Hooke (mezzo soprano), Georgina Dobree, Ronald Moore, Wilfred Hambleton (clarinets), ed. Gerald Abraham, *The History of Music in Sound*, Vol. 10/2, "Modern Music 1890–1950." EMI HLP 27, n.d.

Davies, Peter Maxwell. *Missa Super L'homme armé*. Vanessa Redgrave (narrator), The Fires of London, dir. Peter Maxwell Davies. L'Oiseau-Lyre DSLO 2, 1972.

— *Eight Songs for a Mad King*. Julius Eastman (baritone), The Fires of London, c. Peter Maxwell Davies. Unicorn-Kanchana DPK (CD) 9052, 1987.

Debussy, Claude. *Syrinx*. William Bennett (flute). CACD 1017A, 1994.

Dufay, Guillaume. *Missa L'homme armé*. The Hilliard Ensemble. EMI CDC 7 47628 2, 1987.

Feldman, Morton. *For Frank O'Hara*. Ensemble recherche. MO 7820 18, 1994.

Finnissy, Michael. *English Country-Tunes*. Michael Finnissy (piano). Etcetera KTC 1091, 1990.

Globokar, Vinko. *Res/As/Ex/Ins-pirer*. Vinko Globokar (trombone). Harmonia Mundi IC 065 99712, 1978.

Górecki, Henryk. *Symphony No. 3, Symphony of Sorrowful Songs*. Sofia Kilanowicz (soprano), Polish National Radio SO, c. Antoni Wit. Naxos 8.550822, 1994.

Gubaidulina, Sofia. *In croce*. David Geringas (cello), Edgar Krapp (organ). Schwann CD 310091 G1, 1991.

— *Seven Words*, David Geringas (cello), Elsbeth Moser (accordeon), Kammerorchester der Jungen Duetschen Philharmonie, c. Mario Venzago. Philips 434 041-2, 1992.

Hildegard von Bingen. *Ave Generosa, "A Feather on the Breath of God."* Gothic Voices, dir. Christopher Page. Hyperion CDA 66039, 1981.

Kurtág, György. *Játékok*. Márta and György Kurtág (piano). ECM 1619, 1997.

Lefanu, Nicola. *Deva*, Christopher van Kampen (cello), Nash Ensemble. Chandos BR1017, 1980.

Ligeti, György. *Continuum*. Antoinette Vischer (harpsichord). WER 60 161-50, 1988.

— *Ten Pieces for Wind Quintet*. Quintetto Arnold. STR 33304, 1991.

— *Volumina*. Hans-Ola Ericsson (organ). BIS CD-509, 1997.

Lutoslawski, Witold. *String Quartet*. LaSalle Quartet. Duetsche Grammophon 423 245-2, 1968.

Lutyens, Elisabeth. *and suddenly it's evening*. Herbert Handt (tenor), Members of London Symphony Orchestra, c. John Carew. Decca ZRG 638, 1970.

MacMillan, James. *The Confession of Isobel Gowdie*. BBC Scottish Symphony Orchestra, c. Jerzy Maksymiuk. Koch 3-1050-2, 1992.

Maconchy, Elizabeth. *String Quartet No. 3*. Hanson String Quartet. Unicorn Records DKP 9080, 1989.

Messiaen, Olivier. *Quatuor pour la fin du temps*. Gawriloff (violin), Deinzer (clarinet), Palm (cello), Kontarsky (piano). EMI CDC 7 474642, 1987.

Mozart, Wolfgang Amadeus. *String Quartet No. 21, 'Prussian No. 1' K. 575 in D Major*. Éder Quartet. Naxos 8.550545, 1994.

Musgrave, Thea. *Horn Concerto*. Michael Thompson (solo horn). The National Youth Orchestra of Scotland, c. Bramwell Tovey. NYOS 004, 1997.

Nielsen, Carl. *Quintet for Winds*. Berlin Philharmonic Wind Quintet: Michael Hasel, flute; Andreas Wittmann, oboe; Walter Seyfarth, clarinet; Fergus McWilliam, horn; Henning Trog, bassoon. BIS CD-1332, 2003.

Près, Josquin des. *Missa L'homme armé*. Laudantes Consort. CYP1630/3, 2001.

Reich, Steve. *Piano Phase*. Nurit Tilles, Edmund Niemann (pianos). Nonesuch 979 169-2, 1987.

Saariaho, Kaija. *Verblendungen*. Avanti Chamber Orchestra, c. Jukka-Pekka Saraste. FACD 374, 1989.

— *NoaNoa*, Camilla Hoitenga (flute). Ondine ODE 906-2, 1997.

Saunders, Rebecca. *Molly's Song 3–Shades of Crimson*. musikFabrik, c. Stefan Asbury. Kairos 0012182KAI, 2001.

Schafer, R. Murray. *Epitaph for Moonlight*. Vancouver Chamber Choir, c. Jon Washburn. Audiocassette, Grouse 101, 1986.

Schoenberg, Arnold. *Verklärte Nacht*. English String Orchestra, c. William Boughton. Nimbus NI 5151, 1988.

— *Wind Quintet*, Aulos Wind Quintet, Koch-Swann 3-1163-2, 1994.

Seeger, Ruth Crawford. *Suite for Wind Quintet*. Schoenberg Ensemble. DG 449 925-2, 1997.

Stockhausen, Karlheinz. *MANTRA*. Alfons and Aloys Kontarsky (pianos). DGG 2530 208.

— *MANTRA*, Yvar Mikashoff, Rosalind Bevan (pianos). New Albian Records NA025 CD, 1990.

Stravinsky, Igor. *Three Songs from William Shakespeare*. Ann Murray (mezzo soprano), Ensemble InterContemporain, c. Pierre Boulez. Philips ABL 3391, 1961.

— *Symphony of Psalms*. Atlanta Symphony Orchestra and Chorus, c. Robert Shaw. Telarc CD-80254, 1991.

Takemitsu, Toru. *Rain Spell*. London Sinfonietta, c. Oliver Knussen. Virgin VC 7 91180-2, 1991.

Tavener, John. *Akathist of Thanksgiving*. Westminster Abbey Choir, BBC Singers, BBC Symphony Orchestra, c. Martin Neary. Sony SK 64446, 1994.

Teodorescu, Livia. *Rite for Enchanting the Air.* Pierre-Ives Artaud (flute), University of Huddersfield Symphony Orchestra, c. Barrie Webb. Editura Muzicala Bucharest, UCMR-ADA Oa 10360, 2000.

Webern, Anton. *Fünf Sätze für Streichquartett, op. 5.* Arditti String Quartet. Auvidis Montagne MO 789008, 1994.

— *Concerto, op. 24.* Ensemble InterContemporain, c. Pierre Boulez. Duetsche Grammophon, 437 786-2, 1995.

Weir, Judith. *Distance and Enchantment.* Domus. Collins 14532, 1995.

Wilkins, Margaret Lucy. *Symphony.* Timisoara Symphony Orchestra, c. Barrie Webb. VMM 3055, 2003.

Williams, Ralph Vaughan. *Sinfonia Antarctica.* Sheila Armstrong (soprano), London Philharmonic Choir and Orchestra, c. Bernard Haitink. EMI CDC 7 47516 2, 1986.

Xenakis, Iannis. *Nuits.* Soloists of the Choir of l'ORTF. Ades 14.122-2, 1988.

Index

A

Abstract ideas, 18
A cappella, 200, 224, 225, 227
Accelerando, 51, 108, 163, 166, 217
Accent, 27, 50, 60, 87, 108, 204
Accented passing notes, 87
Acciaccatura, 106, 141
Accompaniment, 91, 107, 158, 161, 177,
    200, 203, 205
Acts, 33
Adams, John, 44, 51
Additive rhythm, 50
Æsthetic, 3, 12, 45, 91, 181
    school, 44
African music, 50
Agnus Dei, 82, 83
Air sounds, 144
Alto saxophone, 55, 145
Anderson, Barry, 32
Andriessen, Louis, 44, 51, 54
    Hoketus (1975–1977), 54, 56
Antiphonal, 55
Appoggiatura, 27, 87
Architect, 24
Arco, 174

Arpeggio, 27, 78, 105, 133, 158, 161, 162,
    236, 241
Artaud, Pierre Ives, 95
    Present Day Flutes, 141
Articulations, 29, 91
Art nouveau style, 24
Atmosphere, 72, 79, 152, 200, 203
Audience, 17, 29, 152
Auditorium, 29
Auld Lang Sine, 61
Aural, 38–39, 76, 110, 149, 226, 236
Avant garde, 44, 45, 82, 94, 233

B

Bach, Johann Sebastian, 9, 236
    Suite No. 1 for Violoncello (BWV
        XXVII.1), 236, 238
Bang on a Can, 262
Barcelona, 24
Bar-line, 17
Baroque, 23, 86, 240
Barrière, Jean-Baptiste, 250
Bartók, Béla, 118, 152, 163, 166, 175
    Microkosmos (1932–1939), 118,
        120–121

Music for Strings, Percussion and Celesta (1936), 16
Sonata for Solo Violin (1944), 240, 242–243
String Quartet No. 6, (1939), 164–165
Bartolozzi, Bruno, *New Sounds for Woodwind*, 141
Basho (1644–1694), 202, 204
Bass guitar, 55
Bassoon, 70, 72, 78, 112, 176, 181
    contrabassoon, 140, 144, 177
BBC Singers, 222
Beat, 16, 27, 50, 57, 163, 217, 236
Beethoven, Ludwig van, 9, 152
    Sonata in C$^\#$, op.27, no.2, "Moonlight" (1801), 21
    Symphony No. 6, *Pastoral* (1808), 16
Bel canto, 200
Bells, 150, 202
    handbells, 84
Benjamin, George, 188
    At First Light (1982), 189, 192, 194, 195
Berberian, Cathy, 200
    Stripsody (1966), 217, 220, 221
Berg, Alban, *Wozzeck* (1917–1922), 144
Berio, Luciano, 201, 245
    Sequenza No. VII for solo oboe (1969), 244, 246–247
Birtwistle, Harrison, 32, 35, 44
    The Mask of Orpheus (1973–1983), 29, 34, 37
Bisbigliando, 144
Blocks, 17
    blocks of sound, 17, 129, 259
Bongos, 55, 145, 150
Boulez, Pierre, 9, 44, 72, 94, 95
    Le Marteau sans Maître (*The Hammer Without a Master*) (1953–1955), 96
Boxes, 171
Brass, 35, 78, 91, 151, 176, 235
Brass band, 11, 144
Brindle, Reginald Smith, *Contemporary Percussion*, 148

British Music Information Centre, 11
Britten, Benjamin, 152, 175, 204
    The Ash Grove, 205, 206–207
    Sea Interludes (1945) from his opera, *Peter Grimes*, No. 1 *Dawn*, 78
    The Trees They Grow So High, 205

C

Cadence, 241
    perfect, 158
Cadenza, 17, 129, 177, 188
Cage, John, 44, 118
    Empty Words, 201
    Silence, 201
    Sonatas and Interludes (1946–1948), 119, 122–123
    Writings, 201
Canon, 79
    Dufay, 82
    Górecki, 16, 86
    mensuration canon, 83, 84
    Webern, 161
Canova, Antonio (1757–1822), 7
Carroll, Lewis
    Jabberwocky, 108
    St. George and the Dragon, 19
    Through the Looking Glass and What Alice Found There (1871), 18, 20
Carter, Elliott, 24, 55, 152, 175
    String Quartet No. 2 (1959), 57, 58–59
Cathedral, 24, 26
Cello, 46, 50, 57, 67, 79, 84, 91, 128, 158, 166
    amplified, 133
    motif, 172
    natural harmonics, 189
    seagull effect, 140
    solo, 163, 236
    strings, 153
    technical possibilities, 133
    as tenor, 162

textural flow, 112
Chalumeau register, 91
Chamber music, 153, 262
Char, René, 94
Character, 15, 23, 105, 180
Choir, 11, 77, 200, 222, 224
Chorales, 17
Chords, 17, 75
  added note chords, 73
  diatonic, 129, 171
  harmonic progression, 76
  pizzicato, 170
  staccato, 185
  tonal, 72, 78
  tremolando, 161
Choreography, 124
Chorus, 16, 227
Christian Church, 9, 61, 79, 226
Chromaticism, 69
Circular breathing, 144, 246
Clarinet, 50, 72, 91, 112, 144, 185, 212
  bass clarinet, 144, 176, 177, 212
Classical era, 9, 159, 175
Clusters, 129, 132, 145
Coda, 29, 106, 158, 203
Commissioners, 24
Common Practice, 87
Components, 45
Compositional process, 26, 149
Composition competition, 3, 255, 262, 263
Concept, 15, 26, 38, 43, 102
Concerts, 10, 12, 145
Concrete poetry, 201
Conductor, 16, 17, 94, 95, 255, 257
Con sordino, 115, 171
Constructed, 45, 46, 73
Contemporary music, 5, 220
  ensembles, 188
  festivals, 12, 263
  scores, 4
Contrapuntal devices, 79
  augmentation, 106
  canon, 106, 161, *see also* Canon
  contrary motion, 106, 132

diminution, 106
imitation, 106
inversion, 106
Coomaraswamy, Ananda K., 119
Copyright, 202, 257
Cornish School of the Arts, Seattle, Washington, 118, *see also* Cage, John
Counterpoint, 17, 45, 79, 82, 87, 106, 177, 213, 241
Cross, 24, 128
Crumb, George, 118, 125, 140, 175
  Makrokosmos I, II, III, IV (1972–1979), 124
  Vox Balaenae (Voice of the Whale) for Three Masked Players (1972), 133, 137–139, 141
Cues, 259
Cunningham, Merce, 118

D

Dallapiccola, Luigi, *Goethe-Lieder* (1953), 212, 214, 215, 232
Darmstadt, 4, 250
Davies, Peter Maxwell, 86, 262
  Eight Songs for a Mad King (1969), 220, 223, 232
  Missa super l'homme armé (1968), 84, 85
Debussy, Claude, 9, 63, 152, 175
  Des Pas sur la Neige, 16
  Douze Préludes Book 1 for solo piano (1910), 16
  La Cathédrale Engloutie, 16
  La Fille aux Cheveux de Lin, 16
  Syrinx (1913) for solo flute, 62, 64–65, 105
  Voiles, 16
Decoration, 24, 26, 193
Dick, Robert, *The Other Flute: A Performance Manual of Contemporary Techniques*, 141
Dominant, 23, 61, 69, 73, 84, 128, 237

Domus Piano Quartet, 192
Dorow, Dorothy, 200
Double bass, 16, 35, 86, 95, 112, 114,
        140, 148, 192, 258
Double-stopping, 153
Drone, 115, 170, 192, 193, 227, 245
Drum, 46, 145, 150
Dufay, Guillaume, (c. 1400–1474), *Missa*
        L'Homme Armé, 82
Duo, 24, 108, 177
Duration, 51
    contract, 16
    decrease, 16
    expand, 16
    increase, 16
    minutes, 78, 86
    seconds, 42, 46
Dvořák, cello concerti, 133
Dyad, 153, 217
Dynamics, 17, 18, 91, 217, 245

E

Echo, 18, 27, 161, 174, 205, 254
Eckhart, Meister, 119
Electric piano, 55
Electroacoustic music, 2, 8, 29, 129
Electronic music, 32, 35, 129
    analog, 51
    studio, 51
Electronics, 29, 250, 254
Elgar cello concerti, 133
English, 18, 202, 216
Enharmonic changes, 110
Ensemble, 84, 144, 151
    instrumental, 11, 217
    mixed, 188
    percussion, 151
Ensemble InterContemporain, 188
Ensemble Modern, 188
Europe, 2, 3, 43, 51, 188, 262
Exercises, 4, 103–115
Experiment, 18, 44, 91
Exploration, 7, 8, 20, 91, 264

Exposition, 86, 167, 241, *see also* Fugue,
        Sonata
Expression, 8, 102, 115, 166, 200, 220,
        262
Extended instrumental techniques, 117,
        193, 250
Extended vocal techniques, 200, 220
Extension, 110, 141
Extra-musical idea, 16

F

False relations, 77, 78
Families of instruments, 112
Fantasia, 84
Ferneyhough, Brian, 44, 152, 175
Fibonacci, 50
    series, 46, 246
Film, 9, 12, 255
Filters, 26, 254
Fingerboard, 133, 159
Fingerings, 245
    alternative, 141
    microtonal, 141
Finnissy, Michael, 118
    English Country-Tunes (1977/1982–
        1985), 126
Fires of London, the, 84, 220, 262
First performances, 263
Flute, 62, 141, 176
    alto flute, 95, 140
    amplified, 133
    bass flute, 95, 140
    flute in C, 95, 140
    piccolo, 84, 95, 140, 176
    speak-flute, 141
Flutter tongue, 115, 144, 250
Folk dances, 46
Folk music, 43, 192, *see also* Melody
    East European, 45
    Scottish, 79
Folk songs, 61, 177, 203
    Auld Lang Sine, 61
    China, 192

Scottish, 61, 192
Serbia,192
Welsh, 205
Forms, traditional, 23, 24
    aria, 23
    binary, 23, 155, 158
    chaconne, 23
    fantasia, 84
    fugue, 16, 23, 86, 87, 240
    minuet and trio, 23, 155
    passacaglia, 23
    rondo, 23, 181
    sonata, 20, 23, *see also* Sonata
    theme and variations, 177
Franck, César, 69
Free composition, 1, 2, 8, 11
French, 82, 225, 251
Frequency, 225, 226
    spectrum, 18
Fugue, 16, 23, 86, 87, 240
    answer, 86, 87
    codetta, 86
    counter-subject, 86, 87
    episodes, 240, 241
    final section, 240, 241
    fugal exposition, 86, 87
    middle entries, 240, 241
    real answer, 86
    subject, 86, 240
Functional rhythm, 45, 46
Fundamental tone, 72, 73

G

Gaudeamus Information, 263
Gaudí, Antoní (1852–1926), 26
    Sagrada Familia (c. 1883–c. 1926),
        24, 25
Gauguin, Paul, 251
Genre, 254, 257
Gershwin, George, *American in Paris*
        (1928), 148
Gesture, 44, 126, 163, 166, 220, 244
Glass, Philip, 51, 175

Glissando, 27, 95, 119, 144, 217, 245, 251
Globokar, Vinko, *Res/As/Ex/Ins-pirer*
        (1973), 245, 249
Goethe (1749–1832), 212
Gongs, Chinese, 17
Gordon, Michael, 262
Górecki, 44
    Symphony No. 3, *Symphony of
        Sorrowful Songs* (1976), 16,
        86, 89
Gothic style, 24
Grace notes, 78, 128, 144
Graphing, 38
Greek legend, 32
Gubaidulina, Sofia, 44, 46, 118, 175
    In croce (1979) for cello and organ,
        128, 131
    Seven Words (1982) for bayan, cello
        and strings, 47–49
Guitar, 94, 235

H

Haiku, 202, 204
Handbells, 84
Handel, *Messiah*, 222
Hand pops, 144
Harmonics, 72, 153, 174, 245
    artificial harmonics, 153, 154
    natural harmonics, 72, 153, 154, 189
Harmonium, 84, 86
Harmony, 43, 45, 72
    chromatic, 87
    harmonic construction, 110
    harmonic fields, 110
    harmonic progression, 72, 76, 107,
        236
    microtonal, 144
    non-tonal, 73
    quasi-tonal, 17
    tonal, 87, 158
Harp, 35, 217
Hart, Roy, 200, 220
Haydn, Josef, 9, 152

Symphony No. 45 in F#, "Farewell," (1772), 21
Heterophony, 193
Hildegard von Bingen, 61
    Ave generosa, Hymn to Saint Mary (twelfth century), 61
Hindemith, Paul, 9, 24
Hirst, Linda, 200
Hoitenga, Camilla, 250
Holliger, Heinz, 244, 245
    Studien zum Spielen Neuer Musik,(Studies for Playing Avantgarde Music), 141
Homewood, S. & Matthews, C., 256
L'Homme Armé (fifteenth century), 82, 83
Homophony, 38
Hoquet, 54
Horizontal lines, 45
Horn, 35, 78, 112, 144, 150, 176
    orchestral, 29
    solo, 29, 180
Howell, Thomas, *The Avant-Garde Flute: a Handbook for Composers and Flutists*, 141
Huddersfield Choral Society, The, 224
Humor, 220

I

Ijsbreker, De, 54
Ikos, 227
Imagery, 16
Imagination, 1, 15, 32, 42, 105, 261
Imitation, 79, 106
Improvisation, 18, 20, 126
Indian music, 51, 62
Inner ear, 10
Instrument, 18, 24, 87, 104, 152, 176, 201, 235, 260, *see also specific instrument*
Instrumental ensembles, 11
Instrumentation, 55, 94, 162
Interludes, 203

International Society for Contemporary Music (ISCM), 11, 263
Intervallic scheme, 41
Intervals, 60, 69, 72, 75, 92, 158, 174, 212
Introduction, 203, 205, 208
Intuitive rhythm, 45
Inversion, 27, 111, 181, 237
    first inversion, 76
    retrograde, 70
    second inversion, 76
IRCAM, Paris, 32
    CHANT programme, 35
Isorhythm, 79, 82

J

Josquin des Près, (c. 1440–1521), *Missa l'Homme Armé*, 83
Joyce, James
    Finnegan's Wake, 201
    Ulysses, 201

K

Kagel, Mauricio, *Match* (1964), 148
Kampen, Christopher van, 189
Kappelmeisters, 9
Keyboards, 12, 220
    celesta, 150, 192, 216, 217
    harmonium, 84, 86, 128
    harpsichord, 118, 132
    organ, 118, 128
    piano, 118, 124
Keys, 78, 148
    key rattles, 144
    key slaps, 144
King George III (1738–1820), 220
King's College Chapel Choir, Cambridge, 222
Klangfarbenmelodien, 91, 115
Klangforum Wien, 188
Kulenty, Hanna, *Air* (1991), 145, 147
Kurtág, György, 118

Játékok (Games) (1979), 126
Kyrie, 82

L

Lang, David, 262
La Scala, Milan, 224
Latin, 82
Layering, 35, 115
Lefanu, Nicola, 188, 189
   Deva (1979) for cello and ensemble, 188, 190, 191
Libretto, 32
Ligeti, György, 118, 133, 177, 188
   Continuum (1968), 132, 133, 135
   Ten Pieces for Wind Quintet (1968), 185, 186–187
   Volumina (1961–1962), 129, 132
Linear, 16, 70, 161, 237
Lingua franca, 43
Listener, 17, 42, 51, 152, 185, 262
Liszt, 69
Location, 18, 263
London Sinfonietta, the, 188, 189
Lutoslawski, Witold, 152, 171, 172–173, 175
Lutyens, Elisabeth, 72, 175
   and suddenly it's evening (1966), 216, 217, 219, 232

M

Machaut, Guillaume de, 79
   S'il estoit nulz, 83
MacMillan, James, *The Confession of Isobel Gowdie* (1990), 78, 79, 80–81
Maconchy, Elizabeth, 152, 166, 170, 175
   String Quartet No. 3 (1938), 167, 168–169
Manet, 91
Manning, Jane, 200
Manuals, 128, 133, *see also* Keyboards

Manuscript paper, 104, 112, 256, 257, 259
March, 19, 46, 163
Mediaeval technique, 54
Melisma, 202, 213, 215, 233
Melody, 43, 78, 84, 106, 236
   folk-like, 16
   melodic line, 17, 35, 43, 61, 79, 91, 107, 158, 189, 227
   melodic shapes, 104
Memory, 20, 115, 152
Mendelssohn, violin concerto, 133
Mensuration canon, 83, 84
Menuhin, Yehudi, 240
Messiaen, 3, 44, 50, 63
   Movement VII *Fouillis d'arcs-en-ciel, pour l'Ange qui annonce la fin du Temps* (*Gatherings of rainbows, for the Angel who announces the end of Time*), 67
   Quatuor pour la fin du temps (*Quartet for the End of Time*) (1940–1941), 50, 52–53, 67, 68
Metamorphosis, 29
Meter, 180
Metric modulation, 55, 57, 63
Microtonality, 44
Microtones, 44, 95, 245
Microtuning, 145
Milhaud, Darius, *Machines agricoles* (1919), 202–203
Minimalism, 44, 51, 54
Minimalists, 50
Mobiles, 171
Modality, 44, 106, 180, 193
Mode, 60, 69, 106, 177, 227
   Aeolian, 61, 62, 86, 192
   Ásávarí, 62
   Bhairaví, 62
   Bilával, 62
   Dorian, 62, 84
   Greek, 61
   Ionian, 61, 62
   Káfí, 62
   Kalyána, 62

Khammája, 62
Lydian, 61, 62, 78, 79, 192
Mediaeval, 61
Mixolydian, 62
modes of limited transposition, 63,
    67
non-Western, 61, 62
Phrygian, 61, 62, 192
Shri, 62
Modulation, 41–42, 236
    metric, 55, 57, 63
Monet, 91
Monodrama, 220
Monody, 153, 235
    plurality in singularity, 236
Monophonics, 141
Monosyllables, 201, 232
Mood, 15, 17, 72, 76, 104, 152, 180,
    200, 205
Motets, 79, 82
Motif, 63, 105, 170, 174, 251
Motive, 26, 163, 166, 180
Moto perpetuo, 237
Motto, 19, 27, 84
Mouthpiece alone, 144
Mozart, Wolfgang Amadeus, 4, 9, 152
    String Quartet No.21, 'Prussian No.1',
        K.575 in D Major (1798),
        155, 156–157
Multiphonics, 141
Murail, Tristan, 44
Musgrave, Thea, Horn Concerto (1970–
    1971), 29, 32
Musical language, 12, 20, 43
    invented, 63, 69
    non-tonal, 43, 73
    parameters, 45
    post-serial techniques, 44
    serial, 72
    tonal, 43, 72, see also Tonality
    twelve-tone, 44, 69, 72, 92
Musical materials, 18, 42, 151, 159, 171,
    236, 254
Music box, 95
Music centers, national, 11

Music copying, 256
Musicology, 2, 5, 8, 12
Music theater, 84, 220
Mutes, 144, 159

N

Nash Ensemble, 189
Neo-classic, see Styles
Nielsen, Carl, 177, 180
Noise, 18, 254
Nomenclature, 128
Non-retrogradable, 50
Nørgård, Per, The Secret Melody
        (Movement I from Libro per
        Nobuko, 1993), 63, 66
Notation, 8, 73, 225, 232, 256
    accuracy of, 104
    newfound sounds, 91
    time-space notation, 144, 245
Note cell, 60, 63, 72, 92, 208
Note unit, 108
Nyman, Michael, the Michael Nyman
        Band, 262

O

Oboe, 86, 141
    cor anglais, 140, 176
Octaves, 50
    divisions, 67
    interruption, 174
    octave displacement, 73, 93, 108,
        171, 208
    vocal range, 220
Oliveros, Pauline, 44
Orchestra, 11, 29, 35
Orchestral layout, 112, 114
Orchestral score, 112
Orchestration, 112, 115
Organ, 118, 128
Original, 8, 46, 84, 108, 110, 193, 226,
    256
Orkest de Volharding, 145

Orpheus and Euridice, 32, 35
l'O.R.T.F., 225
Orthodox Christian Church, 226
Oscillators, 35
Ostinato, 82, 181, 205
Over-blowing, 245
Overtone series, 72, 95

P

Paganini, 133
Palindromic, 19, 50, 161, 162, 217
Panpipes, 55
Parameters, 15, 38, 45, 213
Pärt, Arvo, 44
Pastiches, 222
Pattern, 77, 162, 237, 250
    arpeggio, 133
    breaking of, 55
    intervallic, 63, 181
    mediaeval mode, 61
    phasing, 51
    quasi-speech, 226
    quintuplet, 57
    rhythmic, 50, 54, 188
    syllables, 202
Pauses, 46, 95, 245, 260
Pedal note, 106, 236, 237, 241, 245
Peers, Peter, 205
Penderecki, Krzysztof, 152, 175
Percussion, 94, 114, 119, 145, 150, 188,
    192, 217
    bells, 150, 202
    bongos, 55, 145, 150
    cymbals, 26, 148, 149, 150, 217
    drums, 145, 150
    flexatone, 148, 150
    glockenspiel, 148, 150
    gongs, 17, 145, 150
    handbells, 84
    indefinite pitch, 145, 148, 149, 150
    lion's roar, 148, 150
    marimba, 51, 148, 150

    metal, 102, 145, 148, 149, 150, 192,
        217
    motor horns, 148, 150
    skin, 145, 148, 149, 150, 217
    sticks, 148
    temple blocks, 148
    thunder sheets, 148
    timpani, 145, 148, 150
    triangles, 149, 150
    tuned, 145, 148, 149, 150
    vibraphone, 35, 94 112, 144, 148,
        149, 150, 258
    wind machine, 77, 148, 150
    wood, 145, 148, 149, 150, 217
    xylophone, 35, 148, 150
Performance notes, 95, 97, 250, 257
Performers, 1, 8, 45, 91, 117, 244, 263
Performing rights society, 203
Permutation, 108, 110, 162, 174, 213
Petrov, Gregory, 226
Phase, 44
Phonemes, 35, 201, 220, 225, 251
Phonetic, 232
Phrases, 27, 46, 105, 177, 212
Piano, 29, 118
    amplified, 124, 133
    electric, 55
    inside, 124
    phase, 54
    prepared, 119
Piccolo, 84, 95, 140, 176
Pissarro, 91
Piston, Walter, *Orchestration* (1979),
    112, 133, 152, 153, 176
Pitch, 45, 72
    curve, 38
    indefinite pitch, 145, 148, 149, 150
    line, 60
    perfect pitch, 105, 199, 212, 225
    relative pitch, 145, 148
    sounding pitch, 69, 114, 176, 189, 213,
        258
Pitch bending, 144
Pitch center, 24, 41, 63, 167, 245
Pitch class, 54, 67, 87, 208, 245

operations, 108, 110, 115
Pizzicato, 35, 94, 112, 159, 162, 170, 174
Plainsong, 82
Plurality in singularity, 236
Pointillism, 91, 115
Polytonality, 78
Postlude, 203, 205
Process, 2, 7, 26, 41, 102, 149
Programmatic, 16, 18, 20
Program note, 257, 261
Prokofiev, 44
Prototypes, 23, 26
Pulse, 185, 188, 193

Q

Quadriad, 155
Quadruplet, 185, 188
Quarter-tones, 225
Quasimodo, Salvatore, (1901–1968), 216
Quasi parlando, 95
Quintuplet, 57, 106, 162, 167, 185

R

Radio, 12, 95, 263
Range, 54, 69, 79, 95, 117, 129
    harmonics, 153
    pitch, 132
    vocal, 200, 204, 220
Rattle, Simon, 189
Ravel, Maurice, 152, 175
Redgate, Chris, 141
Refrains, 189
Register, 54, 76, 102, 133, 162, 205
    chalumeau register, 91
Registration, *see* Organ
Rehfeldt, Phillip, *New Directions for Clarinet*, 144
Reich, Steve, 44, 51
    Clapping Music, 102
    Drumming (1970–1971), 51, 102
    Four Organs, 102
    Music for Pieces of Wood, 102

New York Counterpoint, 102
Piano Phase (1967), 51, 54, 55
Resolution, 236, 237
Reverberation, 254
Rhythm, 43, 108
    additive, 50
    advanced, 113
    augmentation, 105, 106, 112
    combination, 109, 113
    complementary, 79, 106
    constructed, 45, 46, 108
    diminution, 106, 112
    exercise, 109
    functional, 45, 46
    Hindu, 50
    intuitive, 45
    irregular, 128
    isorhythm, 82
    machine, 18
    organization, 16
    retrogradation, 109, 112
Rhythmic unison, 46, 177, 226
Romantic epoch, 23
Rounds, 246–247
Row, 70, *see also* Twelve-Tone
    inversion, 70
    original row, 70, 72, 92
    retrograde, 70
    retrograde inversion, 70
Russia, 44, 226

S

Saariaho, Kaija, 254
    NoaNoa for solo flute and electronics
        (1992), 250, 253
    Verblendungen for orchestra and tape
        (1982–1984), 38, 39
Saint-Saëns, 133
Samba, 46
Sarabhai, Gita, 119
Saunders, Rebecca, 44, 201
    Molly's Song 3: Shades of Crimson,
        (1995–1996), 95, 97, 98, 99

Saxophone
    alto, 55, 145
    tenor, 145
Scales, 60, 61, 103–104
    chromatic, 63
    expanded, 29
    invented scales, 63, 69, 72
    major, 61, 62, 205
    melodic minor, 61, 77
    non-Western, 62
    octatonic, 63
    pentatonic, 63, 118
    quarter tone, 63
    whole tone, 63, 240
Scelsi, Giacinto, 44
Scenes, 19, 33, 220, 222
Schafer, Murray, *When Words Sing*,
    Epitaph for Moonlight (1966), 224
Schnittke, Alfred, 44
Schoenberg, Arnold, 44, 72, 94, 159,
    175
    Pierrot Lunaire (1912), 95, 217
    Verklärte Nacht (*Transfigured Night*)
        op. 4 (1917), 87
    Wind Quintet (1924), 69, 70, 71, 181
Score, 4, 11, 28, 31, 95, 112, 124, 126,
        132, 148, 171, 213, 225, 245,
        250, 255, 257
Scottish Music Centre, 11
Sculptured textures, 40, 226
Seagull effect, *see* Cello
Seeger, Ruth Crawford, 175, 177
    Suite for Wind Quintet (1952), 181,
        182, 183, 184, 185, 192
Sehr langsam, 159
Semitones, 63
Sequence, 105, 107, 111, 189, 236, 244
Serial, 44, 181, 208, *see also* Musical
        language
    serial variants, 60
Seurat, 91
Shostakovitch, Dmitri, 44
Sisley, 91
Sketchbooks, 26

Society for the Promotion of New Music
        (SPNM), 3, 4, 11, 263
Soloist, 17, 95, 153, 220
Sonata, 20, 21, 23
    development, 24
    exposition, 24
    first subject, 24
    form, 167, 181
    recapitulation, 24
    second subject, 24
Song, 82, 192, 202, 208, 212, 233
Song cycle, 212, 213
Sonic colors, 87, 91
Sonic composition, 44
Sonic events, 26
Sonic textures, 91, 94
Sounding pitch, 69, 114, 176, 189, 213,
        258
Soundscape, 77, 129, 149, 192, 226
Sound of the sound, the, 91, 102
Sound spectrum, 189
Sound world, 39, 129
Spatialization, 44
Spectral music, 44, 95
Speed, 16, 55, 84, 132, 180, 185
Spiral binding, 258
Staccatissimo, 188
Staccato, 27, 86, 94, 126, 163, 185, 226
Statement, 27, 86, 166, 180, 240
Stockhausen, Karlheinz, 44
    MANTRA (1970), 26
Stow, Randolph, 220
Straus, Joseph, *The Music of Ruth
        Crawford Seeger*, 185
Strauss, Richard, *Alpine Symphony*
        (1911–1915), 148
Stravinsky, Igor, 44, 209
    L'Oiseau de Feu (1909–1910), 133
    Symphony of Psalms (1930), 16, 86, 90
    Three Songs from William Shakespeare
        (1953) for voice, flute,
        clarinet and viola, 208
String quartet, 57, 151, 152, 155, 163,
        175, 201
Strings, 35, 46, 155

open, 152, 153, 154, 170, 189
Structure, 10, 15, 23
    concept, 26
    free flow, 26
    graphing, 38
    intellectual control, 26
Styles
    experimental, 44, 132
    minimalism, 44, 51, 54
    modernist, 181
    neoclassic, 44, 177
    new complexity, 44
    new tonality, 44
    polystylicity, 44
    post-modernism, 44
    sonic composition, 44
    spectralism, 44
Suite, 20
    allemande, 23
    bourrée, 23
    courante, 23
    gavotte, 23
    gigue, 23
    minuet, 23
    sarabande, 23
Sul ponticello, 115
Summer schools, 4, 263
Syllables, 141, 202, 204, 232
    monosyllabic, 201, 232
    multisyllabic, 232
Symphony, 20, 39
Synchronize, 171

T

Takemitsu, Toru, *Rain Spell* (1982), 143,
    144
Talea, 82
Tango, 46
Tape, 38, 39
Tape recorders, reel-to-reel, 51
Tavener, John, *Akathist of Thanksgiving*
    (1988), 226, 231, 232

Technique, 4, 6, 7, 35, 44, 108, 115, 117,
    264
Temporal, 55
Teodorescu, Livia, 44, 95
    Rite for Enchanting the Air (1998),
        101, 141
Tessitura, 149, 193, 204, 220
Text, 20, 200
    bilingual, 82
    choice of, 201, 224
    copyright, 202
    multitextual, 82
    structure, 203
    underlay, 232
Texture, 17, 40, 87, 94, 102, 158, 174,
    185, 212, 225
Theme, 26, 129, 163, 166, 177, 220
Theme and variations, 177
Thomas, Mary, 200
Timbre, 44, 45, 54, 87, 91, 119, 144, 188,
    217, 254
Time
    compound, 57, 163, 179
    simple, 57, 179
Time signature, 57, 104, 108, 173, 245
Time-space notation, 144, 245
Tippett, Michael, 24, 152, 175
Titles, 20, 21, 105
Tonality
    bitonality, 63, 78, 106
    dominant, 23, 69, 167
    mediant, 167, 171
    microtonality, 44
    new tonality, 44
    polytonality, 78
    root, 167
    submediant, 177
Tones, 174, 227
    fundamental tone, 72, 73
Tongue, 204
    flutter tongue, 115, 144, 250
    slap tongue, 144
    tongue-stops, 250
    triple tonguing, 177
Tonic, 23, 24, 42, 61, 69, 129, 180, 237

Transformation, 29, 112, 119
Transition, 57, 163, 166, 244
Transposing instrument, 106, 114, 258, 260
Transposition, 67, 92, 108, 110, 115, 167, 217
Tremolando, 144, 159, 161, 162, 226, 245, 254
Tremolo, 27, 112, 128, 132
    throat *tremolo*, 144
Triads, 73, 76, 78, 227
Trills, 124, 141, 245
Trio, 23, 82, 145, 155, 185, 225
Triplet, 105, 106, 162, 178, 214
Triplicity, 32, 84, 92
Trombone, 112, 144
    bass trombone, 145
Trumpet, 91, 92, 112, 144, 258
    piccolo trumpet, 192
Tuba, 95, 144
Turetzky, Bertram, *The Contemporary Contrabass*, 140
Turner, *Norham Castle: Sunrise* (c. 1845), 189
Twelve-Tone, 44, 92, *see also* Musical Language
    inversion, 70, 76
    original row, 70, 92
    retrograde, 70
    retrograde inversion, 70
    row, 69, 159, 181, 213
    variants, 70

U

Ulstvol'skaya, Galina, 44
Unison, 46, 50, 78, 158, 193, 226

V

Van Gogh, 91
Varèse, Edgard, *Ionisation* (1929–1931), 148
Variants, 70

Variation, 29, 106, 108, 177, 180
Veal, Peter and Claus-Steffen Mahnkopf, *The Techniques of Oboe Playing*, 141
Verse, 18, 19, 73, 108, 205
    strophic, 203
    through composed, 203
Vibraphone, 35, 94, 112, 144, 148, 150, 258
Vibrato, 141
    key vibrato, 144
Viola, 78, 166, 170, 192
    alto clef, 155
    strings, 152
    technical possibilities, 133
    textural flow, 112
Violin, 50, 63, 87, 118, 163, 216, 236, 244
Virtuoso, 45, 117, 128, 153, 188, 220, 226, 244
Vischer, Frau Antoinette M., 132
Visual arts, 51
Vivaldi, Violin Concerto, *The Four Seasons* (c. 1730), 16
Voice, 7, 11, 82, 84, 91, 95, 199–233
    falsetto, 220
Volharding, *De*, 54, 145

W

Wagner, 69
Waltz, 46
Webern, Anton, 44, 94, 152, 161, 162
    Concerto, op.24 (1934), 92, 93
    Fünf Sätze für Streichquartett (*Five Pieces for String Quartet*), op. 5 (1909), 159, 160, 175
Weir, Judith, 44, 188
    Distance and Enchantment (1988), 192, 196–197
Western Europe, 2, 12, 43
Wilkins, Margaret Lucy, Symphony (1989), 40–41
Williams, Ralph Vaughan, 3

Sinfonia Antarctica (1949), 76, 77
Wind, 11, 77, 148
    wind machine, 77, 148, 150
    wind quintet, 151, 175–177
Wolf, Julia, 262
Woodwind, 35, 114, 140, 149, 188, 235
    auxiliary instruments, 176, 177
    subsidiary instruments, 140
Word painting, 200, 202, 205, 213
Word stress, 204
Workshops, 3, 4, 10, 264

X

Xenakis, Iannis, 44, 226
    Nuits (1967–1968) for twelve solo
        voices, 225, 229, 233

Xylophone, 35, 148, 150

Z

Zamarin, Roberto, 220
Zinovieff, Peter, 32
Zodiac, signs of the, 124
    Gemini, 124